RICHARD G. COX LIBRARY
UN. OF SOUTHERN MISS.—GULF PARK

The Soviet Economy

The Soviet Economy

How It Really Works

Constantin A. Krylov
U.S. Army Institute for
Advanced Russian and East
European Studies

Lexington Books
D.C. Heath and Company
Lexington, Massachusetts
Toronto

RICHARD G. COX LIBRARY
UN. OF SOUTHERN MISS.—GULF PARK

Library of Congress Cataloging in Publication Data

Krylov, Konstantin Arkad'evich.
   The Soviet economy.

   Includes index.
   1. Russia—Economic   conditions—1965-   2. Russia—Economic
policy—1976-   I. Title.
HC336.25.K79   330.9'47'085   78-22286
ISBN 0-669-02743-X

Copyright © 1979 by D.C. Heath and Company

All rights reserved. No part of this publication may be reproduced or transmit-
ted in any form or by any means, electronic or mechanical, including
photocopy, recording, or any information storage or retrieval system, without
permission in writing from the publisher.

Published simultaneously in Canada

Printed in the United States of America

International Standard Book Number: 0-669-02743-X

Library of Congress Catalog Card Number: 78-22286

Contents

List of Figures and Tables

Acknowledgments

The peculiarities of Soviet economy, which are without precedent in the history of mankind, make the description and explanation of the Soviet economy an unusually difficult task even in Russian. Translating these peculiarities into English is probably even more difficult. Thus, for instance, the external similarity but internal difference between Soviet economic terms and economic terms in the English language makes this task even more difficult. One can cite many other complex problems of translation.

Nonetheless, I am convinced, and I hope that the future reader will be similarly convinced, that all my former students of the US Army Institute for Advanced Russian and East European Studies who translated this text have successfully dealt with this difficult task. I tender my deepest, sincerest gratitude to all of them—William W. Allen III, Galen L. Clark, John J. Dykstra, Earl E. Keel, Jr., Michael G. Pond, and Everett A. Rice. I am especially thankful to William W. Allen III, who not only translated parts of the book but also edited the entire English text.

The commander of the Russian Institute, Lieutenant Colonel Roland Lajoie, and the directors of instruction, Lieutenant Colonel Jim E. Hinds and Major John C. Reppert, have given me much support in this very time-consuming work. I am sincerely grateful to them for their support.

I would also like to express my appreciation for the long-suffering patience of Ann M. Parker, who typed the text, the corrections of the text, and the corrections of the corrections.

Introduction

The Soviet economic system is unique. Its creators have set as their goal not only the establishment of a new economic system but also a new social order based on that system.

In almost all its salient features the economic system that they have created bears no resemblance to a market economy system. Completely different stimuli and conditions of economic activity prevail: the criteria for evaluating the results of economic activity for the most part possess either a crudely quantitative or noneconomic character. Determination of the actual results achieved by the Soviet economy not only requires significantly more detailed and penetrating study but is often impossible using economic methods alone. Ambiguity is also a peculiarity of the Soviet economic system. Words frequently contradict reality; the portrayal of facts contradicts their essence. The desired result is very often passed off as reality; anachronistic approaches survive within the framework of clearly contradictory reality. This distinctive, disorienting ambiguity also exists in terminology; thus, the term *profit* may be understood in two ways: as a term used in Soviet planning as well as the way it is used in an ordinary market economy.

All of this requires a special approach to its study, an approach based primarily on the strict investigation of facts and only facts. To isolate the most important of these facts, those that determine the nature of the phenomenon under consideration, is the basic complexity and the primary necessity confronting the researcher.

These views serve as the basis for this work. Moreover, diligently selecting and checking facts, the author of this study has limited himself almost exclusively to the writings of Soviet scientists, economists, and individuals directly involved in various branches of the economy. As a result, the author writes as if he were the moderator of a wide-ranging conference at which are expressed only practical, scientifically based, objective, and honest opinions about the substance of each issue.

Many thoughts and assertions are expressed using quotations. No quotation was chosen by accident. Moreover, none is intentionally taken out of context; all convey the main idea of the cited article.

The Soviet economy is undergoing a complicated and controversial stage of development. This process is reflected to a greater extent in Soviet economic periodicals than in extensive basic studies and scientific treatment. For this reason, this "conference" is based almost exclusively on periodicals of the last fifteen years. It is precisely these years, which may be called the creative period in understanding the Stalinist economic system, that offer the material essential to the researcher.

The main goal of this work is to show not only what but also how and why a particular action occurs within the framework of the overall system. Necessarily considering the system in parts, the entire work is constructed so that the reader can form an impression of the Soviet economy as a coherent, integrated entity. Only such an approach, I believe, can explain the system and demonstrate its laws, motivating forces, and organizational principles and indicate its peculiarities and problems as they relate to and influence each other. Special attention is given to unresolved problems of economic laws and price formation, all of which run like threads through this entire study.

1

Formation of the Present-Day Soviet Economy

Historical Background

More than half a century has passed, and the formation of the Soviet economic system is still not complete. It occasionally appeared, especially during Stalinist times, that the transformation process was finished and that ahead lay only gradual, evolutionary modifications and improvements. However, history introduced new variables which created quantitatively different stages of development. As each stage became a part of history, it left a certain mark and, at the very least, taught the creators of the Soviet economic system something new, thus influencing the further development of the economy.

Until it seized power, the Bolshevik party had not developed an economic program. Moreover, the realities of Russia with its predominantly peasant population, its high rate of illiteracy, and its underdeveloped and war-torn industry, differed sharply from the Marxist conception of a country in which a proletarian revolution could occur. The discrepancy turned out to be so great and so acute that in the interests of historical legitimization and justification of the Bolshevik Revolution, Lenin created the theory of "the weakest link in the chain of imperialism." This theory makes it possible for a proletarian revolution to occur in any country, regardless of its level of economic development.

The history of Russia itself determined the first major economic measure of the Bolsheviks: the Land Decree. Published 26 October 1917, this decree had more political than economic significance. A land-hunger psychology had long been forming among the peasantry in the important, heavily populated central regions of Russia. Constrained by landlord ownership for centuries, the poor and virtually landless peasants of these regions (comprising more than half the peasant population of the country) saw their expanding ownership of land as the only way out of this disastrous situation. The Land Decree, signifying the nationalization of all land, the expropriation of land from the landlords, and its distribution among the peasants immediately brought the great majority of the peasants into the Bolshevik camp. Despite all the friction which was to arise in the future between the Bolshevik regime and the peasants, Lenin justifiably said after the Civil War: "We won the Civil War after having settled the peasants' war for land." This lesson entered into Communist party strategy; in the small-scale wars of the present day, this "settlement of the peasants' war for land" has become a necessary prerequisite for success.

Other economic decrees followed the Land Decree in rapid succession. On

1

14 December 1917, the Bank Nationalization Decree was published. Decrees on the nationalization of the railroads (even though they already belonged to the government) and the merchant marine fleet followed later. Early in 1918, a decree was issued on the abrogation of czarist Russia's state debts to foreign governments, and on 28 June of the same year a decree on the nationalization of heavy industry was issued. All these nationalization decrees followed logically from the teachings of the classic Marxists and destroyed the old order. However, in its place something new would have to be created. As early as 2 December 1917, a decree was published on the organization of the Higher National Economic Council (VSNKh), which was followed by the system of workers' control. The workers' control groups became the real managers of the industrial enterprises.

However, the break with the old, customary ways brought about by both decrees and other measures of the regime predestined economic chaos. The Civil War which had just begun and the loss of experienced personnel in which the local workers' control system played no small role increased the chaos in the economy, particularly in industry.

The sharp decrease of industrial production and the circumstances of the Civil War were the chief, but not the only, reasons for the economic policy which was given the name War Communism. The main slogan of the period of War Communism, which was directed at justifying any and all actions of the regime, was "Everything for the front!"

In industry the policy of War Communism was expressed by total nationalization and mobilization and by the creation of centralized management through so-called *Glavks* (chief directorates, organized according to branches of the economy). Centralization of management, the branch principle of organization, and the *Glavks* exist to this day.

However, the situation that developed led to a continuing drop in industrial production. Industry worked for the necessities of war and, in fact, produced almost no consumer goods. The state had nothing to sell and, more important, nothing to offer the peasants in exchange for agricultural commodities. Rapid inflation spread throughout the land. The economy was increasingly transformed into a natural, primitive system with direct exchange of goods for goods. Speculation increased and the campaign against it became one of the tasks of the organizations created for suppression (the *Cheka,* Extraordinary Commission). According to a decree of 21 November 1918, which followed directly from the teachings of the classic Marxists, all trade was nationalized and goods were distributed among the population on a class basis: workers received more; the so-called nonlaboring groups received practically nothing. To save the system from total famine, the so-called *prodrazverstka* was introduced by a decree of 9 May 1918, as the new regime's element of economic policy in the countryside. *Prodrazverstka* was a policy of forcing the peasants to supply agricultural produce to the state without compensation. It was conducted according to class principle: the wealthier peasants (the *kulak*) had to give more, and their deliveries were monitored more stringently. Peasants of average wealth (the *seredniak*) gave less. The rural proletariat (the *bedniak*) gave nothing and helped the regime collect produce from the others. The regime's official point of view affirmed that only "surpluses" were being collected from the peasants, that is, that which the peasant family itself did not consume and did not require for the continued functioning of its household. However, in practice, the confiscation of surpluses meant the confiscation of the greater portion of produce, and the nonfulfillment of deliveries brought about severe measures. Especially severe measures were applied to the *kulak* households, which then numbered about 4 million. During War Communism these *kulak* households practically vanished.

The peasants resisted the policy of *prodrazverstka,* and the confiscation of produce became possible only by force of arms. For this purpose, the so-called *prodotryad,* armed groups with extraordinary authority, were formed. Central Committee detachments, which included Chinese and Latvian units, conducted large-scale punitive actions. In response, the peasants cut back on livestock and by almost 40 percent on cultivated land.

By 1920, the crisis of the Civil War had passed and it was time to switch to a peacetime economy. However, the devastation became greater, and the policy of War Communism continued. By 1921, an intolerable situation was developing in the country. It was no longer justified by either the circumstances or the logic of events. Among the population, and primarily among the workers, disturbances began. Rebellions flared in their wake. The most important of these were the Kronstadt sailors' revolt and the Tambov (or Antonov) peasants' revolt. It is still too early to judge, but it is quite likely that the Kronstadt revolt will someday be recorded as one of the most important turning points in the history of Russia.

At the beginning of the revolution (1917-1918), these sailors supported the Bolsheviks in the most decisive manner. It was certainly not without reason that Trotsky affirmed that "they were the pride and glory of the revolution." However, on 2 March 1921, the sailors of the Baltic Fleet in Kronstadt rebelled against the Bolsheviks. Soviet history disparagingly refers to this revolt as a "mutiny," and describes the event in general terms in the following manner. The fleet in 1921 was composed of different people—farm boys irritated by *prodrazverstka* who were led in the revolt by White generals supported by agents of the Entente. The mutiny had nothing in common with the true feelings of the masses of sailors or the country's population.

The official interpretation of the events and their meaning does not correspond to historical facts. Within the Provisional Revolutionary Committee, which consisted of fifteen men under the chairmanship of Senior Clerk (senior sergeant) Petrichenko, there was only one sailor from the ranks who probably had only recently become a member of the fleet. The remaining fourteen were cadre sailors of petty officer rank and civilians connected with the Baltic Fleet. There were no generals among the leaders of the revolt. One or two artillery generals who were chosen by the soldiers and sailors commanded the artillery positions of Kronstadt. Nor did the revolt have a reactionary (White) character; rather its purpose was to restore revolutionary freedoms which had been usurped by the Bolsheviks.

A proclamation issued by the Provisional Revolutionary Committee characterized the Bolshevik regime and the reasons for the revolt as follows:

> To the Population of the
> Fortress and City of Kronstadt!
> Comrades and Citizens!!
>
> Our country is going through a difficult period. Famine, cold and economic ruin have been holding us in an iron vise for three years. The Communist Party ruling the country has lost touch with the masses and has proved itself unable to lead the masses from a situation of general ruin. It has not taken into consideration those disturbances which have recently occurred in Moscow and which have clearly shown that the Party has lost the confidence of the working masses. It has not heeded those demands which have been presented by the workers. It considers these demands to be intrigues of counterrevolution.
>
> Kronstadt, March 2, 1921. Battleship "Petropavlovsk." Chairman of the Provisional Revolutionary Committee: Petrichenko. Secretary: Turkin.[1]

Defining its political character, the Kronstadt revolt propagated the slogan "Soviets without Communists," which proved to be very popular. The Tambov (Antonov) revolt which took place at almost the same time adopted the same slogan. It was adopted by the Northern Caucasus (Kuban) and Altai revolts during collectivization in 1931 and finally by the independent (that is, non-Moscow-controlled) partisan movement (the so-called Green Movement) and the Vlasov Movement of the Second World War.

The Kronstadt revolt greatly disturbed Moscow. Within a few hours of the publication of the Provisional Revolutionary Committee's proclamation, Moscow responded with radio broadcasts of slanderous allegations. The rebelling sailors were called imperialists, reactionaries, and mercenaries of the Entente. However, the Bolsheviks understood and feared the danger and the force of the revolutionary spirit of the sailors' revolt. Three hundred delegates to the Tenth Party Congress (headed by Voroshilov), military school cadets, the notorious Latvian riflemen, and the most reliable regular units of the army were sent to suppress the revolt. The revolt was put down after twenty days. Kronstadt was bathed in blood. Some of the rebels, including Petrichenko, escaped to Finland, but in 1945 on demand of the Soviet government, they were turned over to the Soviet Union and vanished without a trace. Bolsheviks never forget their enemies!

The second revolt, the Tambov or Antonov revolt, also began in 1921, but in Tambov Province (now *oblast'*). Antonov, the organizer and leader of this peasant revolt, was a professional revolutionary, a former member of the military (terrorist) organization of the Social-Revolutionary Party. He had great experience in conspiratorial and guerrilla operations. Knowing the enemy, Antonov prepared two groups to launch the revolt. The smaller group began the uprising. Bolshevik punitive detachments swept down on them and thereby gave away their plan and disposition. Antonov then committed the second, significantly larger wave of the revolt which encircled and annihilated the "pacification" forces. In a very short time, the revolt encompassed the entire Tambov Province and spread to Riazan', Tula, and Kaluga. Antonov deliberately pushed the revolt toward Moscow. At its peak, the revolt almost reached the borders of the Moscow Province.

To suppress the Tambov revolt, Tukhachevsky was sent in command of selected cavalry units. However, each blow of Tukhachevsky's forces was like hitting water with a stick—the water parts and then flows together again. Antonov had worked out the theory of flexible guerrilla warfare before Mao Tse-tung. The details of the desperate reports Tukhachevsky must have written to Lenin remain unknown, but it is known that despite all his efforts, the revolt continued to spread like a malignancy toward the heart of the organism. Evidently it was thus perceived and evaluated by Lenin. Under the pressure of circumstances and in order to save the system, Lenin proclaimed the New Economic Policy (NEP) against the wishes of the Party, which was still caught up in the "flush of the proletarian revolution." Within the Party NEP caused a wave of suicides. In letters left by the suicides one idea resounds: Lenin sold out the revolution; he is restoring capitalism. All of this attests to the great force of the hidden pressures that compelled Lenin to take this step. However, the decision was correct. As Tukhachevsky later acknowledged, "Not my forces, but NEP liquidated the Antonov revolt."

The period of War Communism was over. From it the Soviet leadership learned a number of hard lessons; chief among them was that the people embarked upon revolution, not for the sake of abstract ideas, but for their own betterment. Many years later (early 1957), in a speech by Khrushchev in Leningrad, this lesson could be heard with all its force.

NEP was proclaimed in 1921. Addressing the entire country, Lenin affirmed that NEP was being introduced in earnest and for a long time. Addressing the Party, Lenin stated: "We must take a step backward in order to take two steps forward."

NEP immediately and sharply changed the situation in agriculture. The *prodrazverstka* was liquidated, and the peasants were given the right and the opportunity to work their land as if it were their private property. In pace of *prodrazverstka,* a limited produce tax (*prodnalog*) was introduced. At first it was a tax in kind, but later it was collected more and more in currency. Addressing the peasantry, Lenin launched the slogan "Enrich Yourself" and thus attempted to erase the shock of War Communism when the wealthier peasants were most persecuted by the regime. Furthermore, only the strong households were able to provide the level of agricultural production needed by the state.

In industry, NEP was characterized by leasing to their former owners first the smaller and later the larger plants. Only the largest heavy and defense industry plants remained in the hands of the state. Private trade was introduced. In a short time almost all internal trade was in private hands, in both the city and the countryside. State trade, represented in the cities by the *Sovrabkop* system, eked out a pitiful existence.

At the end of 1921 a monetary reform was conducted. The Soviet government issued the *chervonets*, paper bank notes worth ten rubles. During the first years of NEP, their exchange rate was higher than prerevolutionary ten-ruble gold coins.

An economic miracle was created by economic measures and by the faith of the people that the object of the revolution for which so much suffering had been endured was finally coming to pass. Industry in 1921 yielded only 13 percent of the production of 1913, but by 1928 the 1913 level had been surpassed. Transportation had been fully restored. In this time agriculture made a colossal quantitative and qualitative leap forward from its low, primitive level. Never in all the centuries of Russia's existence had agriculture reached, nor does it reach today, a level as high as that of the last years of NEP.

However, midway in the NEP period an unpleasant problem arose for the government, a problem that became known as the "scissors" crisis. The intensification of government influence in industry led to a continuing increase in prices for industrial goods. The tremendous successes in agriculture created overproduction and a drop in prices for agricultural products. The prices diverged as the points of an ever-widening scissors, finally reaching an inevitable conflict. Trade with the government lost meaning for the peasantry. Although the agricultural commodities intended for trade (the surpluses) were still being produced, it became increasingly difficult for the government to obtain these necessary products. Official Soviet history, presenting a number of factors that made collectivization inevitable, indicates that the small, scattered peasant farms of NEP did not yield enough trade products, especially grain. However, this fabricated explanation is directly contradicted by a resolution of the Fifteenth Party Congress that refers to the necessity for organizing the export of agricultural products.[2]

Lenin died at the zenith of the NEP "step backward," and therein lies one of the reasons for the legend surrounding his name. To take the "two steps forward," Stalin had to demolish NEP. The liquidation of NEP took several years; it was first liquidated in the central regions of the USSR and later in the outlying areas. Official Soviet history states that the liquidation of NEP occurred as a result of peaceful competition and the economic victory of socialism over capitalism within the country. In fact, NEP was liquidated first by taxation policies amounting to the arbitrary imposition of prohibitive taxes on the NEP men. Second, a great role was played by police and administrative measures, such as the arrest of the most wealthy NEP men or their banishment from large cities. This entire process is brilliantly described in the book *Minus Six* by the Soviet writer Matvei K. Roizman. The impossibility of an *economic* victory of socialism over capitalism within the country was a fact of life learned by the Soviet leadership from NEP. Not surprisingly, this experience is secretly but realistically taken into consideration in the present Soviet policy toward the coexistence of the two systems.

The changeover to the building of socialism demanded that Stalin create a clear concept of an economic policy for both industry and agriculture. From the teachings of the classic Marxists it followed that both the industrialization of the country and the creation of a vigorous, advanced industry, which could guarantee the country's industrial and defense needs were imperative. Among the Soviet leaders there was no ambivalence concerning the need for industrialization. Much more complex and painful was the question, On what sources should industrialization be based? The Soviet leadership had no single, unified concept on this issue; there were two conflicting schools of thought, those of Bukharin and Trotsky. Bukharin advanced the idea, as it was later formulated, of the peaceful assimilation of the *kulak* into socialism. Bukharin proposed the extension of NEP within agriculture and the creation of industry from taxes collected in trading with the now-wealthy peasantry. As could be expected, the scissors phenomenon rendered the Bukharin proposal unworkable. In essence, Trotsky's concept held that it was necessary to expropriate the peasantry. Both points of view focused on the peasantry, for at that time peasants still made up approximately 80 percent of the population, and the mass accumulation of resources was possible only at their expense. Stalin, not having a concept of his own, adopted Trotsky's concept. Bukharin's concept required the development of commodity production first; but Stalin was interested in heavy and military industry and developing these industries required free capital—capital not tied up in the production of trade goods. Thus, the concept of expropriation was significantly better suited to Stalin's requirements.

However, industrialization, particularly its initiation, was unthinkable without significant foreign assistance which would have to be paid for in hard currency. To obtain the necessary hard currency all the country's resources were mobilized. Paintings from the Hermitage were secretly sold, some of the state valuables were sold, and the last remaining church treasures were confiscated. Finally, during collectivization's most severe years of famine, trade with foreigners (*torgsin*) stores were opened in the cities. At these stores Soviet citizens, surrendering gold and valuables (wedding rings, crucifixes, and so forth) at 1913 prices, could purchase foodstuffs and other goods.

However, even all these measures proved insufficient. Thus in 1930 a reform of Soviet finances was conducted, and the turnover tax was introduced. This measure marked not only the intensification of the expropriation of the peasants, but the beginning of the expropriations of the rest of the country's population as well. From this moment on, every Soviet citizen paid a turnover tax which at times reached huge proportions on almost every product.

The mobilization of the country's resources and forces during the first two five-year plans (1928-1932 and 1933-1937) yielded significant success. During this period Stalin definitively shaped both Soviet industry and, through collectivization, Soviet agriculture. Much turned out differently than originally desired, however, and the phrase "that which developed," meaning that which turned out as it did, found increasing use in Soviet literature. It was during precisely this period that the forms, principles, and traditions of the national economy were formed. The principles of planning that would stand unchanged for more than forty years were also formed at this time.

According to official history, cooperation in agriculture dates from the first days of the Soviet regime, and collectivization represents a further stage of this development. After the revolution, farming cooperatives of the poorest peasants, the so-called communes and associations for working the land (*TOZ*) were created from the former estates of the landlords. However, at the beginning of the Stalinist collectivization, only 1.7 percent of the peasantry was included in all the production cooperatives.

Collectivization was a complex and tragic process and a subject of unresolved controversy. The organizational forms of the *kolkhozes* (collective farms) were designed to facilitate state control of all farm activities and offered ideal opportunities for exploitation. The rate of collectivization was determined by the ever-increasing scissors phenomenon and by Stalin's methods of operation. However, why did Stalin succeed in collectivization, despite the resistance of an enormous section of the population and a number of large rebellions? This question cannot be fully answered even today. I believe that Stalin was successful primarily because at the beginning of collectivization a significant part of the population, urban as well as rural, believed in it. And why not believe, if there was an unknown on one hand, while on the other hand experienced propagandists extolled the future? In this vision of the future, agriculture would be controlled by science; every farm would have excellent machines and use fertilizers; operations would be controlled by agronomists, livestock specialists, and experienced managers; the "idiocy of rural life" (Marx) would be ended; the peasantry would be exposed to culture; and their burden of heavy labor would become much lighter. Even the initial horrors of the suppression of peasant resistance failed to convince everyone. The propagandists recalled the Potato Revolts during the reign of Catherine II, when the peasants were forced to plant potatoes under the supervision of armed soldiers. These potatoes had proved beneficial, and the same would be true of collectivization. Backward people do not comprehend their own good fortune. By the time the whole lie became clear to the absolute majority, it was too late; the resistance of the peasants had been broken.

Stalin's collectivization began in the first months of 1929. Force and threats had coerced 58 percent of the peasant households into *kolkhozes* by March. However, the violent resistance of the peasants forced Stalin to retreat and to place the blame on those who had carried out his will. The retreat was announced in Stalin's writings "Dizzy with Success" and "An Answer to the *Kolhkoz* Comrades," as well as in a letter to the Central Committee entitled "Concerning the Struggle with Distortions of the Party Line in *Kolkhoz* Building." As a result, collectivization fell to 21 percent by September of 1929. For a time, collectivization was at a standstill. After using this "breathing space" to reorganize the control and suppression apparatus, Stalin launched a decisive offensive conducted under the slogan "Total Collectivization Based on the Liquidation of the *Kulaks* as a Class." In the countryside, 5 million peasant households were liquidated. The history of this entire process is full of savage violence against the peasantry. The instruments of this violence were unbridled terror and devastating famine. This famine was deliberately created by the regime in the areas of the most stubborn resistance, that is, in the most prosperous agricultural regions. In a conversation with Churchill at the beginning of the Second World War, Stalin said that collectivization had cost 10 million lives. The entire country was starving, and agriculture was totally destroyed. Some idea of what occurred is provided by the losses in livestock during the period from 1928 through 1932. During these four years overall livestock losses were horses, 52.5 percent; cattle, 31 percent; sheep and goats, 66 percent; pigs, 61.5 percent—several times more than the losses of the First World War and the Civil War combined.

Between 25 million and 27 million people vanished from the countryside. Collectivization cost 10 million lives, but the most enterprising peasants did not wait for direct repression; instead they fled to the construction projects of the First Five-Year Plan. Most of these peasants became *kulaks* precisely because they did know some profession other than farming. Directors of construction projects who needed workers to fulfill their plan would accept the fleeing peasants for work and legalize their situation by issuing primitive documents (the passport system had not yet been initiated). The biographies of both parents of one of the cosmonauts, for example, follow this model. An astonishing paradox was created—the proletariat of the first proletarian state was formed from its most consistent, savage, and uncompromising enemies.

The Stalinist Soviet economic system had been formed by 1937 or at least by the beginning of the Second World War. What had Stalin created with his own hands and intellect during this period, replete as it was with its many social, collective, and individual tragedies? What was created as a result of the terrible struggle within the Party and the loss of millions of lives in "the war against the people" (Yevtushenko)?

These questions are answered in many ways. The official Soviet viewpoint is that the system is a socialist system because all means of production now belong to the people in the form of the state. All bourgeois exploiting classes in the land have been liquidated, and there now exist only two friendly classes, the working class and the *kolkhoz* peasantry (and their affiliated working intelligentsia). The Soviet economic system is the first scientifically organized system in the history of mankind. It is controlled, not by the chaos of the market, but by scientifically based planning. This economy does not have crises or trauma; it is the most progressive economy in history and has led the country from one economic victory to another. The official Soviet version always emphasizes that full harmony of production forces and industrial relations exists in this socialist system.

The official version in its pure form is no longer propagated, although it occasionally finds its way even now into the writings of the most orthodox Stalinists. The official version has been greatly changed by fact and lively economic discussion. However, no one has tried to create a modern official version as a unified whole.

Another version, based on objective consideration of facts and only facts, is almost diametrically opposed to the official Soviet version. The principles of this system have nothing in common with science in general and with economics in particular. The means of production belong, not to the people, but to the elite of a new class. It is a system of both classes and conflicts. These conflicts have many variations. The form and character of production forces do not correspond to the character of industrial relations. The Stalinist economic system while under the leadership of Stalin himself can be defined as Party-police monopolistic voluntarism. Such a definition is based on (1) placing the economy in complete subordination to and at the disposition of the Party elite and Stalin personally; (2) the threat of police terror behind every coercive stimulus for economic activity (the fulfillment of a planned assignment); (3) the existence of a single, nationwide monopolistic authority with the ability to implement monopolistic measures (the turnover tax, for example); and (4) the fact that the economic system was not based on any unified economic theory and was therefore a product of Stalin's will and arbitrary experiments.

A simple comparison of the planned and the actual rates of growth of Soviet industry during the years of the First Five-Year Plan[3] reveals the fantasy and voluntarism involved in compiling these plans. The First Five-Year Plan is no exception in this regard.

Nevertheless, the outbreak of the Second World War quickly demonstrated that the Stalinist system also had significant advantages. The high degree of centralization of control and planning, the large defense industry, and the broad prewar militarization of the economy had a positive effect. Despite the devastation that occurred during the first months of the war, 1,360 plants, including almost all defense industry plants, were evacuated from the occupied regions to the east. They quickly set up operations at their new locations, and from mid 1942 armament production grew without further interruption. Especially rapid growth took place in the Urals (about sevenfold) and in

Kazakhstan. In the final years of the war the Urals produced 40 percent of all armaments. The country was deprived of its chief coal and metallurgical base which produced almost two-thirds of all metal. However, the specific nature of the Soviet system in general and its economy in particular resulted in the Soviet Union's ability to produce more weapons than the Hitlerite bloc. Noneconomic measures imposed on the labor force (forced mobilization) made it possible to replace the labor of millions of men with the labor of women and children. During the war years women accounted for almost 60 percent of all workers, and this fact deserves the closest attention. During the second phase of the war the rapid reconstruction of industry and transport in the regions recaptured from the Germans played a great role in building the Soviet military potential. However, all the successes of the war period, economic as well as military, resulted from the abrupt change in attitudes among most of the population. This change in attitude was caused by German policies during the first year of the war. In the Soviet Union it has only recently been acknowledged that "the moral factor [defense of the homeland against fascism] acquired paramount significance."[4]

There is not the slightest doubt that the Soviet leadership learned an important lesson from the Second World War, that is, that although their centralized system is one of the best military systems, the "moral factor" is even more important.

Reconstruction of the economy, which was begun while the war was still in progress, accelerated as the war drew to an end. However, it took three years (until 1948) to restore industry and transportation to their prewar levels. It has been officially confirmed that agriculture did not attain its prewar level until 1949.

The abrupt cutback in production of commodities during the war years led to financing the war through inflation. According to official data, more than four times as many bank notes were placed in circulation during the war than had been in circulation before the war. Thus a monetary reform was carried out in 1947. Ten old rubles were exchanged for one new ruble, and the prices of retail goods were adjusted accordingly. Three years later (1950), in conjunction with the foreign trade requirements of the Socialist Bloc, the new ruble was backed by gold or, more precisely, expressed in terms of gold. This was the first time in the history of the Soviet system that this had happened.

The Fourth (or first postwar) Five-Year Plan (1946-1950) further restored the economy and provided for its future growth. The plan was fulfilled in general: "As early as the Fourth Five-Year Plan, despite the speed of the restoration process and the significance of industrial growth, there had appeared precisely that inattention to qualitative indicators of our industrial growth that led to the presence of enormous underutilization of resources and to the artificial retardation of the potential rates of development of our industry."[5]

The fifth and last Stalinist five-year plan, which still contained elements of economic restoration, was in effect from 1951 through 1955. The first three years of the Fifth Five-Year Plan, that is until the death of "the Boss," as Stalin was called in the Soviet Union, are characterized as follows, according to the present official version: "The rough planning drafts were not supported by the necessary economic and organizational measures and as a result, it was impossible to fulfill the goals for the first years of the Five-Year Plan. Industry [as it was subsequently established in the July 1955 Plenum of the CPSU Central Committee] was not provided with the proper technical and organizational progress. Even agricultural production marked time for a prolonged period."[6]

With Bulganin's report on the economy, the July 1955 plenum censured Stalin as a manager and economist but in no way touched or changed the Stalinist economic system. The plenum merely provided a forum for the discussion of the issues and problems of the system. The discussion changed neither the system nor its principles of control and planning.

These circumstances, more than any others, provided the reasons that the Sixth Five-Year Plan (1956-1960) was rescinded after three years. It proved even more unsuccessful than the two preceding postwar plans, and it was unable to survive in an atmosphere of discussion and Khrushchevian experimentation. In 1957 the branch principle of industrial organization was discontinued, and in its place the territorial principle was introduced—the *sovnarkhozes*, which in turn became the object of further experimentation until 1965. All of this made economic chaos inevitable.

Although an exact date cannot be fixed, it was during this period that the Stalinist system lost its police character, at least in principle. Administrative measures replaced the pure police repression that during Stalinist times made it necessary to work in accordance with the orders of the system. Instances that would previously have cost the Soviet director or manager his head (literally) now resulted only in administrative punishment. This punishment included dismissal and, in the rarest cases, exclusion from the *nomenklatura* of managerial personnel (listing of Party-sanctioned executives). This had a negative effect on the so-called planning discipline of middle- and lower-level Soviet management.

The last two years of the Sixth Five-Year Plan and the next Five-Year Plan were combined in a single plan, the Seven-Year Plan of 1959-1965. This plan is still the only one of its kind in the history of Soviet planning. The Seven-Year Plan not only attempted to correct accumulated mistakes but also tried to make up for past neglect associated with the expanding scientific and technical revolution in the economy. However, this plan again proved unsuccessful. The March 1964 Plenum of the Central Committee of the CPSU adopted a resolution about the formulation of a new, Seventh Five-Year Plan (1966-1970) and about the fundamental restructuring of the plan for the final two years of the Sixth Five-Year Plan (1964-1965). The October 1964 Plenum of the Central Committee of the CPSU removed Khrushchev from the leadership of the Party for a number of reasons. (Among these reasons economic failures played no small role.) Following the October 1964 Plenum, Khrushchev's nearly ten years of economic activity received a new and honest evaluation. Thus *Ekonomicheskaia gazeta* wrote: "The urge to solve a number of problems of building communism by reorganization causes great damage. The management system for the national economy must have a firm scientific foundation. It is important that elements of subjectivism in this sector be completely eliminated."[7]

Throughout the postwar years, experimentation took place not only in industry but also in agriculture, which became greatly distorted during Khrushchev's time. Despite all these experiments, the principles of organization and management of the system remained unchanged. These principles became officially known as administrative, and it is apparent that one of the most important economic lessons that the Soviet leadership learned from the postwar period is the following: "Is it possible to improve production and the quality of commodities and to generally move ahead using administrative methods? Yes, it is possible. Proof of this is the successes of our industry. . . . Yet what an ineffective way this is!"[8]

It is for precisely this reason that the reform begun by the new leadership at the September 1965 Plenum of the Central Committee of the CPSU made its overall goal to replace the administrative principles of management by economic principles. However, the administrative principles were not actually replaced; the reform measures went only halfway and were inconsequential. Concerning the "hidden reserves" of the economy on which so many hopes had been placed, the reform made it possible to use only the surface reserves without touching the deep reserves of technical and technological progress and the improvement of product quality. After the first few years, the momentum of the reform subsided.

At the same time, Brezhnev's report on the state of the economy at the December 1969 Plenum of the CPSU Central Committee was never published. At that time the report served as the basis and the reason for a letter addressed to all workers of the USSR. This was the first time in the history of the Soviet regime that such a letter had been signed by the CPSU Central Committee, the Council of Ministers of the USSR, the VTsSPS (the leadership of the Soviet trade unions) and the Central Committee of the VLKSM (*Komsomol*). From the "nationwide discussion" of the letter at the beginning of 1970, it was evident that the letter appealed to the workers to improve their work quantitatively and qualitatively, to observe the strictest economy in all aspects, to strengthen and expand socialist competition, and to strengthen work discipline at all levels. From the continuing reform all that can be ascertained about the letter is that it presents a Stalinist-Khrushchevian recurrence of wordy exhortations instead of the creation of economically effective measures.

As expected, the Soviet leadership learned a significant and by no means final lesson during the years of the economic reform. The meaning of the lesson may be reduced to the following: the demands of time and circumstances cannot be postponed or ignored with impunity. The long-standing Soviet experience with total centralization and control conflicted with both demands. The problem consisted of finding a balance between a rational measure of centralization on the one hand and economic freedom on the other. However, experience warns that economic freedom involves political freedom. How can the two be combined? Where must the border be drawn and the barrier erected? There are no answers. Recent experience shows that it is no longer possible to control a huge, complex economic system by decrees alone. It is necessary to have some economic stimulus, a certain self-regulation and self-stimulation of economic activities and processes, all of which are mutually reconciled within a unified economic concept. "Under present-day conditions such mutual regulation may occur only when based on monetary and commodity relationships."[9] The campaign for gradual improvement (*uluchshenchestvo*) that the Soviet leadership had been conducting in the economy during recent years was a complete fiasco.

The leaders of the CPSU cannot avoid searching for answers to these problems. Whatever may be said or written to the contrary in the USSR, the economic teachings of Marx have been found bankrupt in practice and have been debunked in theory in the Soviet Union. The anathematized idea of convergence of the systems impedes widespread adoption of the experience of modern-day capitalism. Who in the inter-Party struggle would dare open himself to the charge of being in the employ of capitalism? The most complex issues must be solved anew; most important, the psychological barriers, which are openly discussed in the USSR, must be overcome. It is necessary to retreat cautiously under the pressure of events as they develop and to adopt "capitalist" experience even more cautiously.

All these circumstances are developing in such a way that the further formation or reformation of the Soviet economic system will be essentially a product of the economic impressions formed by Soviet Party leaders on the basis of their individual economic experiences. This is why I devoted particular attention to this question when considering the formation of the Soviet economic system.

The economic problems awaiting solution will determine the fate of the system. Among the various "managerial comrades" are several interpretations of the methods and possibilities for solving them. Therefore the 1980s will undoubtedly be a period of intense inter-Party struggle based essentially on economics, regardless of the nature of its external manifestation.

Problems Arising from Marxist Theory

The classic writers of Marxism did not leave a single finished work on the economic system of socialism. Isolated thoughts on the characteristic features and peculiarities of the new economic form are scattered throughout their writings. The actual creation of socialism took place without an approved plan but with a need for carrying out all their basic instructions.

The creators of the Soviet economy implemented instructions that they found practical. These included the nationalization of production, planned management of the economy, restructuring of agriculture, and the principle of distribution under socialism. However, the instructions given by the classicists concerning the elimination of trade and the conversion to direct distribution based on labor under socialism nearly resulted in disaster toward the end of the War Communism period and were rejected for good. Other instructions—for example, the elimination of the contrasts between city and country and between physical and mental labor, as well as the principle of distribution under communism—not only were never implemented but have never been fully explained. This is one aspect of the problem.

Another aspect results from the fact that the creators of the Soviet economy, and above all Stalin, looked at economic problems through the eyes of Marx, a man who was obsessed with violent criticism of the capitalist market economy. In *Das Kapital* Marx repeatedly emphasized that the economic laws that he had discovered were laws of a capitalist economy and capitalist commodity production only. According to Marx, the basic law of the capitalist economy is the law of surplus value, from which the law of value is derived. Capitalist exploitation is possible only when there is surplus value, and it manifests itself in the capitalist's appropriation of a portion of the surplus value. Surplus value, or profit, is a portion of value that first appears in the market but is created during production. "As a union of the process of labor and the process of creating value, the production process is a process of commodity production. As a union of the process of labor and process of increasing value, it is a *capitalist process of production and a capitalist form of goods production*" (italics mine).[10]

In an attempt to obtain a maximum profit (maximum surplus value) the capitalist tries to lower the cost of producing goods by all means available to him. In particular, "the capitalist makes sure that work is done properly and that the means of production are used efficiently. Therefore, he ensures that raw materials are not wasted and that implements of labor are treated with care, that is, they are expended only as much as is required by their use on the job."[11]

In the end, the market mechanism of a capitalist economy determines the profit norm and its distribution among individual capitalists or groups of capitalists. The craving for personal gain leads to a clash of interests among capitalists in the market economy. This clash creates chaos in market relations. According to Marx, the chief result of chaos in market relations is an increase in the exploitation of labor by the capitalist.

It is now evident that in his approach to building socialism, Stalin spurned Marxist teachings on capitalism. Soviet socialist production, in principle and in contrast to the capitalist version, is not a commodity production system; for this reason, the laws of commodity production discovered by Marx do not apply to it. Under socialism, as is well known, there is no exploitation of man by man. Socialist production has no surplus value and therefore does not need to strive for a maximum profit. Consequently, under socialism the law of surplus value has no place, and as a result neither does the law of value. On the strength of this logic all value categories were discarded—optimal production cost (the minimum attainable), cost, price, profit. This is how its creators looked at the situation: the socialist system must produce material goods (products) but need not consider how much it costs to produce them or how profitable this production is.

Thus, on the one hand, the laws of commodity production discovered by Marx were not suitable, in Stalin's view, for socialist production in general and for socialist commodity production in particular. On the other hand, every economic system must have economic laws, and if the classic writers of Marxism did *not* formulate the economic laws of socialism, then someone would have to discover and formulate them. Stalin assumed this responsibility and created a number of "laws" for the socialist system. One of them, the law of balanced proportional growth, is still alive today.

In the early 1960s, the Institute of Economics of the Academy of Sciences, USSR, evaluated the meaning, nature, and consequences of Stalin's activities in economic theory and science as follows:

> Having started down the path of libertarianism and arbitrariness in running the economy, having grossly violated the demands of economic laws, having personally invented dogmas contradictory to the demands of life, Stalin did not want to admit the determining influence of economic science on practice and even tried to substantiate his position by an erroneous juxtaposition of socialist political economy with scientific planning and economic policy.[12]

> He simply postulated his own theses as the infallible truth, demanding no proof. He did not support these theses with either economic calculations or a deep and comprehensive analysis of actual practice, or with any amount of detailed argumentation.[13]

> And all this was presented as program directives, which needed only rapturous commentary and the broadest propaganda. It was presented as a major "scientific discovery." Many of Stalin's theses were directed at theoretically justifying and concealing the gross deficiencies in actual economic practice.

> Despite magnificent personal declarations about the importance of objective laws, arbitrary rule and libertarianism showed a marked increase in the last years of Stalin's life, as did a tendency toward adventuristic directives in economics.[14]

Dogmas and disregard for value categories always led to enormous wastes of materials and manpower. This was felt as early as the 1930s. However, the situation was tolerable because of the following circumstances:

1. The country was undergoing the initial, comparatively primitive stages of its development after a number of years of devastation and was lacking all types of products.
2. Production links in industry were still relatively simple and lent themselves more readily to review, guidance, and planning.
3. The country possessed enormous labor resources with its many millions of peasants. However, the low skill level of this labor force created severe problems from the very beginning of the five-year plans.
4. The turnover tax, which was introduced in January of 1930, provided the government with enormous monetary resources. The high rate of assessment provided the government with unencumbered revenues through the process of goods reproduction. The revenues could be used for any type of capital investment or to indemnify any losses.

However, just before World War II, the problem of low economic efficiency began to bother economists and economic managers. The idea was advanced in 1940 that commodity production in the USSR must also adhere to the Marxist laws of commodity production. Of course, the war brought to a halt the realization of an economic system unique to the USSR. However, during the postwar rebuilding of the economy, the problem of falling economic efficiency arose with a new, significantly greater and threatening force. Its acuteness was emphasized drastically by the following:

1. The significant growth and increasing complexity of the economy led to complications in production links, to a growing complexity in planning and management, and to a growing lag between both planning and management and the demands of reality.
2. Labor resources were clearly being exhausted. This was attributed not only to economic growth and losses suffered during the war but also to the waste of labor that arose from not taking value categories into account.
3. The new technological revolution which had begun in the West around 1950 showed that in its average technological level the USSR was falling further and further behind other leading countries. At the same time, it became obvious that the technological revolution itself was the product of calculating value categories and that its final goal was an increase in the efficiency of the economy.

Under the pressure of circumstances, Stalin had to acknowledge that Marx's law of value and the law of commodity production existed in the Soviet economy.

"In this regard, problems such as the question of economic estimates and profitability, production costs, prices, etc., are of pressing significance for our enterprises," wrote Stalin in his last pamphlet, *Economic Problems of Socialism in the USSR* (p. 20).

Stalin's vague and extremely general formulations hindered the further development of new ideas until the July 1955 Plenum of the Central Committee.

The July 1955 plenum marked the start of the economic discussion which has continued to this day. An end to this discussion is still not in sight, since the problems around which the discussion has centered have still not been resolved. Much of the discussion is already history; much has lost its former urgency and significance. Therefore, I shall examine only the main points and basic ideas of the discussion and their evolution.

Stalin's dogmas in economic theory left in their wake, not merely a vacuum, but a certain negative value. One has to begin a discussion of economics by reestablishing the elementary concepts, by turning them right side up again. Thus, as a counterforce to the dogmas, it was established that an economic law objectively exists outside our consciousness and acts automatically, independent of the desires of the participants in the economic activity. Cognizance of the law and an ability to use the automatic nature of its action is the only way to attain real success in economics. No peculiarities or exceptions in socialist economies, such as Stalin always pointed out, can exclude the action of universal and general economic laws in the socialist economy.[15]

Expressing the predominant point of view among Soviet economists, Strumilin maintained that a more universal, general law is the law of conservation of work time. Setting this law against the strong-willed and administrative nature of the Soviet economy, Strumilin emphasized that "this law of conservation does not need the sanctions of external coercion, since it itself contains internal stimuli."[16] These stimuli consist of the opportunity to create more physical assets per unit of time and to create an abundance. Insofar as socialism, in its current interpretation, equals abundance, Strumilin maintained that the law of conservation of work time is particularly important under socialism.

In a complex economic system, conservation of work time can be achieved only by measuring the expenditure of various types of labor in attaining the same economic effect by various methods. The only way to measure and compare the expenditures of labor that differ in character, qualification, and other indicators is by measuring them in monetary terms (expenditures for wages, cost of labor). In this regard the law of conservation of work time comes close to Marx's law of labor value.

After the all-union conference concerning the problems of the law of value in 1957, the view was finally established that the law of value is a universal law of economics, that it has existed for five thousand to seven thousand years, beginning with the fall of primitive society and ending with socialism.[17] Since the law of value was accepted as a law of the market economy, the idea of establishing an "automatic mechanism of market relations" in the Soviet Union could be expressed for the first time at this conference.

During the course of the discussion, it became increasingly clear to Soviet economists that the labor concept of value (Marx's concept) gave no answers to very important questions in economic practice. Following this theory, the supposedly cost-free status of the country's natural resources leads to the squandering of those resources. In mining industries, mineral losses underground reach enormous proportions; complex minerals are used inefficiently. The same thing happens with timber resources and arable land. The word *labor* disappears from the name of the Marxist law. Furthermore, if the law of value explains commodity production, it is not able to grasp the entire mechanism of commodity-monetary relationships in the market economy. Since Marx defined his law as a law of the market economy, Soviet economists concentrate their attention on the effect of the market mechanism and on the problems of establishing prices.

The market mechanism and its effect are depicted by Soviet economists to a considerable extent according to Marxist theory, and they deliberately simplify it to the extreme. However, one should not think that they do not comprehend the complexity of the real market and are not familiar with non-Marxist theories. The problem is not one of a lack of information or knowledge. The primitive and somewhat idealized market scheme that they have created pursues well-defined objectives.

First, there is no market in the Soviet economy, and there are no market relationships. Generations of Soviet citizens are unfamiliar with these concepts; thus, they must be explained in a simple and comprehensible manner. The idea of a market must become the domain not only of managers and economists but also of the mass population, for "an idea once grasped by the masses becomes a force in reality."

Second, the idea that the market mechanism represents the only absolutely indispensable instrument of economic activity in the entire history of mankind must be affirmed and popularized. It has to exist irrespective of ideological or sociopolitical concepts that form the basis of a given society or its government.

The third objective is to use the scheme of a market as a standard for comparing and monitoring, as well as for criticizing the theory and practice of the present Soviet economy. The existence of a blueprint frees Soviet economists from a dangerous comparison of the Soviet system with the capitalist market system and gives them a theoretical basis for and an integrated concept of the contrasts between the two systems.

There is reason to believe that the proponents of the market concept are having success in dealing with the problems before them. It is directly due to their influence that "the sharp rise in interest in economic problems is considered one of the more significant phenomena of recent times." This sharp rise in interest contains dangerous notions from the Party leadership's point of view. Chief among them is the notion that "the economist must be guided in his work by that mechanism that will, first, give him complete information on consumer interests and, second, quickly and automatically correct mistakes made in planning. Currently the only such mechanism is the market commodity-monetary mechanism."[18]

From the Soviet leadership's point of view, there is an even more dangerous by-product of this entire process—the destruction of the myth about the scientific nature of the Soviet economic system and about economic planning in its contemporary form.

Based on different economic views, two opposing groups exist in the USSR today. Neither one opposes planning or the necessity of allowing for economic laws. The argument concerns which concept should be dominant and definitive.

The larger group, which is better trained in both scientific and general terms, includes almost all the economic scientists. Their opponents call this group "the marketeers" (*rynochniki*), a more or less scornful nickname in Soviet circles. The smaller group, which includes the political and economic leaders of the country, has been scoffingly called "the improvers" (*uluchshentsy*) by the first group. (In the 1960s the majority of the resolutions of the CPSU Central Committee and the USSR Council of Ministers began with the words: "Concerning improvements. . . .")

The first group generally summarizes the Soviet economic system by saying, "As experience shows, the normal operation of an economic organism under conditions of strict centralized planning cannot currently provide a radical solution to the economic and social problems facing socialist society."[19] The viewpoint of the second group is basically: "The methods of planned economic management developed through a half century of experience have stood the test of time and need not be changed. We should only talk about perfecting these methods."[20]

Strictly speaking, the argument involves the requisite optimal combination of plan and market. The first group attempts to prove it necessary for commodity monetary relationships and the market to be predominant over the plan. The second group states its viewpoint in this way: "The ideological and Party content of planning is a manifestation of its scientific nature."[21] This group insists on preserving the absolute predominance of the directive plan over commodity-monetary relationships and limits planning-market relationships to the sphere of internal trade. This viewpoint is not well-founded and is not shared by a large segment of those interested in economic problems. But the proponents of this view hold the power in their hands. For this reason alone, they were victorious at the All-Union Economic Conference in 1968.[22]

Over time the viewpoint of the first group has attracted more and more followers, and by 1965-1966 it had gained wide popularity. The realities of Soviet life in general and of economic life in particular accelerated this process. By demanding basic, logical, and consistent changes in the economy [for example, Nemchinov's system of "self-supporting" (*khozraschet*) socialism or the Liberman proposals], these viewpoints formed a new, very critical view of the existing economic system and formed objectionable new concepts and moods. M. Roshchin's story, "From Morning 'til Night" (*S utra do nochi*), characterizes them very well.

> No matter what type of people got together or where ... no matter how the conversation got started ... in the end they got around to the hue and cry about what was going on and when it would be settled. Doctors complained about their own problems; engineers complained about theirs. Teachers, workers, journalists, even the military, no matter who it was—each one told of some sort of nonsense and everyone's spirits were low. Everyone saw and understood the disorder; everyone knew how to make it better. Everyone saw, but could do little. Of these people, the strong ones boiled with rage. The weak ones generally gave it up for a lost cause. "To hell with it all! It's no use. You can't fight City Hall!" It was as if some sort of god were over everything. What they say is true; a higher thought binds everyone hand and foot. A god is over everything, and you can't get rid of him.[23]

This phenomenon reached frightening proportions and content. The Soviet leadership, it seems, did not understand the current situation and tried the old methods, bringing back bad memories of the Zhdanov era. Ideological suppression on the one hand and dogmatic brainwashing on the other are the principles of this method.

By late 1966 the Press Committee of the USSR Council of Ministers, the censorship organ of the CPSU, scrutinized the activities of the Ekonomika publishing house and practically prohibited it from discussing the most important questions concerning theories of the Soviet economy.[24] However, the marketeers were able to get around the prohibition formally. The process was slowed but not stopped. The second blow to the marketeers was struck in 1967 by a resolution of the CPSU Central Committee, "Measures for the Further Development of Social Sciences and for Increasing Their Role in the Building of Communism."[25] However, the ideas of the marketeers continued to catch on among the populace. To counter this, in the second half of 1971 the Central Committee passed a resolution, "Improvements in the Economic Education of the Worker."[26] The resolution provided for the general involvement of the adult population of the USSR in economic "education." Designs of typical model lesson plans for a system of economic education can be divided into two basic groups: for management personnel (four different levels) and for all other workers.[27] Lesson plans for management personnel, amounting to a vindication of the existing system, included certain elements pertaining to raising qualifications. The course material for all other workers, "Foundations of Economic Knowledge," was almost exclusively a simplified vindication of the present system in various aspects and viewed from various angles. Problems were not treated. Even the most superficial examination of the course materials showed that their chief, if not only, aim was to drive economic freethinking from the workers' minds by filling them with orthodox economic "science."

Finally, in December 1971 the leaders of the CPSU felt it necessary to strike a blow against the chief pocket of marketeers within the Institute of Economics of the Academy of Sciences.

The resolution of the Central Committee, "The Function of the Party Organization of the Institute of the USSR Academy of Sciences in Carrying Out the Resolution of the CPSU Central Committee, 'Measures for the Further Development of Social Sciences and for Increasing Their Role in the Building of Communism,' " tried to depict events as a natural consequence of the 1967 Central Committee resolution. However, a brief summary of the content of this resolution does not support that stand, and the fact that a new resolution was published raises a number of questions. First, it was passed in December 1971 but was not published in the Party's central press organ (*Pravda*); and it was not until January (possibly due to technical reasons, although this is unlikely) that it appeared in *Kommunist*. Even then it was not a complete text but only an abridged descriptive account. Second, not until February 1972 did the same text appear in the journal *Voprosy ekonomiki* (the institute's press organ) with the comment, "Reprinted from the text of *Kommunist*, no. 1, 1972." The questions arise: Since when can the Academy of Sciences *not* publish a resolution of the Central Committee until two months after the fact? What circumstances or which forces made this possible? How did the editors of *Voprosy ekonomiki* dare to make this significant comment about the reprint? Finally, why did the Central Committee itself deem it necessary not to publish the full text of the resolution? Putting this all together in light of what has taken place in the Soviet economy, one may ask one more question: Has the "economic reform" spent itself, and is the position of its creators as strong as it seems? These questions are all the more justified in view of the fact that in 1973 it was "difficult to name another economic problem that evokes as many differences of opinion and differing viewpoints as the problem of commodity production and the effects of the law of value under socialism. *It has been and remains the center of attention of Soviet economists*" (italics mine).[28]

Prior to the appearance of the resolution, according to the official version, "serious mistakes of a theoretical nature" had been made in "certain books and articles published by employees of the institute."[29] The resolution obliges the institute's Party organization to "remove said deficiencies," among which was "serious neglect in the selection, placement, and use of personnel." Along with other assignments, the Presidium of the Academy of Sciences was charged with "straightening out the structure of the institute." The institute underwent a purge, and their neglect in the placement of personnel would be corrected by promoting orthodox Party members to positions of leadership. These events signified an attempt to destroy sources of lively economic thinking in the country. The institute's press organ was cut back from more than 200 pages to 160 and the orthodox *Planovoe khoziaistvo* was increased from 60-80 pages to 160 pages.

Under sober scrutiny, all these measures by the Soviet leadership seem void of logic. The original cause for economic discussion with its new theories, as well as the source of the mood and opinion of broad circles of the populace, is the

Soviet economy itself and this economy in action. In this discussion we find the source of intellectual contacts among moods, an evaluation of the present economic system, and new economic theories. An attempt to stifle analytical, critical, inquisitive thought obviously only worsens the situation. First, a certain spin-off will disappear, such as minor improvements (a review of prices, the all-union goods classification system, partial implementation of computers). Second, an answer to the people's question, and just when will this be corrected? will be eliminated or postponed indefinitely. All this is part of the prerequisite, according to the predominant conviction, that the only barriers in the road to this "correction" are artificial, psychological ones. "Overcoming Psychological Barriers" is the headline of an article in *Novyi mir*. The barriers are actually in the minds of Soviet leaders ("decision makers").

Notes

1. *Bor'ba*, no. 1-2 (1951):7-8.
2. *Directives of the CPSU and the Soviet Government* 1 (1957):614.
3. See *Planovoe khoziaistvo,* no. 9 (1967):69.
4. Ibid., p. 74.
5. *History of the National Economy of the USSR*, pp. 206-207.
6. Ibid., p. 219.
7. *Ekonomicheskaia gazeta,* no. 1 (1965):3.
8. *Oktiabr'*, no. 8 (1966):173-174.
9. "Overcoming the Psychological Barrier," *Novyi mir,* no. 2 (1971):151.
10. *Das Kapital,* vol. 1 (Moscow: Sotsekiz, 1931), p. 135.
11. Ibid., pp. 125-126.
12. *Voprosy ekonomiki,* no. 11 (1962):5.
13. Ibid., p. 7.
14. Ibid., p. 5.
15. Refer to articles by Corresponding Member of the Academy of Sciences A. Pashkov, in *Voprosy ekonomiki,* no. 9 (1960):19, and in the compilation *Problems in the Political Economy of Socialism* (Moscow: Gospolitizdat, 1960), p. 33.
16. *Vosprosy Ekonomiki,* no. 7 (1959):124.
17. Ibid., no. 9 (1960):21.
18. *Novyi mir,* no. 8 (1970): pp. 167, 184.
19. "Overcoming the Psychological Barrier," p. 151.
20. *Planovoe khoziaistvo,* no. 10 (1968):77.
21. Ibid., 75.
22. Ibid., 77.
23. *Novyi mir,* no. 8 (1967):97.
24. *Planovoe khoziaistvo,* no. 3 (1967):94.

25. *Voprosy ekonomiki,* no. 9 (1967).

26. *Pravda,* 16 September 1971, p. 1.

27. See *Ekonomicheskaia gazeta,* no. 5 (1972):7-8; no. 6, pp. 7-8; also no. 7, p. 10.

28. *Planovoe khoziaistvo,* no. 1 (1973):142.

29. *Voprosy ekonomiki,* no. 2 (1972):4.

2

The Soviet View of the Market Economy

This will not be a discussion of the theory of market economy or of the operation of the market mechanism in general. I would just like to describe in more detail the simplified and somewhat idealized abstraction of the market economy that has been created by Soviet economists. This abstraction is only an instrument for understanding the present-day Soviet economic system and, most important, the problems facing it.

Commodity Production

When starting production, the manufacturer must first decide which product he will produce and at what consumer value he will produce it in order to be successful in the market. The consumer value of a product is not an expression of value. It is an abstract concept, defined as a product's degree of usefulness for a consumer, under the assumption that its usefulness must be optimal. The optimal consumer value is logically connected to a series of questions, including the final market price. Obviously, a product that has no consumer value should not be produced. But it is just as senseless to manufacture a refrigerator that will last only one year as it is to make a woman's dress projected for six years' wear. In addition there is the problem of quality categories for products, and all these problems are viewed in light of the market prospects of the product.

After this difficult and sometimes risky decision, the manufacturer calculates the production cost of the product; that is, he determines the cost of manufacturing the product. This calculation involves many expenses, but all of them can be divided into two groups: the first is *external supplies,* that is, everything that comes from outside sources, for example, raw materials, semifinished goods, items for assembly, and energy. The second group is *internal expenses,* for example, wages, depreciation, tools, auxiliary materials, and administrative and marketing expenditures.

On the one hand, the unit cost of expenses is determined by the market, since unit cost shows the market price, which the manufacturer is powerless to change. On the other hand, in order to maximize profit and increase his competitive position, the manufacturer strives for minimal production costs. External supplies can be decreased only by well-considered conservation or by replacing old, expensive materials with new, cheaper ones. Internal expenses can be lowered only by improving technology, equipment, and organization, both in the manufacturing process and in the management system. Expenditures for labor (the extent of labor used and its cost) must be as small as possible. Thus, for commodity production in a market economy, the very laws of commodity production automatically ensure uninterrupted scientific-technical progress of production in all its sectors, as well as an economical and rational use of materials and manpower. From a purely economic standpoint, it is most important that the production cost be as low as possible under any given conditions; in other words, it must be optimal.

Based on the production cost obtained, the manufacturer makes a percentage computation of added costs, which represent taxes, marketing costs, average rate of profit, and other costs. The rate of these extra charges is determined basically by government legislation and to a degree depends on the rationality of the social and governmental structure. As a result of these computations, the manufacturer arrives at the value of his product, and since the rate of extra charges on the optimal production cost is determined objectively by established conditions, the value determined by the manufacturer is also optimal. Thus, production cost forms the basis for value, and both of these value categories are created during the production process. They operate during the manufacture of all products and determine the comparability of the cost of producing various types of goods. However, at the same time, the value represents a calculated price, and when selling the goods at this price, the manufacturer receives an average rate of profit in a given economy.

The Market Mechanism

A product whose value has been determined enters the market and becomes subject to the market mechanism. The chief manifestation and tools of this mechanism are supply and demand, along with competition. The market mechanism sets the final price of the product, which usually differs from its value. If the price is lower than the value, the manufacturer-marketeer receives a below-average profit.

When the price is set below the value of the goods, the financial difficulties that arise can threaten the manufacturer or firm with bankruptcy. If this situation spreads to an entire sector (*otrasl'*) of industry, production is curtailed and the process of withdrawing capital from this sector begins. The sector decreases production to a level corresponding to the demand for its goods. When the price is above the value, individual enterprises boom and receive additional material stimulation (superprofits). The entire sector of industry has a chance to reinvest part of its superprofits, and free capital is directed toward it. The sector expands to a level of production that corresponds to the demand for its products. The result of this process is the formation of proportions in the economy. These proportions correspond to demands, forming optimal, socially necessary proportions.

Thus, the market itself is a businesslike mechanism. It is necessary for activity in any economic system, and according to the skillful definition of Soviet economists, it creates a self-adjusting, automatic system of market relationships. This mechanism leads to both gains and losses, the magnitudes of which depend largely on the awareness of and the ability to deal with this mechanism. As years of experience in economic activities have proved, the most important thing is for gains to exceed losses, for the final symbol of operations to be a plus sign.

The chief instrument by which the market fulfills its function as an automatic regulator of economic activity is the deviation of price from value. The automatic mechanism leads to deviations of price from value in both directions, striving toward a reduction of the gap between price and value. When the deviation is negative this narrowing occurs either by reducing production to the level of demand or by further optimizing a product's use value and by increasing demand for it. When there is a positive deviation, the price-value gap can be narrowed through competition that ensures a rise in production to the level of demand.

The supply and demand mechanism makes the automatic system of market relationships very flexible in solving the problem of production and resources. Every manufacturing process quickly receives its necessary resources. The necessary amount of resources is provided for by rapid changes in the structure, nature, and rates of production.

An automatic system of market relationships cannot exist without competition. Any monopoly that excludes competition destroys the automatic market system, bringing immense negative factors and losses to the economy and leading inevitably to technical and technological stagnation. An automatic system of market relationships is just as impossible without a free play of supply and demand for both traditional and new goods. Without this free play of market forces, the formation of optimal national economic proportions is inconceivable.

The Functions of Prices

Prices developed by the market mechanism, as current Soviet economics maintains, assume three main functions: stimulative, accounting, and allocating. Only the accounting function is a function exclusively of price; the other two come about as a result of the deviation of price from value. But the term *price function,* which has become deeply rooted in economic science and literature, also includes this phenomenon.

The stimulative function of prices is demonstrated by the fact that higher stimulation (profit) is attained by the manufacturer who can minimize the cost for his goods, including production cost, and whose goods have reached the optimal use value in their group. Under any circumstances, the manufacturer who minimizes the cost of a product is the one who has most efficiently organized its manufacture. Under present conditions, efficient organization is impossible without broad scientific research in production, without continual improvement in technology, equipment, and organization of the production process, and without rational management and utilization of manpower. The national economic effect of the stimulative function is that every manufacturing process proceeds under optimal conditions, thus increasing the effectiveness of the national economy to the optimum.

The accounting function of prices determines the possibility for an efficient exchange of goods, since the manufacture of all goods is based on the principle of reducing expenditures to the minimal socially necessary (or optimal) level. Second, only this function permits calculations of the optimum in all economic undertakings, which includes decisions in economic planning, distribution of capital investment, and calculations of the optimal production cost. Last, this function makes it possible to compare the effectiveness of various types of expenditures for socially necessary labor. This analysis can be made on a national scale in both the productive and nonproductive spheres.

The allocating function of prices expresses itself in the allocation of man-hours in relationship to social demands. In the production sphere (that is, in the economy as a whole), the allocating function of prices formulates optimal proportions in the national economy. In the regional aspect of the economy, the role of the allocating function includes the formation of optimal complexity of the regional economy. This role is greater the more a given economy, or government, or economic bloc of governments is organized territorially, and the more natural-geographical, ethnographic, and other peculiarities differentiate economic regions from one another.

These three inseparable functions of prices exert an absolute determining influence on the productive sphere of the economy. In the nonproductive sphere (government, management, social organizations), prices are not the only determinants, but they are nevertheless an important influence on the number of man-hours expended and the distribution of social man-hours among sectors of the nonproductive sphere.

Soviet economics has often emphasized that prices developed by the market mechanism contain indecipherable information as well as information that cannot be separated into its individual factors. This information allows one to decide the products to manufacture, the value level (the limits of socially necessary expenditures of labor), the levels of production, and the level of use value at which it pays to manufacture a product at a given time. Second, a price, which contains an enormous amount of economic information, reflects the actual processes at work in the economy. This actual reflection is an indispensable condition for the use of market prices in economic estimates made with computers. No economy or system of price determination allows one to translate into machine language all the factors in a complex economic decision, but market prices and the entire market mechanism represent a system of self-regulation that eliminates gross miscalculations and corrects all other miscalculations. To minimize potential miscalculations, the market economy has the price mechanism as well as many other means, including psychological means (advertisements or influence on taste and style).

Planning in the Market Economy

The market economy has employed planning in making decisions on both current and, to an even greater extent, future problems. In fact, long-range planning was developed in the market economy systems and not in the so-called classic planned-economy systems, where economic prognostication was created from the bottom up. Cursory examination of the historical process led to rash conclusions concerning replacement of the market mechanism by a planning mechanism and gave birth to the notorious theory of convergence. On the other hand, a deliberately unconscientious examination of this phenomenon is used as one more piece of evidence in favor of the inevitable victory of the socialist "planned" system over the capitalist system.

Neither is correct. A plan in a market economy is put into effect by the market mechanism. It is monitored and corrected by the market mechanism and therefore always strives toward the optimum. Only government investments in a market economy bear any resemblance to a directive; as such, they sharply lower the optimizing influence of the market mechanism. Examples of this influence are the enormous losses and mistakes that result from economic assignments by various governments. Nevertheless, planning in a market economy does not make it a planned economy, nor does it transform the economy into an instrument for fulfilling a plan full of directives, as is the case under a socialist system. External resemblance does not signify blood relationship. In the socialist economy planning results in directives and is a dominant factor. If there is also a market, then the directives govern the market and monitor it. In comparison with planning in a market economy, directive planning is planning turned upside down. This is the actual starting point of the theory of convergence.

3 National Economic Planning in General

General Principles

A general theoretical principle of a socialist economy is that "inherently, the single goal of a socialist economy is development. This involves maximum satisfaction of social needs (an increase in well-being and the creation of conditions for the unimpeded and complete development of the individual, but applicable to all members of society). This maximizing of the satisfaction of social needs is the highest criterion in evaluating the effectiveness of social productivity."[1] However, as we shall see, this principle is not reflected in economic practice.

The law actually in effect in a socialist economy is the law of systematic proportional development. The concept of the way that it functions has been modified in the past few years. A more up-to-date and orthodox description of this law and the way it functions was put forth by L. Abalkin.[2] His description was aimed specifically at fulfilling the resolution of the CPSU Central Committee about improving the economic education of the worker. Abalkin writes:

> As you know, the law of systematic proportional development of the national economy is in effect in a socialist economy. Does this law implement itself regardless of planning and guidance? Absolutely not! Planning can prove more or less complete. It can either completely or relatively poorly take into account progressive changes in science and technology and foresee necessary changes in the structure of production sectors. Depending on these factors, this law will be implemented for better or for worse. However, if there is no planning, the law loses its force, and the economy will begin to develop spontaneously. To allow laws to exist without the effect of human activity is the same as hoping that the economy will develop systematically even without planning.[3]

The following questions naturally arise: Can an objective law lose its force? And if this is possible, is it really a law? Who governs whom? Does the law of systematic proportional development govern planning, or is this law governed by planning, the planning organs, and above all by the State Planning Commission (*Gosplan*) as it fulfills the will of the CPSU leadership? These questions are answered by both actual practice and a group of documents, of which I shall point out only two.

1. A report on a *Gosplan* conference attended by A.N. Kosygin, who, in less than flattering terms, evaluated some of the most important features of *Gosplan*'s work.[4]
2. A report on *Gosplan,* order no. 35 of 18 April 1972. The order establishes the general requirements for *Gosplan* departments. Each requirement refers to *perfection, improvement,* or *increased efficiency.* Eight additional paragraphs, consisting of fifty subparagraphs, explain the general requirements in detail. Only one of these, paragraph VI-3, does not mention *perfection.*[5]

Realizing the precariousness of his theoretical position in light of actual practice, one author contends that "economics today is faced with the task of a higher synthesis [or 'the negation of a negation']. Theoretically, it must give meaning to a combination of objective economic laws and human activities to make these laws reality and to draw the necessary practical conclusions from this combination.... We cannot repeal the law of value. [Although] economic laws by their very nature are objective, independent of the will and wishes of the people, planning organizations determine and correct proportions and checks and balances ... we plan and perfect prices."[6]

Thus (and this is confirmed both by actual practice in management and by hundreds of sources in Soviet economic periodicals), the socialist system lacks general principles based on objective economic laws. The system lacks instruments of internal self-regulation and self-adjustment or any sort of automatic system of optimizing economic decisions and actions. This does not mean that other principles are also lacking. They exist, but they are not of an economic nature and they function without coordination, both for and against the interests of the Soviet economic system and the policy that determines the path of the Soviet economy.

The Price Mechanism in a Planned Economy

Prices in the Soviet Union are also planned, or, more exactly, established arbitrarily. Lately, however, certain restrictions have been placed on arbitrary price setting.

In explaining the level of various prices in the 1967 reform, the chairman of the State Pricing Committee, V.K. Sitin, correctly noted that "we cannot build a price system in a vacuum. New coal prices are 1 1/2 times higher than the world price. If the price of coal were raised not by 78 percent but by 360 percent, prices in Soviet heavy industry would have nothing in common with either world prices or prices in the other socialist countries. In such a case, many price problems in foreign trade between socialist countries would never be solved." The necessity to take world market prices into consideration in all foreign trade is the chief limiting factor in the free establishment of prices. Here, too, is an internal "price reaction." Having set prices for coal that are high but nevertheless lower than cost, one has to set completely artificial prices for possible replacements for coal. Therefore, prices "for petroleum and natural gas are set with the idea of bringing the low prices for these products up to the price of coal."[7] The explanation is that all calculations of efficiency are made according to the price-list prices. Maximum efficiency is required, which means the use of minimum prices. However, the strained fuel balance of the Soviet Union, for now at least, does not allow it to stop using coal.

The system and method of price establishment would be very complicated if an attempt were made to show the whole picture. Therefore, I shall dwell only on the main points. The price policy forms the basis for establishing prices. Under this policy, prices for the means of production are set lower than cost, and prices on consumer goods are set higher than cost.[8]

The price policy is actually put into practice with the aid of extra-charge coefficients which are added to the cost (for example, 0.8, 1.0, or 1.3). These are applied either to a sector of industry as a whole or to a group of goods. "The basic methodological principle presently in use in establishing prices is that the *branch-average cost of production* serves as a basis for prices" (italics mine). But distortions occur even in the process of calculating production cost. V. Dyachenko counts six groups of expenditures that go into calculations of production cost in distorted form. The chief one is "the variance between production cost calculations for means of production and their actual cost."[9]

The method of setting prices makes it impossible to compare wholesale industrial prices. The turnover tax is figured on these wholesale prices and is reflected mainly in the prices of consumer goods (72 percent of all taxes collected in 1970).[10] As a result, "it becomes even more difficult for consumers to compare prices."[11] In summary, Soviet price-list prices (prices for industry) and retail prices for goods do not express socially necessary expenditures (in other words, economic reality) proportionally, nor are they conducive to comparison.

Many organizations are involved in the actual setting of prices. The *Ekonomicheskaia gazeta* mentions eleven levels of organizations.[12] Of course, prices for the more important items are always set by all-union organizations. The situation had become so complicated that in December of 1969 the State Pricing Committee of *Gosplan* was reorganized into the Union-Republic State Pricing Committee under the Council of Ministers.[13] This "promotion" not only increased the importance of the committee and broadened its rights and perspectives but also placed the chief price-setting organizations of the union republics under its direct subordination. However, the centralization of the price-setting and price-monitoring mechanism does not change the essence of the problem. Even after this streamlining took place, it took "months" to go through "thirteen to fifteen different offices to set the price on a new product." If the "grand total of all the different prices currently approaches 10 million," and if "a large portion of the pricing information is still processed by hand" or with the aid of primitive machines, one can easily imagine the unwieldy structure and inflexibility of the entire system.[14]

Planned prices have already undergone several reforms. The most important was the wholesale-industrial price reform of 1967. This was followed by a series of supplementary reviews and addenda. The reforms did not substantially change planned prices. In the opinion of Chairman of the State Pricing Committee V.K. Sitin, "the prices in effect do not meet the demands of the economy in many ways and need further improvement." Sitin feels that "in the meantime, *the chief method of correcting prices remains the introduction of certain corrections into the price list*" (Sitin's italics).[15] More radical economists feel that "in order to accomplish economic reform, prices must approach socially necessary labor expenditures to an increasingly greater extent."[16] Others propose a stepped price system, which will promote technical progress and a rise in product quality.

Price setting for agricultural products does not differ greatly from price setting for industrial products. Unfounded and arbitrary practices in price setting are just as common in agriculture, and "the marketing of many agricultural products at current prices does not cover socially necessary expenditures. The production of several of them continues to operate at a loss."[17] On the other hand, the cultivation of many crops (sunflowers, grapes, and practically all grains) is unjustifiably profitable. In dealing with the selling prices for agricultural products, one must consider the balance of income and expenses for *kolkhozes* and *sovkhozes* in a totally self-supporting operation. One must also consider political factors such as the mood of the populace.

There are also many problems with prices for transportation services (tariffs). The greatest problem is that transportation costs for some goods are included in the price-list price (free-on-board at receiving station), while for others the costs are added to the price (free-on-board at shipper's station). In many other cases, the rates are lower than actual shipping costs, and there is no clear or direct connection between the difficulties in shipping certain loads and the remuneration for them.

Still another important peculiarity of the planned method of setting prices is that this method is theoretically based on Marx's labor theory of value. According to this theory, value is determined only by labor expenses in actual production. In principle, anything that is not produced by human labor cannot have a value and therefore cannot be assigned a price. By this logic, all natural resources and lands in the Soviet Union—all forest resources, arable land, and minerals—are free. In a planned economy, only the cost of exploiting these resources is considered.

Having described the principles, methods, and organization of the planned method of price setting, I shall try to formulate the basic characteristics and internal qualities of planned prices. I shall also try to reach a conclusion about the degree of suitability of planned prices for normal economic activities.

Economic development is regulated and guided by economic planning. At the same time, the law of value operates in a planned socialist economy. On this basis, "it is improper to either underestimate or overestimate the regulatory role of market relationships under socialism."[18] This interdependence, the chief requirement recognized by everyone, determines the necessity for first-rate economic decision making, both in planning and in management. All similar decisions can be made only on the basis of a price assessment. However, planned prices, as the Soviet scientist N.N. Novozhilov, pointed out, "contain far less economic information than they are supposed to according to the law of value and the theory of optimum planning. Prices do not tell an enterprise what it should produce, what the quality should be, or what the limit of socially necessary expenditures in production is. The very lack of prices for material resources means that prices do not explain how to use production inventories, working capital, and natural resources, nor what the minimum level of profitability of their use should be." However, planned prices have their own information, which "often differs from the plan directives." This divergence demands that the directive be reinforced by sanctions. Be that as it may, planned prices with their information are included in planning estimates and create an illusion of correctness. As a result, "a mistake in the principles of planned price setting is the source of massive miscalculations and losses."[19] This mistake is the source of great economic conflict arising from the difference between social, governmental, group, and private economic interests. The consequences are the social problems that obliged the Soviet leadership to discuss social-economic planning at the Twenty-fourth Party Congress.

Planned prices do not fulfill any of the functions that should be inherent in them according to the law of value. This characteristic expresses itself repeatedly, and almost always negatively, in all economic activity because in reality consumer goods are subject to a market economy and their manufacture should be subject to the effects of the law of value. Products used by the state and distributed through a supply system only on a governmentwide or national economic scale are not and cannot be considered commodities. However, at the highest distribution level (between ministries and departments) and down to the producers, these products are commodities of a specific distribution market with all its consequences. Economic reforms have already strengthened the influence of this fact with the requirement for a completely self-supporting production operation.

Later I shall return repeatedly to the problems of planned price setting in relation to various facets of economic activity in order to explain its influence on a given sector of the Soviet economy. This planned price-setting procedure is the basic cause of general disproportions in the national economy. These disproportions occur between industry and agriculture; within industry, they occur between groups. At the same time, it is universally recognized that unbalanced development must be eliminated "to do away with some of the losses suffered by the national economy."[20] Planned prices do not reflect economic reality, because they contain distorted economic data. Planned prices are unsuitable for economic estimates made through computer processing. While it is still possible to adjust planned prices through manual processing of valuable economic estimates, machine solutions yield errors of unknown proportions and plus-or-minus deviation.

A discussion of the problems of planned price setting more than fifteen years ago led the Institute of Economics of the Academy of Science to conclude that "the main political and economic problems of the Soviet state revolve around the question of prices."[21] Only when the Soviet leadership carries a clearly expressed protectionist policy toward some branch of industry or group of industries (for example, the defense industry) does planned price setting play a definitive role. By setting prices for this industry significantly lower than cost, the Soviet leadership creates the fiction of low prices or very high efficiency in the use of products from this industry and thus artifically forces its development. This is what took place with the price of natural gas and the construction of gas pipelines.

Notes

1. *Voprosy ekonomiki,* no. 10 (1967):116.
2. "Aids for the Economic Education of the Worker," in *Planovoe khoziaistvo,* no. 12 (1972).
3. *Planovoe khoziaistvo,* no. 12 (1972):77-78.
4. Ibid., no. 11 (1972):7.
5. Ibid., no. 7 (1972):153-157.
6. Ibid., no. 12 (1972):78.
7. *Voprosy ekonomiki,* no. 5 (1968):29-30; *Planovoe khoziaistvo,* no. 9 (1972):47.
8. *Voprosy ekonomiki,* no. 2 (1969):93; also *Planovoe khoziaistvo,* no. 10 (1969):31.
9. *Voprosy ekonomiki,* no. 3 (1970):57; no. 2 (1963):48.
10. Ibid., no. 1 (1970):48.
11. Ibid., no. 11 (1969):66.
12. *Ekonomicheskaia gazeta,* no. 39 (September 1969):8.
13. *Pravda,* 31 December 1969, p. 3.
14. Ibid., 10 July 1970, p. 1; *Ekonomicheskaia gazeta,* no. 5 (1972):9.
15. *Ekonomicheskaia gazeta,* no. 11 (1970):5.
16. *Voprosy ekonomiki,* no. 3 (1972):41.
17. *Voprosy ekonomiki,* no. 1 (1970):68.
18. *Planovoe khoziaistvo,* no. 11 (1965):6.
19. *Ekonomika i matematicheskie metody,* no. 3 (1966):328, 338.
20. *Planovoe khoziaistvo,* no. 2 (1968):60.
21. *Voprosy ekonomiki,* no. 11 (1962), lead article.

4

National Economic Planning in the Soviet Union

General Comments

The planning of an entire national economy (and here I shall discuss only economic planning) is a key element in its development. If it is possible to draw a parallel to a market economy, then it is planning that must perform all functions performed by a market mechanism. Moreover, a plan, at least as expounded in theory, should perform these functions better, more scientifically, more purposefully, and more harmoniously.

The very nature of the problems in an economy reveals the complexity and magnitude of the work involved in national economic planning. Therefore, in this section I shall speak almost exclusively about the planning of industrial production and shall return to planning in other areas of the economy later in this book. The planning of industrial production in itself has many complicated and contradictory problems. Production planning is only part of the process, for it is inseparably linked with the planning of resources. The complete process is a delicate and controversial question in national economic planning and is rarely mentioned in Soviet sources. It is almost never examined as a unified, interconnected process. I shall devote serious attention to this problem.

The plan created by national economic planning is the primary instrument that puts the Soviet economy into motion in all of its operations and manifestations. The internal peculiarities of the plan determine everything in a decisive manner.

National economic planning in the USSR has been total in scope for some time. First, it encompasses all economic life. It is characterized by complete centralization of control and management according to the Party-spirit principle, or the unity of politics and economics. "Plans for the development of the national economy are drawn up in accordance with basic regulations of policy and directives of CPSU congresses, which spell out the policy of the Communist Party of the USSR. Policy regulations of basic Party documents establish goals for the national economic plans, set the structure of the economy, and provide guidelines for the use of society's resources."[1] Second, national economic planning is absolute; under the influence of the demands and conditions spelled out in the plan, the principles of economic activity and the actions of those who execute policy are made almost completely uniform. As a result, economic activity is uniform at all levels in the economic hierarchy. This is true even when external factors may appear completely different. Third, planning is fully centralized within itself. A low-ranking planning or economic organization has practically no legal recourse to exert influence on a higher-ranking organization. The higher-ranking organizations, however, have the legal authority to abrogate the decision of a lower-ranking organization and then to dictate their own decision.

A production plan is not important just because it determines the day-to-day activity and perspective of the economy and is primarily an economic document. Even more important, while created by Party directive, at a certain point it becomes a state law, with all the attendant consequences. The primary consequence is that the nonfulfillment of a plan is a crime, a violation of the Party's will.

National economic planning is officially considered the practical expression of the law of balanced and proportional development. Earlier I discussed the extent to which this corresponds to reality. Planning is considered scientific in that "society's need for material and spiritual happiness necessary for the total development of the individual is scientifically substantiated in the plan, as are the needs of current production, capital construction, and scientific work for material, labor, and financial resources and society's needs in the realm of control, defense, and the state's foreign policy."[2] This same source provides a long list of topics that are either "under study" or are "subject to scientific basis." This official definition of planning deserves close attention so that we may later compare and analyze several problems.

Modern political economics of socialism firmly establishes that the primary indicator of a system's progress is the uninterrupted growth "of material and spiritual happiness necessary for the total development of the individual"; thus a change in terminology has taken place. Before the Twenty-fourth Party Congress, the adjectives *national economic* and *economic* were applied to planning; but since the Twenty-fourth Congress, the term *social economic* planning has been used more frequently.

Historical Development

The State Commission for the Electrification of Russia (GOERLO), which was formed in 1920 under the direct control of Lenin, must be considered the first plan in Soviet history. No matter how insignificant it may seem, it was the first long-term plan. Today this fact allows the Soviets to proclaim that "the scientific principles of planning were first developed by Lenin."[3] It is also officially felt that GOERLO was the forerunner of modern planning. This is absolutely untrue because modern principles and methods of planning came into existence much later, without the slightest noticeable influence from the ideas and people who drew up the GOERLO plan.

Gosplan was created in February of 1921, and the gradual strengthening of the planning principle in Soviet economics began at this time. A new stage in the development of planning took place, both qualitatively and methodologically, in the period 1928 to 1932 when the First Five-Year Plan was developed and introduced. The principles and methods of this type of plan, preserved with no significant changes in the ten-year plans, were Stalinist principles and methods. Today these principles and methods are known as directives. These principles and methods, which Stalin created and enforced by means of terror, worked much better under him than they do today. The great post-Stalin "ameliorating" activity in the field of planning has not yet led to the slightest conformity of Stalinist methods to the present needs of the national economy.

The principles of the five-year plan, the annual operational plans, and the omnipotence and uncontrollability of *Gosplan* with regard to all lower-ranking organizations were formulated under Stalin. The *branch principle* of planning, which still exists, was formed at this time. The concept is that plans are worked out in branches (*otrasl'*) or in offices (*vedomstvo*) (for this reason this planning principle is also known as the *office principle*), starting at the enterprise and reaching the ministry level. The final plan is then submitted to the branch department of *Gosplan*, USSR. During the formation of planning under Stalin, *Gosplan* became one of the most important links in the functioning of the Soviet economy. From the beginning of economic discussion, the work done by *Gosplan* has been subjected to sharp criticism. Kosygin's speech at a *Gosplan* conference toward the end of 1972 is only one of many recent examples.[4]

Planning Organizations

Soviet planning organizations can be divided into two groups: state planning organizations and branch planning organizations (figure 4-1).

State planning organizations are structured on a territorial basis, but they preserve the branch internal structure, particularly at the higher levels. The state planning organizations include USSR *Gosplan,* union-republic *Gosplans*, district (*krai*), *oblast'*, region (*raion*), and city planning commissions. Only the USSR *Gosplan* and the union-republic *Gosplans* are considered central planning organizations; all other levels of planning commissions are considered local planning organizations. The entire *Gosplan* system has a union-republic structure, that is, the union-republic *Gosplans* are subordinate directly to the USSR *Gosplan* as well as to the council of ministers of the appropriate republic. USSR *Gosplan* is subordinate directly to the USSR Council of Ministers.

The branch planning organizations include the planning economic departments of the ministries, the chief directorates (*glavk*), the directorates (*upravlenie*), the trusts (*trest*), the associations (*ob"edinenie*), and the plants (*predpriiatie*). Each branch organization plans exclusively for its own branch.

The union of these two groups of planning with the branch principle means that the work of the local planning commissions and that of the branch planning organizations in the same area are essentially uncoordinated. The chairman of the Brest *Oblast'* Planning Commission complains that "it has come to the point where we learn about the union offices' plan for the *oblast'* only from data provided by the statistics directorate after the first quarter has already ended."[5]

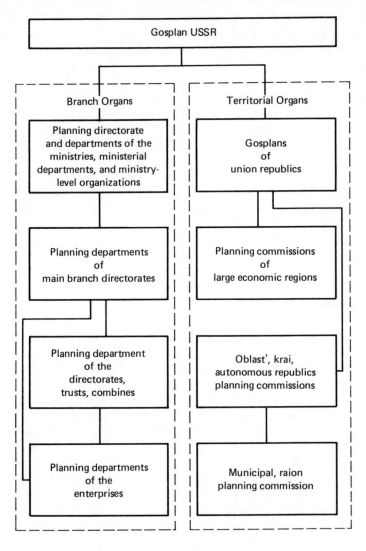

Figure 4-1. The Planning Organs

Types of Plans

The totality of planning, the fact that it encompasses all aspects of economic activity, naturally gives rise to many different plans. First, plans must pass through many people and organizations; this in itself means that a huge list of ministries, offices, and special state tasks (target plans) is compiled. A second reason for the large number of plans is related to the period of time that plans are in effect.

All this means that a large number of organizations, not part of the system and not subordinate to planning organs, are brought into the planning process. Here I have in mind such organizations as the various committees of the USSR Council of Ministers, the Ministry of Finances, and the State Bank. The state planning organizations receive the results of the planning work of all these organizations (especially *Gosplan*, USSR) in the most general form. *Gosplan* always retains the right to change and correct any of these plans; but in principle the sum of the plans represents a logical unity, which is defined by the unity of the nation's economic organism. Therefore, the coordination of all these elements, which appears disjointed but is logically connected, is a primary and essential condition. This includes the initial organizational technical requirement for correct planning. However, just balancing all the parts of the plan does not solve the most important problem: increasing the effectiveness of the Soviet economy. This can be solved only when the national economic plan becomes optimal. However, "not just any balanced plan is optimal. It becomes optimal when it ensures a proportional development of the economy by the most effective use of available resources and increased labor productivity and when the production of goods corresponds to public demands for them," writes Kovalev, the chief of the computer center of *Gosplan*, USSR.[6] Optimal planning is the primary problem officially recognized in the entire planning system.

The influence of new ideas and economic requirements has led to changes in the periods of time covered in plans and the interaction between them. At one time, economic forecasting was rejected as a "bourgeois false science," but today more attention is being given to it, at least in economics. Long-term plans have been an exception and have generally concerned only some branch or group of branches. Five-year plans bear some similarity to national economic long-term plans, but annual changes to the five-year plan violate its integrity and frequently change its general trend. Today "long-term plans are worked out on a centralized basis for fifteen years and are then broken down into five-year periods; the five-year plans, the basic kind of long-term plans, are then broken down into yearly periods. Five-year and yearly plans are compiled at all levels, from the plant and production association to the national economy as a whole. Plans for the extended future are developed at the level of the USSR and the union-republics. They are also developed at the level of branches of the national economy, the production interbranches and production-territorial complexes, the large economic regions, and the branches of industry."[7] In this way, the outlook is increased, and the internal intercommunication and interdependence of time plans are reinforced.

Of all these time plans, however, only the yearly plan is an operational plan. It is put together in the same sections as a five-year plan but in significantly more detail. Only this plan includes complete material balances, earmarked to match resources and amounts of production, as stipulated in the plan. Only in an operational plan is the most important section included: the plan for material-technical supply. A yearly plan is divided into quarters (three-month periods) and months.

Although both the five-year plan and the yearly plan are confirmed by the Soviet government and thereby have the power of law, the five-year plan is a law for compliance and general management. The yearly plan is a law for action and is compulsory for everyone involved in economic activity.

The yearly operational plan tells all plants what must be done. To show how the task will be accomplished, the plant writes up its own internal plan, the technical-industrial financial plan (*Tekpromfin Plan*), which is a detailed plan for production-technical and financial-economic activity. The technical-industrial financial plan is made up of many sections and indicators (a large machine building plant uses about forty thousand indicators) and is often broken down by department and shop. To summarize, the technical-industrial financial plan must answer the question, How will the task outlined in the yearly plan be completed?

Planning Indicators

The measuring devices for planning tasks are called planning indicators. These can be cost indicators, that is, estimates of what it will cost to produce a particular product, or physical indicators. There is a fairly wide range of physical indicators, and when possible, they are adapted to the type of production or to the job at hand. Physical indicators include items, weight, length, area, volume, or a combination of these. For example, one of the most important indicators in transportation and shipping is the weight per unit distance of the goods being shipped.

For many years gross output volume, expressed in rubles, was the primary indicator. This indicator is known as a multiple indicator, meaning that it passes through the entire national economic system from *Gosplan* to the plant. This indicator has made it possible to use various measures that are "economically not expedient but advantageous for creating the illusion of well-being and for exceeding the gross output plan." In conjunction with other conditions this indicator has opened up "additional loopholes for disguising and falsifying the actual state of affairs relevant to the fulfillment of economic plans."[8]

Therefore, the economic reform of 1965 came up with a new multiple indicator, the volume of market output, which is expressed in cost. However, in the muddle of a centralized distribution and inadequate supply for the basic mass output, this indicator has not lived up to expectations. "Just as any other cost indicator, it promotes production that is advantageous for the enterprise to the detriment of less advantageous production that is necessary for the national economy and the populace."[9] However, this failing is characteristic of all cost indicators and stems from the Soviet system of price setting in planning.

This new indicator has not led to the anticipated increase in output quality or to the discontinuance of combining lists of manufactured articles according to the principle of "advantageous or disadvantageous"; neither has it led to an increase in the production of new and technically better output.

The unsatisfactory nature of the realized output indicators led to the introduction in 1974 of a new multiple indicator, the volume of normative net output. "This indicator is based on stable norms which are, in turn, based on operating wholesale prices by subtracting material expenditures from the wholesale prices. Similar to 'gross output' and other such indicators, 'net output' is a cost gradient. However, it differs from them in that it represents only a newly created cost."[10]

It is still too early to judge how this new indicator will be reflected in planning and economic practice, but it has many of the shortcomings inherent in all Soviet price indicators. It is also supposed to strengthen the economic significance of the labor productivity indicator, particularly for associations and plants.[11]

The economic reform reduced to nine the number of indicators for which the enterprises must obtain approval from higher authority.[12] Before the reform, there were anywhere from twenty-two to thirty-six or more, depending on the branch of production. However, besides the direct indicators, there are several indirect indicators. For example, in the creation of a wage fund, the old volume of gross output is established.[13] As D. L'vov asserts, "The tendency to increase the number of central indicators with which the enterprises must work has increased noticeably in recent times."[14]

The second main indicator is the list of manufactured articles (*nomen-klatura izdelii*), which is expressed in the actual number of units of a given output. The most important output having economic significance includes nomenclature indicators. "Altogether, a centralized plan is confirmed for the production and distribution of approximately forty thousand kinds of industrial output."[15] This planning indicator is particularly important when it comes to compiling material balances.

The nature and results of a branch's work depends to a large extent on the unit (meter, ton) chosen to measure the physical indicator. Often the indicator selected has a negative effect on the branch's work (for example, the ton in metallurgy). Physical indicators are an attempt to improve this situation; however, the process of improvement is very slow.

When discussing all planning indicators, most Soviet economists conclude that "no matter how good the system of indicators may be, it cannot provide the necessary effect unless something is also done to improve price setting."[16] Only in this manner can the practice of dividing output into "advantageous" and "disadvantageous" be eliminated, and can goods-currency relations influence output quality.

Planning Methods

"The resource-branch principle completely dominates" national economic planning methods. ("From 1957 through 1965, this was known as the resource-territorial principle.") The balanced planning of the output of resources and products, as well as the provision of resources and raw material, equipment, and labor force, is based on this principle. This balanced planning is derived from branch projections.[17]

The following basic balances are now compiled: the labor-resource balance, material balance, financial balance, and a national economic summary balance.[18] The summary balance has been drawn up only twice, for the year 1959 and for the year 1966 (in 1968, two years after the fact).

Of particular importance are the material balances compiled in both physical and cost expressions. "The products list by which *Gosplan*, USSR, works out material balances and yearly plans of distribution . . . consists of . . . approximately nineteen hundred designators."[19] The number of the various material balances developed by *Gosplan* and *Gossnab* (State Committee for Material-Technical Supply) exceeds fifteen thousand."[20]

The Plan in Theory

"The planning of the USSR's national economy, as in all the Soviet government's economic organizational activity, is determined and controlled by the Communist Party, the leading force of our society."[21] This is why the initial data for drawing up five-year plans are CPSU directives. The Twenty-fourth CPSU Congress provided the directives for the Ninth Five-Year Plan. Control figures representing (with some variation) a portion of the assignments outlined in these directives, covering the year being planned, are used to compile yearly plans. These documents express the Party's wishes regarding economic development; the documents are prepared by the economic departments of the CPSU Central Committee.

Along with the document that outlines the desires is a document that indicates the realistic ability of the national economy to fulfill the stated desires. This document, the national economic estimate, is prepared by the USSR Central Statistics Directorate.

After comparing and analyzing these two documents in conjunction with the absolute priority of the control figures, the USSR *Gosplan* issues instructions for the preparation of the yearly operational plan. These instructions are very general; they show only the main trends and rates of development according to the plan's basic indicators. Along with the instructions, *Gosplan* distributes forms (tables) for preparing the plan. These instructions and forms are supposed to facilitate the process of planning and make all plans uniform. However, as is self-evident, standardized forms cannot reflect the diversity of the branches or plants. Therefore, every plant appends an explanatory note to its forms, indicating the plant's unique features and its specific situation for the year being planned. This explanatory note is usually more voluminous than all the forms, that is, more voluminous than the plan itself.

The compilation of the yearly operational production plan begins as soon as the plant completes its forms and writes its explanatory note, that is, when it prepares its draft plan. This process ordinarily starts in June of the year preceding the year being planned. A plant's draft plan is drawn up using price and physical indicators. There are so many physical indicators in this plan that they virtually cover the entire list of the main manufactured articles produced by a given plant.

The plant passes its draft plan to a higher-ranking organization. After receiving plans from all its subordinate organizations, the planning department of this organization summarizes these plans in its own national economic draft plan. The plans of the lower-ranking organizations are broken down and synthesized in this new plan. In this process, the lower-ranking organization "coordinates" its plan with the higher-ranking organization. This coordination represents the foundation and justification of a proposed plan before a higher-ranking organization or authority; the higher-ranking authority has the right to make a final decision, a decision that cannot be appealed.

In this manner, the draft plan moves from one rung of the departmental ladder to the next. As a draft plan goes higher, physical indicators disappear from it, and an increasingly larger part of output is expressed in cost. The final branch plan is formulated by the appropriate ministry.

The plans of the ministries and the union-republic *Gosplans* then go to the USSR *Gosplan* where they serve as the basis for the preparation of a single national economic plan. It is at this phase of the planning process that other organizations, not subordinate to *Gosplan,* become involved. This involvement creates significant difficulties in coordinating individual parts of the plan. Through mutual efforts and coordination, a final national economic plan comes into being. Formally, the plan is still a draft plan, but in practice it is never changed.

The completed draft plan is then sent to the USSR Council of Ministers for examination. It is confirmed by the USSR Supreme Soviet and the Council of Nationalities. This process converts the draft plan into a plan-law.

The plan-law now moves downward through the same stages that the draft plan moved upward. At each level, the plan-law is distributed among the executors, who give their "approval." As the plan-law descends, more and more physical indicators reappear, and many price indicators disappear. At the plant level, the physical indicators are again specified in order to catalogue the list of the main manufactured articles. Later these indicators serve as the basis for concluding agreements with other plants for delivery of finished output.

The shuffling of plans upward and downward and the "coordination" and "approving" in the planning process all take place with "no unified system for the legal regulation of national economic planning." At the same time, "the sequence for coordinating a plan's sections and indicators and for eliminating possible violations in a given area is not stipulated by legislation."[22] These problems introduce additional difficulties in the planning sequence and thus lead to many conflicts.

Notes

1. *Voprosy ekonomiki,* no. 12 (1972):112-113.
2. Ibid., p. 113.
3. Ibid., p. 112.
4. *Planovoe khoziaistvo,* no. 11 (1972):7.
5. *Ekonomicheskaia gazeta,* no. 24 (June 1968):9.
6. *Planovoe khoziaistvo,* no. 5 (1970):35.
7. *Voprosy ekonomiki,* no. 12 (1972):116.
8. *Planovoe khoziaistvo,* no. 7 (1961):6.
9. Ibid., no. 8 (1971):50, subsector chief of *Gosplan,* USSR, D. Ukrainsky.
10. *Ekonomicheskaia gazeta,* no. 12 (May 1974):13.
11. *Planovoe khoziaistvo,* no. 3 (1974):9.
12. See *Ekonomicheskaia gazeta,* no. 2 (January 1969):36.
13. See *Voprosy ekonomiki,* no. 9 (1969):83; also *Planovoe khoziaistvo,* no. 5 (1971):27.
14. *Planovoe khoziaistvo,* no. 5, (1971):27.
15. Ibid., no. 3 (1968):12.
16. Ibid., no. 9 (1969):83.
17. *Voprosy ekonomiki,* no. 3 (1971):17, Academician Fedorenko and E. Mainimas.
18. Ibid., no. 10 (1961):61.
19. *Planovoe khoziaistvo,* no. 7 (1969):5.

20. *Voprosy ekonomiki,* no. 2 (1970):124.
21. *Planovoe khoziaistvo,* no. 2 (1971):13.
22. Ibid., no. 8 (1971):124, 62.

5   The Plan in Practice

General Comments

In all its manifestations, planning in practice is considerably different and more complicated than the idealized official version. First, "there is a basic contradiction in our economic theory and practice. We all realize that the goal of socialist production is to best satisfy the needs of the total development of the individual, as well as to create the conditions for that development. However, when it comes time to implement economic and other measures, we are never directly governed by this goal," writes A.G. Aganbegian.[1] "In our opinion the starting point for a national economic plan must be tied directly to the ultimate goal of socialist production."[2] In practice no such tie exists.

Planning has been lagging behind the requirements of a developing and increasingly complicated economy. Its forms, methods, and traditions belong to the mid 1930s, when it was first organized. The majority of Soviet economists believe that planning in its present form is unable to solve the Soviet government's economic and social problems. "The entire system presently in effect for developing and confirming plans is cumbersome, labor-consuming, and time-consuming."[3] The system has acquired a way of doing things "in general" and "on the average." It has acquired a style of "scholasticism, of remote abstractions, of too broad figures."[4] "In essence, planning bears the characteristics of an art form [by which] the overwhelming part of planning procedures . . . is based on the individual know-how, experience, knowledge, and intuition of the planner." Thus, with the introduction of mathematical methods into economics, "electronic computers and economic mathematical methods have proved incompatible with the existing sequence of planning." In each of the organizations helping to prepare the national economic plan, each "planner has his own things to add to the plan, either an indicator or a group of indicators. There is almost no specialization in basic production."[5] Departmentalization (*vedomstvennost'*), which makes it impossible to balance a plan even at the highest level, stems from this. A.N. Kosygin is justified in demanding that "the departmental approach to working out state plans be totally eliminated."[6]

Radical changes are needed, and the sooner the better. However, complicated obstacles stand in the way. The tragedy is that these planning problems cannot possibly be resolved within the framework of present-day principles and the existing organization of Soviet economics.

Planning must be a process for economic decision making, directed at raising

49

the effectiveness of the national economy. In other words, optimal decisions must be made which result in an optimal plan. This is at least in theory the primary task of planning.

The national economic plan and the planning process have been put in the position of having to solve all the main economic problems of the Soviet government. Included here are optimal national economic, territorial, inter-branch, and intrabranch proportions; the direction and rate of scientific-technical, technological, and organizational-directoral progress; questions concerning the placement of branches, industrial complexes, and plants; problems dealing with a more complex use of natural and other resources, as well as many analogous matters that determine the effectiveness of the national economy.

An optimal solution for all these problems is possible only by thorough analysis and comparison of many plausible solutions. The most effective solution is then selected and calculated in cost expressions reflecting economic reality. However, planned price setting makes such calculations impossible. As early as 1967, the late Strumilin noted that "an increase in the effectiveness of national economic planning is, without doubt, becoming the most important problem in economics." However, to increase effectiveness and to introduce electronic computers and economic mathematical methods, "we must first completely eliminate the confusion in price setting that causes prices to deviate from their cost base by tenths or even hundredths of a percent. Until that time, and as long as even initial data for planning tasks and long-term prognoses are so unreliable, the far-reaching conclusions that result from them cannot be reliable. Even the most sophisticated electronic computers will not make them more precise."[7]

In this regard, Khachaturov points out that "we are still unable to compile an optimal plan with electronic computers, and I do not know when we shall be able to do so."[8]

Therefore, "in economic practice indicators are used to measure the effectiveness of a plant, a branch, and all material production [and, it follows, to measure the effectiveness of decisions being made for the future]. However, by using these indicators, it is almost impossible to measure the results of the work of a plant, and it is certainly impossible to compare the results of the activity of two or more enterprises or branches."[9]

Khrushchev, understanding the illusory nature of such calculations in day-to-day planning practice, stated that "the rates of development of individual branches and economic regions are based on developed proportions, or at times on 'visual methods' alone."[10] The practice of compiling plans based on "developed proportions" and "the attained level" means that required growth percentages are added to the attained production level. Kosygin had precisely this practice in mind when he said that "the statistical approach to solving even the most important matters very often predominates" in *Gosplan.*[11]

Crucial changes in plans, such as new trends in development, the appearance of new branches, or a change in proportions, always have either a "subjective" nature or are an imitation of some foreign development. There are dozens of examples of subjectivness, the influence of which even Baibakov, the chairman of *Gosplan,* has cited.[12] Here I have in mind the imposition of the "leader's" will on a plan. Many examples of crucial changes under the influence of foreign developments (largely those of the United States) might also be cited.

Such are the practical and real starting points of planning. The absence of any scientific basis is an important, though not the only, reason that "plants must use caution in formulating and executing a plan."[13] Everyone who compiles and must later fulfill plans is cautious. This is true up to the ministerial level.

Coordinating the Parts of a Plan

Coordination is based on two main premises. First, many high-level organizations participate in the formulation of a national economic plan. Each of them pursues its own departmental interests. Moreover, each is influenced by its own special situation. Second, the planning organizations themselves, and especially *Gosplan* are structured according to the branch principle. Inter-*Gosplan* departmentalization has led to a situation in which "not a single *Gosplan* department is responsible for coordinating tasks."[14] Furthermore, *Gosplan* "branch departments have become 'small ministries' of their own. Their workers are concerned only with their own branch and do not wish to think of anything else."[15] This intolerable situation is repeatedly discussed from many angles. Some Soviet economists feel that coordination and balance are carried out at the highest level of planning; others deny such thinking. At a USSR *Gosplan* conference, A.N. Kosygin shared the point of view of the latter group.

Of course, there are balancing departments within *Gosplan* which enjoy equal footing with branch organs, but they work with data and information provided by the branch organs. In the end, the balances are compiled. However, as the chief of a *Gosplan* department, N. Lebedinsky points out, such balances are "nonoptimal balances." As an illustration, Lebedinsky presents data showing that in accordance with the plan, there is an overproduction of 10 million to 15 million tons of cement per year, because of a bad transportation and storage system as well as the backwardness of the building industry.[16] Similar examples of "nonoptimal balancing" could be cited for nearly any other branch of Soviet industry. At the same time, "the greater the use of such methods for balancing plans, the lower the effectiveness of public production."[17]

Such is the very tangled beginning by which many organizations are linked in the process of ever-continuing coordination. Coordination moves downward from level to level within the organizational planning structure. In a discussion of optimal planning, R.O. Khalfina takes the position that plans are fully coordinated at the highest level. He states that "plans are balanced at the

RICHARD G. COX LIBRARY
UN. OF SOUTHERN MISS.—GULF PARK

Gosplan level, then pass through a multitude of levels, both subordinate to one another and independent. They arrive at a plant as separate, unbalanced plans which are then corrected by adding funds, orders, and so forth."[18]

As we shall see later, at no level of planning is there a balance between production and material-technical supply. Frequently there is no balance between production and financing. This lack of balance presupposes that the planning leadership's management is of a production-control nature rather than a scientific nature and that corrections to a plan appear almost as soon as the plan itself. The absence of coordination and balancing is another important reason that prompts future executors of plans to compile scaled-down plans for themselves and not to reveal their so-called hidden reserves under any circumstance. Thus, even several years after the economic reform, Deputy Chairman of *Gosplan* Bachurin admits, "This year, as in previous years, the ministries have presented *Gosplan* with reduced plans for production volumes and other economic indicators."[19]

No amount of subsequent correction to a plan during its execution can make it more balanced, more coordinated, or more complete. "So many corrections are made to a plan that by the end of the year, the plan is in no way the plan that was put together by the planning organizations or the one which was confirmed by other organizations."[20] Figure 5-1 shows how a plan is coordinated.

Technology and the Use of Labor

The technology of planning, as E.Z. Maiminas and many other sources point out, has come to the point that "the process is 'manufactured': it is based on manual labor . . . the automation of labor has been poorly developed and is based almost exclusively on the use of simple computing devices used as individual units. Electronic computers operate 'above the line.' "[21] This results in "enormous labor expenditures for making planning calculations and large expenditures of time to arrive at a single version of a calculation. In many cases, it is impossible to make the necessary calculations in the allotted period of time. . . . The result is single-variant planning which requires a great deal of time for plan development. Because of inadequate analysis of the dynamics of economic development, subjective evaluations can creep into the plan. This has a negative effect on the development of the entire economy."[22] Khachaturov also alludes to the single-variant problem in modern-day planning.[23]

Because of the enormous labor expenditures and the impossibility of automating planning calculations, a great many people are involved in planning. There are about 135,000 people working in the USSR *Gosplan* system alone.[24] Several million people work in planning organizations, and more than 10 million people work in planning, calculation, and administration.[25] The number of people working in these areas is constantly increasing, a fact not readily

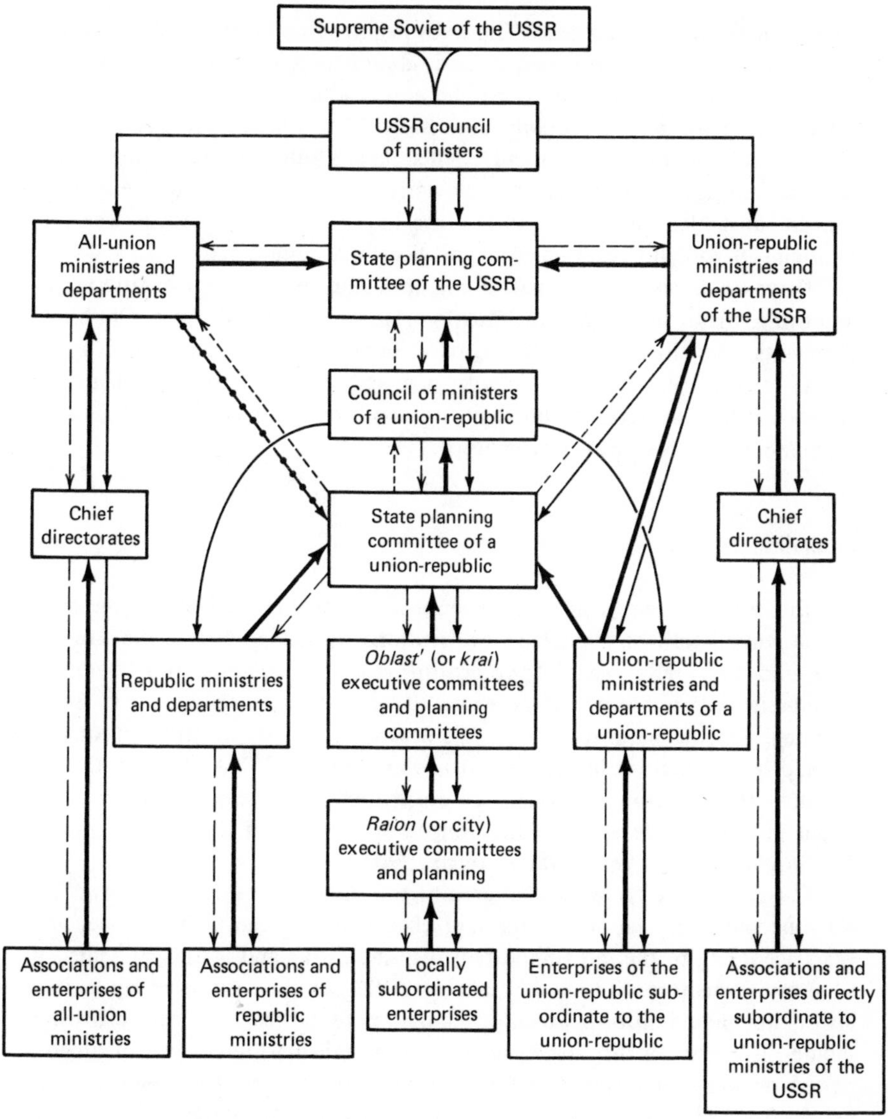

— — → Tasks of directives according to the five-year plan or control figures according to the annual plan

━━▶ Projects of the plan

•••••▶ Copies of the projects of the plans for USSR ministries for economic units spread across the territory of the union-republic

——▶ Ratification of the plan

- - - -> Proposals of the republic state planning committee according to the project of the plans of the USSR ministries

Figure 5-1. Coordination of the Plan

discernible from Soviet statistics. Glushkov believes that "if the level of technical equipment in planning, calculation, and administration remains as is, with no decrease in quality, then by 1980 the entire adult population of the Soviet Union will have to be working in this field."[26] Of course, this is only a demonstration of the general trend, cited as an absurdity. Increasing the number of people engaged in planning will only worsen planning because of the resultant increase in subjective errors made by the larger number of people. The only solution is to switch to econometrics and electronic computers.

However, if one accepts that raising optimality is the ultimate criterion for improving planning, then the situation has not changed since Glushkov's comments. The chief of the USSR *Gosplan* computer center, Kovalev, feels that "some economists have incorrectly asserted that economic-mathematical methods and computer technology are used by planning organizations in conjunction with the optimality concept."[27]

Compiling the Plan

"As the result of long years of experience in planning in the USSR, three stages in the compilation of plans have evolved: the overall prognosis, the five-year plan, and the yearly plan."[28] Forecasting was once considered a "bourgeois pseudoscience," but now, of necessity, it has been incorporated into Soviet planning. As Khachaturov puts it, "Forecasting methods are still inadequately developed, and there is limited experience in their use."[29] As a result, the first attempts at even private forecasting were extremely unsuccessful.[30] Work was begun in 1969 to develop the first long-term forecast for the entire economy. This would cover the years 1985 through 1990.[31]

Changes in the five-year plan are a significant and positive step forward in planning practice. The most important change is that the plan is divided into years according to the most important plan indicators and is then presented to all future executors. This should eliminate the past practice of yearly leaps in plans and should inform executors about more far-reaching perspectives. It should also serve as the first decisive step in realizing the concept of uninterrupted planning (it might be referred to as a sliding planning), by which the switch from one yearly plan to another is accomplished smoothly, with no planning surprises.

The yearly operational plan is the only plan for practical production, but no production is possible without resources. Therefore, if in principle only planning organizations draw up long-term plans, then again in principle the operational plan is drawn up by two organizations: *Gosplan* and *Gossnab*. Both on the USSR level, they are equal in stature and neither is subordinate to the other. V. Seliunin, special correspondent for the newspaper *Sotsialisticheskaia industriia*, aptly describes the dilemma that arises in compiling an operational plan. He also presents a solution to this dilemma.

"Each plant is at one and the same time both a supplier and a consumer of goods. As a supplier, the plant requires that it first receive the orders for output so that it can put together a feasible plan. In its role as a consumer, however, this same plant insists on the opposite: first, it must have a precise production plan so that it can make reliable requisitions for everything needed to fulfill the plan.

Thus, two mutually exclusive demands are made simultaneously, and both are justified. The situation is reminiscent of the age-old question of which came first, the chicken or the egg. Either answer is more or less logical. In practice the vicious cycle is broken in the following manner. Between April and June of the current year, the plants must present their requisitions for materials and equipment needed to fulfill next year's plan. Before this time, the production plan is an unknown, for only the sum of the requisitions tells what the total requirement for each type of production will be. If this is the case, the customers [the plants] must accept a proposed plan rather than an actual one as a basis. Subsequent corrections to requisitions change very little. Only after the final plan has been approved (this usually occurs in December or January) are computation errors discovered."[32]

The plants' requisitions for material and technical supply proceed step by step through the *Gossnab* system and make up a plan-requisition. This is similar to the movement of the draft plan described earlier. The office-level stages of movement remain, but supply organizations take the place of the planning organizations. Since the requisition is based on an unknown plan (or at least a hazy one) the plant managers always strive to present an inflated requisition. The economic reform that permitted the plants to exchange material costs has only bolstered this practice. In principle, the less available an item, the harder people try to acquire it. The movement of the plan-requisition upward is accompanied by a reduction of requisitions in the supply organizations and by "trade" intended to justify and vindicate the submitted requisitions. The plan-requisition is coordinated and compiled in *Gossnab*, USSR. At this point it becomes a supply-funds plan; or, to put it differently, it becomes an actual production plan for output in which production and resources are organically joined, although this balanced relationship is far from perfect. The supply-funds plan, although important, is not confirmed by higher-ranking USSR state organs, nor does it become law.

The operational yearly production plan is compiled according to the principle "from the attained level." However, the actual outcome of the current year's plan is still not known when the draft plan is compiled, nor is it known when the plant receives the plan-law. As a result, a plan is based on a plan. "When the ministries' account for the previous year is confirmed in April or May, changes are incorporated into the current year's plan based on data from this account. This is called 'correcting planning indicators by means of the accounting base.' Just as before, things are still done in this way."[33]

In compiling the draft plan, receiving plan-law tasks, and making corrections to the plan at a later time, all executors of plans have one primary goal: to complete as small a plan as possible.

The substantiation of both versions of the plan, the *Gossnab* version and the *Gosplan* version, are about the same. Not only are both unscientific, but both are poorly founded statistically. Nonetheless, the *Gosplan* version becomes a law that must be carried out and adhered to. The *Gossnab* version is much better balanced in resources production. The demand that these plans concur shifts the final decision to the executors. This comes about in the following manner: "A ministry or *sovnarkhoz* [since replaced] when compiling plans for branch plants, suddenly discovers that they have not made allowances for 1 or 2 percent of the projected rate. That is, for the current year, it should have increased output volume in rubles by 8 percent, let us say; but according to the totals of plant plans which have been confirmed and provided for by orders and materials [the plan-requisition], only 7, or worse still, 6 percent was actually achieved. A state plan is law. If it says 8 percent, it means there must be 8 percent. The missing 2 percent, somewhere in the neighborhood of 1 billion rubles, has to be divided among the plants. Nobody knows what the gross output will be, nor how the missing billion will be handled. Nobody knows what kind of output there will be and who will buy it. Everything is ephemeral, invisible, and imponderable—a breath of air, an ethereal gross product."[34]

When there was a change to "market output" or "realized volume" during the reform, the "ethereal realization" came into existence.

This indefiniteness and lack of coordination of plans in practice is the main reason for the enormous reserves of material goods that for long periods of time do not circulate in the nation's economy. "Altogether, throughout the country, the worth of excess reserves alone is greater than 4 billion rubles. This represents one-tenth of all reserves concentrated (perhaps it would be better to say 'scattered') among the industrial plants."[35] Thus, the total "reserves," are greater than 40 billion rubles.

Planning practice today convincingly demonstrates that the plan is actually an empirical attempt to solve several different national economic problems, frequently without a unified concept and a reliable connection between the decisions being made. (For example, the supply plan never corresponds to the production plan.) The main tasks that planning attempts to perform are

1. To provide "Party spirit" for economic development by subordinating this development to the will of the Party leadership or "leader."
2. To provide absolute managerial centralization and complete control over all economic life.
3. To establish, only approximately, the rate, nature, and trend of the economy's development for the period being planned, with the overall tendency to "squeeze out" the greatest possible output.
4. To coordinate, as far as is feasible under existing conditions, essentially

through administrative measures, the contradictory economic, departmental, social, and other interests that come up in economic activity.

5. When possible, to reduce to a minimum control interference by *Gosplan* and
other state organs in the process of executing a plan by the national
economy. For the most part, this is achieved by shifting all problems to the
shoulders of those who execute plans (at the lower levels of the economy).
This is extremely difficult because of the single-version aspect of all
planning.

Receiving and Fulfilling the Plan

The plan-law moves downward through each lower-ranking level of executors. In
practice several factors determine the receipt of the plan. First, the plan is
peculiar to itself. As a rule, the plan's most important parts are not tied together.
This leads to corrections and thus loss of time. Second, "the supply system does
not function smoothly. Mild punishments for suppliers compel the producers to
keep excess reserves of raw materials and power on hand to assure that the plan
will be fulfilled even if deliveries are not made." Third, "nonfulfillment of a plan
is punished more severely than overfulfillment is encouraged." Fourth, "plans
are frequently changed and increased 'from above.' Reserves must be kept on
hand for this as well as for additional obligations." Fifth, the acceptance of a
high plan often leads to the revision and tightening of norms for material
incentives (bonuses), and in essence, "all moral incentive for plants is based on
the indicator of a plan's fulfillment, regardless of its level."[36] An evaluation of
the collective's labor, the moral and material incentives, the awarding of bonuses
to management personnel, engineering-technical workers, and common laborers
depends on the plan's being fulfilled, not on the level of intensity of the plan
received."[37]

The receipt and fulfillment of plans takes place under conditions whereby,
in the minds of the executors, "the feeling is firmly ensconced that 110 percent
will give him esteem and a banner [the 'traveling' victor's red banner in socialist
competition which goes from one 'victor' to another]. A mere 99 percent will
win him only sidelong glances, reproaches, and a sharp reprimand in the *raion*
committee."[38]

It is easy to understand why every executor tries to obtain a minimum plan
for himself. There are several ways to do this. First, every executor tries to
compile a minimal draft plan and have it approved at higher levels. If this does
not work, or if it appears that nonfulfillment of the plan is likely, then the
ministries and departments (*vedomstvo*) attempt "to obtain a so-called amend-
ment to the plans at the end of the year. In other words, the plans are
lowered."[39] Within the ministries and departments, planning tasks are redistributed among plants that are functioning well and those functioning poorly in
order to "save" the general plan.

The plan must be fulfilled at all costs. Thus, "in striving to fulfill the plan for realized output volume at any cost, some managers occasionally disturb the order of deliveries and inflate calculation indicators."[40] To this same end, they change the lists of manufactured articles in favor of "advantageous" articles (high-cost and highly profitable items) which have been produced for a long time. The method of inflating prices of articles for no reason is in wide use. Naturally, this is an easy way to raise the chief indicator, the volume of market output. There are also a number of quasi-legal methods and "tricks" for fulfilling a plan (for example, demanding payment not only before the product is shipped, but before it is even produced). When all other possibilities have been exhausted, some managers resort to outright forgeries, which are punishable by law.

In general, the fulfillment of all plans at all levels falls under the universal motto, "All is good that helps to fulfill the plan; all is bad that hinders." In the eyes of those who execute plans, no national economic, state, Party, social, or other consideration has any meaning when placed alongside this motto.

Notes

1. *A Discussion of Optimal Planning* (Moscow: Ekonomizdat, 1968), p. 41.

2. *Planovoe khoziaistvo,* no. 3 (1971):54.

3. Ibid., no. 6 (1969):89.

4. Ibid., no. 9 (1966):10.

5. E. Mainimas, *Planning Processes in the Economy* (Moscow: Ekonomika, 1971), pp. 337, 338.

6. *Planovoe khoziaistvo,* no. 11 (1972):7.

7. *Voprosy ekonomiki,* no. 1 (1967):146.

8. *Ekonomicheskaia gazeta,* no. 25 (1968):11.

9. *Voprosy ekonomiki,* no. 4 (1972):126.

10. *Krasnaia zvezda,* 20 November 1961, p. 5.

11. *Planovoe khoziaistvo,* no. 11 (1972):7.

12. *Pravda,* 29 October 1965, p. 2.

13. *Planovoe khoziaistvo,* no. 8 (1967):38.

14. *Pravda,* 5 October 1962, p. 3.

15. *Planovoe khoziaistvo,* no. 12 (1962):3.

16. Ibid., no. 10 (1969):24.

17. Ibid.

18. *A Discussion of Optimal Planning,* p. 177.

19. *Planovoe khoziaistvo,* no. 11 (1969):10.

20. Ibid., no. 7 (1962):3.

21. Mainimas, *Planning Processes in the Economy,* pp. 337-338.

22. *Voprosy ekonomiki,* no. 4 (1966):67.

23. *Ekonomicheskaia gazeta,* no. 25 (1968):11.

24. *Tekhnika molodezhi,* no. 7 (1967);1.

25. *Planovoe khoziaistvo,* no. 8 (1963):49.

26. *Tekhnika molodezhi,* no. 7 (1967):1.

27. *Planovoe khoziaistvo,* no. 5 (1970):35.

28. *Voprosy ekonomiki,* no. 5 (1971):26.

29. Ibid., no. 3 (1971):5.

30. Ibid., no. 2 (1968):22-23.

31. *Planovoe khoziaistvo,* no. 4 (1970):21.

32. *Sotsialisticheskaia industriia,* 15 January 1971, p. 2.

33. *Pravda,* 28 June 1967, p. 2.

34. *Novyi Mir,* no. 11 (1966):181.

35. *Sotsialisticheskaia industriia,* 5 January 1971, p. 2.

36. *Voprosy ekonomiki,* no. 3 (1970):60.

37. *Pravda,* 14 January 1969, p. 2.

38. Ibid., 3 June 1968, p. 2.

39. *Planovoe khoziaistvo,* no. 5 (1971):9.

40. *Pravda,* 19 June 1970, p. 1.

6 Militarization of the Economy

The problems of preparing the country for possible military conflict involve more of the economy than just industry. Therefore, if one limits oneself to the economy, one must speak, not of the military-industrial, but of the military-economic complex of the USSR. If one goes beyond the economy and examines the entire system from the viewpoint of "its ability to defend itself," one invariably concludes that the entire system is more adaptable to solving the problems of war than those of peace. Historical precedence is graphic evidence of this.

Soviet leaders have always devoted enormous attention to raising the defense posture of the country. In a system where the attention and will of the leader (or leaders) are the decisive criteria in all development, such treatment speaks for itself in a most positive way. From the very beginning of the five-year plans, military (defense) industry has belonged to group A industries (production of the means of production). Within group A, defense industry tops the list and grows faster than the rest of group A. During the Second Five-Year Plan (1933-1937), production in defense industries rose by 286 percent and more than doubled in just three years.[1] In recent years, repeated outstanding achievement in the growth of defense industries has continued without interruption.

The official Soviet point of view has, perhaps, a certain basis in fact, that "socialist production relationships even in peacetime allow us to solve military-economic problems, strengthen the material base of defense, and raise the level of the economy's preparedness for mobilization with smaller military expenditures and with greater effect than can be done in the capitalist countries."[2]

However, the great amount of military production is a heavy burden on the Soviet economy and the standard of living. If the current volume of military production in the Soviet Union and the United States is equal, then this puts a minimum of 2 to 2 1/2 times more pressure on the Soviet economy. Nevertheless, one cannot expect a cutback in military production. Theoretically, official Soviet views on future war and armament come to the same conclusion. First, "the Soviet military doctrine maintains that given the current means of armed conflict, a war can be over quickly or it can be prolonged."[3] Second, "under current conditions, it is difficult to count on a significant increase in military production at the beginning of a war, as was the case previously." Therefore, "while still in peacetime, industry must be prepared" so that it is in a position to create government-mobilized reserves and necessary military reserves." Thus, three very important tasks are placed before the military-industrial complex (arms production):

1. To provide the necessary level of armament for contemporary armed forces.
2. To stockpile reserves of armaments, the amount of which is based on the supposition "of large material losses in the armed forces" during a prolonged war.[4]
3. To continually update the more complex and labor-consuming types of armament, for the reserves in the event of war, as well as for the active forces.

Whether it will be feasible in the long run to perform these tasks is a question to which research can give only an approximate answer. Particular attention must be given to a new point of view (for the Soviet Union), that is, that a high defense posture must not be created if disproportions exist. These disproportions already exist in the Soviet economy. General conclusions cannot be based solely on past experience in solving clearly defensive strategic problems. Past experience has demonstrated great success in solutions, as well as complete failures and insufficient strength to change an unfavorable situation. For example, the continued concentration of industry in large cities is a complete failure, whereas the long-term shortage in ferrous metals demonstrates a lack of strength.

The state economic plan plays an enormous role in the militarization of the economy. "The entire job of planning the national economy is inseparably tied to the task of national defense. A peculiarity of all national economic plans lies in the unity of economic and defense tasks."[5]

All plan tasks and measures projected by them are evaluated according to their suitability for raising the national defense posture. This evaluation usually exerts the dominating influence on the final solution to high-level national economic problems such as the rate and direction of technical progress, the proportion of development in the various sectors of industry, and the overall rate of development in the industrial forces of the land. In solving problems on a smaller scale, the dominant role of the military viewpoint is even greater and often decisive.

The attempt to militarize the entire economy and especially the leading sectors of industry has an all-embracing character. This stems directly from the unity of economic and defense tasks in all national economic plans. The extent of this penetration is well illustrated by the following example. Shells, bombs, and mines are machined on lathes. One has to cut thread on them, and both their diameters and their lengths are usually large. In 1966 76.4 percent of the 2 billion common items machined on lathes had diameters of less than 100 millimeters, and only 3.6 percent had diameters of more than 250 millimeters; but "a large share of the lathes produced continue to have large measurements between the centers" because the lathes are used for defense purposes. Of the 2 billion parts machined, only 19.5 percent required that thread be cut, but the "majority of lathes produced had guide screws."[6]

Many similar examples in practically every sector of Soviet nonmilitary industry, transportation, or communications can be cited. Also falling into this category is the high proportion of *sovkhozes* in agricultural production, although they are less profitable to the government than the *kolkhozes*. However, the attempt to make *sovkhozes* the backbone of the nation's agriculture did not alter the fact that agriculture remains the weakest link in the military-industrial complex. Its weakness casts doubts on the nation's ability to carry out a large-scale, prolonged war.

The basis for militarization and for planning a military economy is, in fact, the defense industry. Embracing a vast complex of involved sectors, it also fulfills the three chief tasks that face the military-industrial complex. In several sectors of industry, special departments of civilian enterprises (so-called special shops) participate directly in solving these tasks. In fact, the basic significance of defense industry is that in cooperation with scientific research and design organizations, it makes new armaments, develops and prepares technological processes for mass production of arms, trains an experienced work force, and thus creates favorable conditions for shifting the whole economy to a military footing in the event of mobilization. The special shops also enable industry to mobilize quickly.

The militarization of capital investments has enormous significance in the militarization of the entire Soviet system. In the construction or modernization of various projects, their possible military applications have already been foreseen in the design stage. Because it occurs on a wide scale, this unprecedented phenomenon greatly raises the level of militarization and has enormous advantages in the event of mobilization and war.

Notes

1. *Planovoe khoziaistvo,* no. 3 (1966):4.
2. *Military-Economic Problems in a Political Economics Course* (Moscow: Voenizdat, 1968), p. 203.
3. Ibid., p. 210.
4. Ibid., p. 211.
5. Ibid., p. 212.
6. *Planovoe khoziaistvo,* no. 4 (1966):33.

7

National Economic Accounting

General Comments

Theoretically, at least, the complete centralization of the economy greatly increases the role played by statistics. Under the Soviet economic system, more than any other, neither sound planning, correctly organized management, nor qualified economic control would be possible without comprehensive governmental statistics. Lenin understood theoretically the extraordinarily important role of statistics in the future socialist system and coined the slogan, "Socialism is accounting."

However, the current discipline of statistics was formulated not during Lenin's but rather during Stalin's time, and presents a rather limited range of information. "It does not meet Lenin's requirements of being supported in actuality by masses of *reliable* facts and figures and by the sum total of materials based on scientific research (italics mine)."[1] As an aspect of economics, statistics is also related to it, particularly in planning and management. Statistics has the very same principles of organization and methodology. It *"still bears the well-known imprint of purely administrative methods of management. Statistical data are excessively numerous and at the same time their content is harmful"* (italics in original).[2] "So, for example, we know how many ski poles were produced and how many baby chicks were hatched, but unfortunately, some vitally necessary information about the efficiency of new equipment is missing."[3] This situation is caused to a considerable degree by the fact that Soviet statistics are "designed to register any deviation from a given plan" and do not pay attention to "a timely reflection of deep-rooted social and economic tendencies until they have matured and developed."[4]

The Stalinist slogan, "Catch up with and surpass America," is currently expressed as "Competition between two systems." This slogan assigned to statistics tasks that were not inherent but completely alien and contradictory to it. It must not only do the accounting but also present the results of the accounting in a more favorable light. Therefore, if some plants did not meet their plan while others exceeded their plan, and if the value of the production of the entire group of plants was higher than anticipated in the plan, the entire plan is considered met, "even though the items produced that exceeded the plan (with rare exceptions) do not replace the items that were not produced by the first group of plants."[5] The "value" of items that were produced includes items that have no use value, that is, items that have no demand, that lie in the warehouses of marketing and trade organizations.

The credibility of Soviet statistical data presents a distinct problem on which the opinions of economists are sometimes diametrically opposed. The two opposing poles are that everything is correct and that nothing can be trusted because everything is falsified.

Those who hold the first view usually argue that one cannot manage an economy on the basis of data prepared for experimental purposes. *Ekonomicheskaia gazeta* (no. 45, 1970, p. 15), for example, cites the opinion of an American economist, V. Katkov. This argument does not stand up to criticism; it does not even deserve consideration. In the USSR not a single economic leader uses publications of the Central Statistical Directorate in making economic decisions.

Neither is the other point of view entirely correct. Falsification is necessary only when the situation has to be pictured as better than it really is, no matter what the cost (embellishment of reality). As one can imagine, the correct approach to official statistical data is that one does not know whether something is correct, and one investigates the problem (or sector of industry) to ascertain as well as possible the accuracy of the figures.

These criticisms apply to the official data published by the Central Statistical Directorate. However, there are also departmental working statistics (of *Gosplan, Gossnab,* and of ministries and departments) that are never published. To a certain degree, these are the statistics used to make economic decisions. On very rare occasions certain figures from these statistics appear in the press. There is almost always a discrepancy between these and the official statistics.

Are these departmental statistics reliable? One statement has already been cited witnessing the low reliability of statistics. The same opinion is expressed in another article.[6] The lack of reliability of departmental statistics is assured by the condition of having to meet the plan no matter what.

Types of Accounting

Accounting for the national economy is divided into statistical accounting, bookkeeping, and operational accounting.

Statistical accounting is the most important, since only it encompasses all sectors and theoretically, at least, gives the complete picture of the economy. There are two parallel lines of statistical accounting: the Central Statistical Directorate system and the departmental system. Industrial and trade organizations produce quarterly and annual statistical accounts. Agricultural organizations and governmental offices produce yearly accounts. Therefore, higher statistical organizations receive the results of departmental statistics only as an overall view on the all-union and republic level.

The bookkeeping account monitors monetary-material values. Accounts for entire sectors of the economy are produced quarterly and, in shortened form, monthly for a stricter accounting of monetary resources. Monthly accounts are presented to statistical organizations and, more important, to the offices of *Gosbank*; they serve as the most effective means of monitoring the activities of any subsector of the economy.

Operational accounting is intended for direct management of sectors of the Soviet economy. "Presently there are the so-called urgent bookkeeping system (sent by telegram) and the routine system (sent by mail)." Urgent telegraphic bookkeeping "is overloaded with thousands of indicators . . . but nevertheless does not contain complete information."[7] Operational accounting actually forms the basis for the administrative management of the Soviet economy.

Statistical Organizations

The highest statistical organization in the country is the Central Statistical Directorate of the USSR, which has an all-union structure. There are statistical directorates at every administrative level of the government, as well as in Moscow, Leningrad, and the capitals of the union republics. The Central Statistical Directorate, USSR, has the status of a state committee of the Council of Ministers, USSR. The statistical directorates of the union republics have dual subordination, both to the Central Statistical Directorate, USSR, and the councils of ministers of the union republics.

Parallel to these organizations are the departmental statistical organizations of ministries and departments, also organized on a territorial basis. These organizations make calculations along departmental lines and are administratively subordinate to their departments. However, in methodology they are subordinate to the Central Statistical Directorate. Departmental statistical organizations at all departmental levels are also part of their respective planning organizations.

The following major tasks are assigned to the Central Statistical Directorate, USSR, as the chief and governing statistical body:

1. To develop methods for the national economic accounting necessary for all statistical organizations.
2. To provide leadership and instruction for all statistical organizations without exception.
3. To perform systematic accounting of the fulfillment of the national economic plan.
4. To take the census.
5. To publish data on all phases of the national economy. The Central Statistical Directorate has its own special publishing house, Statistika, to perform this task. (See the breakdown of the Central Statistical Directorate in figure 7-1.)

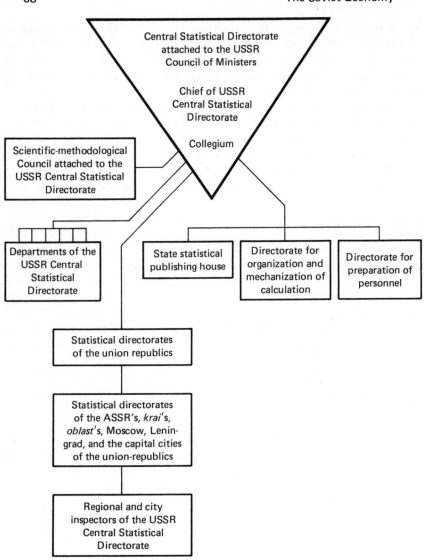

Figure 7-1. The Central Statistical Directorate

Accounting in Practice

Official Soviet economic science feels that "statistics provide initial data for developing governmental national economic plans" and that "the inseparable unity of governmental statistics and national economic planning find concrete expression in a united system of indicators, and by a unified method of determining these indicators."[8]

We spoke earlier of how statistics and national economic assessments provide initial data for planning. Concerning a unified system of indicators or designators, these designators must coincide throughout the *Gosplan, Gossnab,* and Central Statistical Directorate systems when compiling an annual operational plan. Table 7-1 shows the numbers of designators for several very important types of products as listed by those three organizations. Even more important is the small number of designators which coincide between the various systems.

Obviously, "a unified system of indicators" does not actually exist. Many years have passed and the situation has not changed. Especially with the current economic reforms, it has remained particularly urgent for the centralized leadership in accounting and statistics to provide unified methods.[9]

As early as 1967, determined attempts were made not only to unify accounting but also to create designators suitable for computer processing. The most important of them was the development of a union-wide classifier of industrial and agricultural products.[10] Each item was given a ten-digit code. The values of the first six places, the classifier supergroup, were drawn up by the central organizations by the end of 1967. The remaining four places in the code were to be worked out by the ministries and departments. At the same time, a question arose about establishing other classifiers which "would constitute an orderly complex of economic data classifiers. This is one of the prime conditions

Table 7-1
Numbers of Designators

	For Gosplan, USSR (1)	For CSD,[a] USSR (2)	For Gossnab, USSR (3)	Those that coincide between		
				1 & 2	1 & 3	2 & 3
Rolled ferrous metals	70	131	55	39	48	27
Products from powerplant machine building industry	122	221	322	21	6	3
Metallurgical equipment	46	34	682	21	21	17
Mining equipment	439	95	444	45	278	69
Petroleum production and petroleum refining equipment	38	44	114	7	28	7

Source: *Voprosy ekonomiki,* no. 12 (1962):107.
[a]Central Statistical Directorate

for the widespread introduction of computer technology and automated management systems into the economy."[11] "However, the original time period [1967-1968] established by the State Planning Committee, USSR, for developing sections of the Unified Product Classifier for each sector of the economy has run out."[12] Issuance of the Unified Product Classifier was set for the end of 1972 or early 1973. "However, before the verdict is in, other projects go on, projects which are labor-consuming and divert many people, but which are obviously devoid of thought or promise. They are inventing their own personal classifiers for use among themselves in their own sectors or plants. . . . Nevertheless, the situation is not as hopeless as it might seem at first glance. Luckily, one can see concrete steps being taken to solve this problem."[13] This procrastination can be explained by the unwillingness of ministries and departments to place themselves under the "computer control" of central organizations. A whole series of classifiers compiled by separate departments turned out to be unsuitable for the governmentwide mechanization of accounting.

As a result, improvements in accounting and the elimination of at least the major shortcomings occur very slowly. In the opinion of Fedorenko, "without meaningful changes in bookkeeping, it is impossible to make economically sound decisions for raising production efficiency or to substantiate planning assignments scientifically."[14]

An even more radical point of view is expressed by B. Kolpakov, the head of the Central Statistical Directorate, RSFSR, and Sh. Kamaletdinov, head of the computer center of the Central Statistical Directorate, RSFSR. They write: *"in our view, the statistical system does not need to adapt to the needs of economic reform or need slow improvement. Rather, the system needs to be completely revamped"* (italics in original).[15]

Notes

1. *Voprosy ekonomiki,* no. 4 (1963):17-18.

2. *Ekonomicheskaia gazeta,* no. 28 (July 1966):18.

3. *Voprosy ekonomiki,* no. 9 (1968):158.

4. Ibid., no. 4 (1968):71.

5. *Pravda,* 18 February 1967, p. 2; see also *Planovoe khoziaistvo,* no. 2 (1968):19.

6. *Voprosy ekonomiki,* no. 4 (1971):156.

7. *Planovoe khoziaistvo,* no. 2 (1968):17.

8. Volodarsky, *Industrial Statistics and Planning Problems* (Moscow, 1958), p. 75.

9. *Voprosy ekonomiki,* no. 4 (1971):72.

10. *Ekonomicheskaia gazeta,* no. 42 (October 1967):29.

11. Ibid.

12. *Ekonomicheskaia gazeta,* no. 11 (1972):8.
13. *Pravda,* 24 September 1971, p. 3.
14. *Planovoe khoziaistvo,* no. 8 (1968):24.
15. *Pravda,* 18 February 1967, p. 2.

8 Computer Technology in the USSR National Economy

The major task of the Soviet economy is to increase its efficiency. Necessity suggests that the primary task after this is to make planning varied, optimal and uninterrupted and to plan not only by sector (*otrasl'*) but to create territorial planning as well.

All these tasks, not only in planning but in the areas of accounting, supply, and management as well, can be accomplished only through the use of computers and econometrics. The insurmountable barrier to the use of econometrics and computers in solving economic problems (above all planning) is the price-setting system. This problem is acknowledged, but it has still not been resolved. Judging from what is occurring in the Soviet economy under the influence of the higher Party leadership, one cannot expect a solution to this problem very soon. Therefore, it is practically impossible to predict how the Soviet leadership will try to solve the basic problems of planning and, for that matter, of the entire economy.

Theoretically the situation is different when computer technology can be used for working with various physical indicators (intrasector planning) and with automated management systems or for automating technological processes and bookkeeping. In areas where the use of computers is possible, they are only partially used in practice. Many technical-organizational problems are artificially created. Glushkov is inclined to consider some of them growing pains.[1] However, the most important of them are ascribed to something entirely different.

There is no common mathematical "language" throughout the Soviet Union when various upper-level offices discuss the same specific items. Here again departmentalism prevails over broad government interests. Perhaps this is only temporary, since the Unified Product Classifier and other union classifiers offer tremendous possibilities. The first experiments with departmental classifiers have shown promising results, although they in no way ensure optimal planning within sectors.

In Soviet management the course has been set toward the creation of automated management systems at various levels, which must be fused into a governmentwide automated system. Some Soviet economists consider the idea of nationwide automated management systems to be utopian, others (Glushkov) consider this problem "one of the most important and of nationwide significance."[2] For the present, computer centers are widespread. Many businesses chiefly in heavy and technologically advanced industries, have automated management systems. As of 1 January 1973 there were about two thousand computer centers in the country at various levels and of varying sizes. There were also 839 automated and automatic management systems. There are still several problems that will require a lot of time and hard work to eliminate. The deputy director of the Central Economic-Mathematics Institute of the Academy of Sciences, USSR, Yu. Oleinikovod, expressed it this way: "The role of computer technology is generally recognized. However, it still has to prove itself. First, plants are not interested in computers for economic reasons. Second, there is a shortage of trained personnel. Third, the quality of the equipment itself is inadequate. Moreover, existing computers are used poorly with regard to the correct distribution among their customers."[3] These concise statements need to be expanded. An enterprise is not interested in computers for economic reasons because the maintenance of computer equipment, as well as the equipment itself, is very expensive. This increases one important planning indicator—the production cost of a product. The situation, however, only becomes worse. "What bothers us is that several third-generation computers with the very same capacity as the 'Minsk-32' will cost several times more than a 'Minsk-32.' "[4] The shortage of trained personnel can be explained by two important factors. First, the training of computer personnel began very late, under conditions of severe shortages in instructors. "Now training of personnel is done at all universities and at many technical institutions of higher education." The programs suffer from growing pains and instruction "is not at a level with today's computer equipment. Many institutions of higher learning that train computer programmers either have no computer centers whatsoever or are outfitted with antiquated equipment and do not familiarize the student with the type of equipment he will encounter on the job."[5] Moreover, the shortage brings about the incorrect use and distribution of the available personnel. The quality of computer equipment is only the most important aspect of the "equipment theme." This problem is discussed repeatedly on the pages of the economic media. The minister of the chemical industry, L.A. Kostandov, writes, "The computers currently being produced have a low reliability in their central computing mechanisms and software assemblies. The operational memory is small, and there is practically no memory function on magnetic disks. There are no pieces of equipment for displaying data on cathode-ray tubes."[6] In addition there is the problem of communication, and there is no simple solution to this problem. The coordination necessary in equipment production is lacking, and many important technical problems are left to their own devices. The incorrect distribution of computers, in effect, means that they are widely scattered. In many cases (particularly in industry) computers are economically unprofitable, but they have become a status symbol. In larger businesses their unprofitability is underplayed while "having an automated management system means that you are in tune with the times. What kind of businessman wants to remain in the horse and buggy days? So they install a jet engine on an oxcart."[7] In spite of all the difficulties blocking the introduction of computer equipment, Glushkov maintains, "the use of computers has already attained a certain systematic character, especially in performing concrete production tasks." Computers are being used more and more "for automating research and scientific processes."[8] The effect of all this is now being felt as the sum of the individual effects on the lower levels of the Soviet economy. However, the overall effect remains an unknown quantity; moreover, an increase in the efficiency of one industry may not necessarily coincide with the demands for efficiency in the entire national economy. Computers may not help at all in solving the problem of raising the efficiency of the entire economy by creating optimal economic plans.

This may be a moot point, but it seems that the rate of introduction of computer technology into the Soviet economy is very inadequate. For the present, this rate is not able to provide the "cybernetic" push forward that would decrease the Soviet Union's backwardness in comparison with the leading capitalist countries. The "cybernetic gap" continues to widen.

Notes

1. *Pravda,* 10 February 1973, p. 3.
2. *Pravda,* 28 October 1971, p. 2.
3. *Ekonomicheskaia gazeta,* no. 27 (1968):13.
4. *Ekonomicheskaia gazeta,* no. 24 (1972):7.
5. *Pravda,* 25 March 1972.
6. *Ekonomicheskaia gazeta,* no. 9 (1972):8.
7. *Pravda,* 28 August 1971, p. 2.
8. *Sotsialisticheskaia industriia,* 8 July 1973, p. 4.

9 Soviet Economic Management

In Theory

The principles of managing the Soviet economy were created and developed during the First and Second Five-Year Plans. According to the official point of view, "the Leninist principle of democratic centralism is the basic principle for managing the Soviet economy." In practice this principle is expressed by the total subjugation of economic life to a single center. "Democratic centralism in the economy is inseparably linked to the principle of Party spirit in management. Party spirit in economic work represents a logical fulfillment of the Party's prime objective, that is, the socialistic transformation of society, the development of incentive for creative labor, and the instillation in each member of society of a sense of economic responsibility for the matter at hand." The Party spirit principle is also evident in the fact that all command positions in economics are filled by managers chosen by the Party (the *nomenklatura,* or list of Party-sanctioned executives). The managers are selected "on the basis of their political and business expertise." Thus, Party requirements are most important.[1]

These general principles, of which the Party-spirit principle is the most strictly observed, have been realized under particular conditions and the influence of very specific factors. I shall discuss only the three most important factors.

The total absence of the incentive function of price has not created the necessary material interest in economic activity, just as the so-called Leninist principle of material interest does not create it. In combination with democratic centralism and other phenomena, this principle not only fails to generate but also kills initiative in the economy. It has become necessary to force people to work. The methods of management that "have been given the name administrative" have developed in this way.[2] The economic growth of the USSR has shown that the economy can be controlled by administrative methods of management. The dominant opinion among Soviet economists is that these methods have determined the ineffective route of economic management. Administrative methods, that is, orders from above with no legal recourse from below, have given rise to irresponsibility in management at the top and an attempt to avoid the responsibility of making a decision at the bottom. It is precisely this avoidance of responsibility that causes the many stages and the long periods of time required to study and confirm almost every economic decision. This is the source of "conference sitting," the purpose of which is to convert an individual decision into a collective decision. "The abundance of conferences and sessions has become a distinctive, serious, and chronic disease, which we are unable to reject. . . . Very often we do not have time to think about what we are doing or how we should do something. We have no time to dream or gaze into the future."[3]

A second relevant factor is the so-called class approach. According to Marxist classification, only the proletarian worker creates value; he is the prime figure in the economy, the physical and ideological base of the system, a kind of persona grata. It is from the proletariat that the leadership ("workers elevated to administrative posts") is formed. The system deals relatively cautiously with workers. Middle-level management workers, that is, the white-collar workers, have found themselves in a very different situation. They are the outcasts of the system, and it is presumed that they are bureaucrats engaged in red tape. They are the first to be let go under the yearly plans for staff reductions. "We have fought bureaucratism and red tape on all fronts and with every weapon. It cannot be said that bureaucratism has been defeated. After many years of battle the maze of clerical specialists has been drastically reduced, and the new breed of office workers has been decreased as well. . . . Many secrets of clerical work have been lost. No one has given any thought to the technology of red tape and to its perfection."[4] Now they are beginning to think about this, but for the present the gigantic management apparatus uses traditional methods, creating, working, and reworking an enormous amount of nonstandardized documents. "If one were to paste together all documents (more than 30 billion pages) passing through our institutions in a year into a single paper ribbon, this ribbon would encircle the earth at the equator more than two hundred times! It is physically impossible to do a good job of reworking all this information by customary methods."[5]

In Practice

In industry the planning-administrative principle of control based on a lack of confidence of one person in another leads directly to a multitude of indicators and bookkeeping forms. These in turn determine the structure of control and the size of the management apparatus. Thus, "the volume of yearly information being reworked by plant management workers at the coal combines of the USSR Ministry of the Coal Industry adds up to almost 60 million indicators, and at the ore management organizations of the Ministry of Nonferrous Metallurgy, almost 50 million. At large machine-building works, there are at times up to 1,200 bookkeeping forms in use, and the yearly volume of document turnover exceeds 250,000 to 300,000. Within the sectors the picture is even more amazing. Thus, the year's volume of information for the Ministry of the Chemical Industry in 1969 came to 1.3 billion indicators. In the Ministry of Power, the Ministry of the Ship Building Industry, and the Ministry of the Coal Industry, this figure came to nearly 100 million.

A further subdivision of management organizations to support the operational management of a complex system of industrial production under such conditions is needed. New chief directorates and new plant management departments and services appear; staffs for the administrative apparatus are continually increasing. However, this does not provide the necessary results or lead to the required effectiveness in national economic management. This is because the problems of the operational receipt and processing of technical-economic information are becoming more complicated. Very rational plans are being developed because many factors regulate production at the enterprise, branch, and national economic levels. This means that calculations should be worked out in several variations. *In reality the information comes, as a rule, after decisions have been made and thus cannot be used to compile plans.*

Because manual methods are used in selecting and processing information, each manager has three to four times more work than he can be expected to handle, leading to serious shortcomings in the organization of production. The most significant is equipment shutdown, which reaches 20 percent according to many businesses that have made studies.[6]

Such is the actual situation in the management of industry. It does not conform to the reform for simplifying management through the creation of industrial and production associations. Are these not the basic causes for the slow, internally contradictory, and disputable progress of this reform?

If the reform were to be completed and the traditional methods of management and bookkeeping were to remain, then reform is not a condensation of the book through deletion of unnecessary chapters but only a cutback in circulation. The management apparatus is being choked to death by the flow of paper. As a result, "it is not uncommon for highly skilled specialists to use most of their working time for paperwork."[7] The diversion of highly skilled specialists to common technical tasks is increasing disproportionately in the management apparatus. Thus, in industry engineering-technical workers represent 11.4 percent of the total, while white-collar workers represent only 4 percent. At the same time in U.S. industry, white-collar workers represent 10.9 percent of the total, which is more than double the number of engineering-technical workers.[8] The battle with bureaucratism and red tape has led to a sharp reduction in middle-level white-collar workers. A significant portion of the necessary work is being done by even more highly qualified people, and the effectiveness of their work is dropping sharply. Thus, in 1971 "one specialist with a higher or medium-level education brings in only half as much national income as did his counterpart in 1913," writes Khachaturov.[9] Such is the effectiveness of their use.

For nearly a quarter of a century the Soviet economy was structured by the terrorist methods of Stalinist control. Administrative-directive methods were reinforced by police terror and people became afraid to take individual initiative or risk. People were taught to carry out blindly the letter of plans and were compelled to seek ways of defending themselves. This became the tradition, the style of work. However, it was not terror alone, although this was the prime reason, that gave rise to playing it safe, that is, the attempt by bureaucrats to surround themselves with a wall of paper and thus provide a defense in the event of failure. Playing it safe only strengthened bureaucratism. The lack of initiative and the fear of risk had an especially strong influence on the deceleration of scientific-technical progress, because the risk of failure and persecution was connected to every innovation and every economic or technical experiment. Previously this meant making oneself liable to terror; now it means making oneself vulnerable to administrative action. This leads to the following line of reasoning: "What kind of director, whether consumate idealist or even a patriot, will allow himself to be persecuted? ... *However, to everyone's surprise*" sometimes a director takes a risk and ends up with a State Prize, a rare exception to the general rule (italics mine).[10]

The influence of these factors, in a complicated interrelationship with many other factors and influences created by the system itself, has spawned the characteristic features of the methods and style of management. This is the essence of bureaucracy in management. These features have become firmly entrenched, become a nearly insurmountable tradition. They are all of a "defensive nature," meaning they serve to soften the sharper edges of administrative-management methods. The main ones are giving priority to local interests (*mestnichestvo*), departmentalism (*vedomstvennost'*), formalism, "window dressing" (*ochkovtiratel'stvo*), and the system of working in spurts (*kampaneishchina*). Giving priority to local interests and departmentalism are in principle related to each other. To give priority to local interests means that local (territorial) interests are paramount even when this is contrary to overall government interests. "It will be more peaceful and better for me if it is better here than in other places." This is the logic behind giving priority to local interests. However, this approach violates the confidence of the central organizations toward local organizations. Even at ministerial levels, this approach "comes crashing down on republic-level ministries like a boomerang: the all-union level office is afraid to extend rights even in those spheres where it might function effectively."[11] In departmentalism, departmental or office interests receive first priority while overall governmental interests are pushed aside. One of the foremost and, for the economy, most unhealthy consequences of departmentalism is the unusual difficulty in coordinating the actions of different offices performing the same national economic task. A decision of the CPSU Central Committee and the USSR Council of Ministers concerning the acceleration of the development of oil extraction in western Siberia provides an outstanding example of departmentalism and its consequences.[12] Formalism, as is apparent from its name, is the purely formal realization of requirements levied by higher-ranking organizations. In this case the measure being carried out has no meaning. Window dressing is just that—the deception of high-ranking organizations by lower-ranking organizations, subordinates deceiving the bosses. This deception has come about for many reasons but largely because of the "fanfare" custom, which has been established by the higher Party leadership to celebrate every accomplishment. The economy also lacks objective means for measuring the effectiveness of the managers. Deception is practiced on a wide scale, beginning with the so-called glossing over reality, when everything is presented in a prettier form than it really is, and ending with "additions" where the volume of produced output or performed measures is simply altered in the books. Although there has long been a law calling for the punishment of additions by up to three years of imprisonment, this practice still continues. Finally in the system of working in spurts, every new requirement levied by a higher-ranking management level is first executed very precisely with displays of zeal and "devotion to duty," but as time passes, the work is done more and more sluggishly and poorly. Eventually, it comes to naught. And this is true not just in economics. On 1 March 1973, the exchange of Party documents began. The Party leadership considered the exchange an outstanding political measure. However, by June of the same year, *Pravda* was writing that in some places people were regarding the exchange of Party documents as yet another routine campaign, meaning that they allowed the matter to proceed without proper attention.

I shall discuss the organizational charts of the direct management of the economy later. Here I shall touch on their intrinsic and principal characteristics. First, there is no adequate legislative regulation of economic activity, and there is no self-regulation. There is no effective economic regulation of interrelationships. In Soviet terms an economic agreement is carried out "as far as possible," and a loss is never compensated by those who inflict the loss. Finally, within the management system there is no clear, strict chain of command, "precisely what is needed to create a rational management system. For the present this is only to be hoped for. In reality we have no such chain of command in the management system of the national economy."[13] In support of her opinion, R.O. Khalfina cites the "extrahierarchial" position of the State Committee for Material and Technical Supply; but beyond the hierarchy are Party organizations and the State Bank with its right of control and sanctions.

The position of Party organizations in the routine work of the economy is unique. On the one hand, they violate the chain of command of the organizational chart and at times even substitute for economic organizations. On the other hand, only the interference of the Party organizations makes it possible to alleviate departmentalism and the granting of priority to local interests and to restrict the administrative arbitrariness of the planning and supply organs. "Experience shows that if a matter is not resolved in the appropriate chief directorate or ministry, the enterprise managers appeal to the local Party

organizations. . . . The Party committees at times become middlemen or medi-
ators, handling matters that can and should be resolved by the offices
(*vedomstvo*)," writes the secretary of the Ivanovsk *Oblast'* Party Committee, V.
Kliuev.[14] It is difficult to overestimate the supervisory role of all levels of Party
organizations in the economy. The need to drastically improve management has
become a nationwide task. "The perfection of economic management at a
modern level is the deciding factor for our further economic growth."[15] At the
same time, "the most important task in perfecting the control of production
under modern conditions is to solve the economic and social problems regarding
the use of human labor in the system of controlling production. It is also
important to resolve the questions of basing the structure and methods of
management on the latest accomplishments of science and advanced technology."[16]

The experience of recent years shows that the main obstacles in the path of
perfecting management are the principles, methods, and style of management
that have become tradition. It appears that the human aspects (psychological
barriers) are placing insurmountable obstacles in the path of introducing modern
methods of management into the Soviet economy.

Notes

1. *Voprosy ekonomiki,* no. 1 (1967):7.
2. *Oktiabr',* no. 8 (1966):173.
3. *Pravda,* 24 March 1967, p. 2.
4. *Novyi mir,* no. 11 (1966):177.
5. *Pravda,* 8 September 1971, p. 2.
6. *Planovoe khoziaistvo,* no. 1 (1974):104.
7. *Pravda,* 8 September 1971, p. 2.
8. *Planovoe khoziaistvo,* no. 4 (1969):19.
9. *Voprosy ekonomiki,* no. 3 (1973):40.
10. *Novyi mir,* no. 10 (1969):198.
11. *Sotsialisticheskaia industriia,* 24 June 1970, p. 2.
12. *Pravda,* 15 January 1970, p. 1.
13. *Discussions of Problems of Optimal Planning* (Moscow: Ekonomizdat,
1968), p. 176.
14. *Pravda,* 13 February 1972, p. 2.
15. *Pravda,* 28 February 1970, p. 2.
16. *Planovoe khoziaistvo,* no. 5 (1970):41.

10 Industry in the USSR

General Comments

Industry, which occupies a central place in the Soviet economy, is significant not just for its economic role. According to ideology, industry performs an important political role because it is based on a higher national form of ownership of the means of production and unites the leading class of society — the working class. In practice, Soviet leadership attaches enormous significance to industry because it is the foundation for strengthening the defense capability and because it plays an exceptionally important role in ensuring the technical-economic independence of the nation. First, it is the practical significance of industry that places it in the center of the Soviet leadership's attention in solving economic problems. The greater the role that a particular branch of industry plays in solving practical problems, the more attention is devoted to it, and the more significant is its development.

All industry belongs to the state, although officially a distinction is made between state and cooperative industry. In reality, cooperative industry, as represented by primitive *kolkhozes*, not only has an insignificant share of the nation's industrial production but also is under the control of the state. This discussion concerns only state industry.

The USSR's industry is characterized by a high level of concentration. Thus, in 1971 the largest plants accounted for only 2.8 percent of total industry but produced 43 percent of industry's gross output. According to this indicator, Soviet industry surpasses even U.S. industry. However, at the same time 36.1 percent of the plants produce 1.9 percent of industry's gross output; in smaller plants technical equipment is much worse than the industry average.[1]

The Subdivision of Industry

Industry is subdivided into two groups: group A and group B, or "subdivision I and subdivision II of public material production." These two methods of subdividing are somewhat different. If group A is heavy industry and group B is light industry, "then subdivision I is the total of all branches manufacturing the means of production, and subdivision II is the total of all branches producing goods for private, or consumer, use."[2] In principle such a subdivision should be useful, but several of the more important branches do not fit into this scheme,

83

nor do they fit into any of the groups or subdivisions. Thus, military industry fits into group A or subdivision I, although it produces no means of production. The enormous size of this industry not only distorts group A but also makes national economic proportions unclear. Khachaturov and the late Strumilin pointed out this fact some time ago, as did S. Khaiman more recently in a very interesting article.[3]

Such a general and imprecise method of subdivision suffers from another important defect: there is no way for it to determine the economic role that a given product will play in the overall economic system. A product's economic role in the Soviet system depends first on whether it is to be a commodity for the domestic or foreign markets or an objective of planned distribution through the material-technical supply system for use by the state. This distinction is important because goods, while having a role in commodity circulation, determine the circulation of currency in its main sphere: state-citizen-state. From this the means for the existence (financing) of the entire Soviet system are derived. By its transfer, the planned distribution of a product among state institutions and enterprises determines currency circulation in the state-to-state sphere, which basically means taking money out of one pocket and putting it into another. Naturally, on a statewide scale, this sphere of circulation does not provide, and in principle is unable to provide, a "mobilization of means into the state budget," as it has come to be expressed in official Soviet economic literature.

At the same time every branch of industry provides a product for both trade and use by the state. Even a single product can be divided by following this important principle: shoes for sale to a consumer are objects of trade, but shoes for the army are objects for use by the state.

From an economic point of view, only the subdivision of industry based on economic outcome of the product is justified. Several Soviet economists have also noted this.

Factors of Development

The accepted division of all industry into groups and subdivisions plays an important practical role. "The Communist Party firmly and consistently pursues the Leninist policy of ensuring the preferential growth of the production of the means of production," as it is expressed in official Soviet economic literature. As a result of this policy, group A has developed considerably faster than group B. For example, between 1928 and 1972 all industry had increased 89.3 times, but group A had increased 182.5 times and group B 31.9 times. As a result the proportion of group A's industrial output to all industrial output has increased from 39.5 percent in 1928 to 73.4 percent in 1972.[4] In addition, official figures do not clearly reflect the actual situation. "The evaluation of national economic ratios in active prices produces results that differ from the real ratios of socialist reproduction."[5] Group A's share is even higher, and the correlation that has currently evolved is acknowledged to be disproportionate. This disproportion must be eliminated by bringing the rates of growth of both groups into closer alignment. The growth rate of group B might even be occasionally allowed to outstrip that of group A. "However, the problem of aligning the rates of growth of groups A and B has still not been completely resolved. During the Seven-Year Plan, the difference in the rates of growth of groups A and B increased. During the years 1951 to 1955, the rate of growth of group A [means of production] was 112 percent greater than the rate of growth of group B [consumer goods]; during the period 1956 to 1960, it was 130 percent greater; and from 1961 to 1965, it was 150 percent greater."[6] During the Eighth Five-Year Plan, the margin was reduced to 104 percent, and according to directives of the Twenty-fourth Congress of the CPSU, in the Ninth Five-Year Plan according to the first time in history group B is to surpass group A by 106 to 107 percent.[7] However, the actual results in only the third year of the Ninth Five-Year Plan made it doubtful that this directive could be carried out.

Thus, an important determinant of the rates and proportions of industrial development has been the "Leninist policy" in the Party's economic policy. A second extremely important factor has been and remains the famous slogan "Catching and surpassing the advanced capitalistic nations," especially the United States. This competition has always been conducted by imitating U.S. knowledge and putting it on a Soviet basis, largely without a systematic approach to the development of any particular branch (otrasl').[8] For example, "the rapid development of chemistry and the oil and gas industry . . . has not been accompanied by corresponding rates of growth in the chemical machine building [industry]."[9]

The so-called subjective approach by which "many economic measures are implemented without being properly thought out and without having an adequate economic basis" is yet another important factor.[10] For obvious reasons this factor is always discussed in the past tense. It might be put this way: in each of the groups a branch develops in the manner and degree that the head of the branch believes is important.

All these extraeconomic factors which have determined the development of the Soviet economy are the sources of national economic, interbranch, and intrabranch disproportions, which lower the effectiveness of the national economy. They are reflected in plans and put into practice by plans in conjunction with the principles of planning "from the attained level" and several other concepts. Some influences vary and are similar to campaigns, but others are constant. As a result, on all levels of Soviet economic leadership a fixed scale has been traditionally established for evaluating the subdivision of industry, its branches, and the measures being carried out. According to this tradition, group A is very important, and group B can wait. To build a blast furnace is important and respectable; to build a concentrating factory (without which the blast furnace cannot function properly in modern times) is something that the Soviet economy has managed to do without until now. Moreover, the construction of the factory is not something that can be celebrated with a meeting and a report about its readiness. This fallacious tradition is gaining strength (or evolves from it) because of a parallel scale of responsibility for the nonfulfillment of tasks. The higher a branch is rated, the greater the degree of responsibility and punishment for the same economic misdemeanor. This tradition is so firmly established in the consciousness of management personnel that even direct demands from the higher Party leadership are unable to eradicate it. Nevertheless, this psychological barrier must be eliminated, if only to make it easier to correct disproportions that have become a great economic danger.

There is one other serious barrier to the elimination of disproportions. Development by new construction programs requires new capital investments for the poorly developed and new branches of production. However, "the length of time for the complete cycle of capital investments (drafting, construction, and the mastery of the rated capacity of the enterprises) frequently requires from eight to twelve years.... However, the constraint placed on investments by projects that have been under construction for a long time makes it difficult to change proportions in order to develop new, more effective branches of the national economy."[11]

The Nature of Siting

The economically based, optimal siting of production forces (that is, determining where a plant or factory might best be built or physically located) is very significant. Under any economic system, it is the most important factor in the effectiveness of the national economy. It is also the most difficult factor to change. Nonetheless, in the Soviet Union "this exceptionally important problem has not been adequately studied. This has a negative effect on the building of socialism. Serious errors in production siting are frequently allowed to occur, such as in selecting a site for the construction of enterprises and defining their size and specialization."[12]

"Basically these errors are connected with calculation errors in territorial planning, *with the absence of a widely accepted scientifically founded methodology of determining the economic effectiveness of the siting of production forces* (italics mine), and with an inadequate development of theoretical questions concerning the siting of socialist production."[13] The absence of a scientifically founded methodology leads to serious errors, and an error in siting one enterprise leads to errors in siting other enteprises."[14] Several Soviet economists feel with complete justification that "it is impossible to seriously discuss the effectiveness of public production until a scientific methodology is created to determine the effectiveness of siting."[15] However, the creation of a scientific theory and a scientifically founded methodology of siting is practically impossible under the conditions of Soviet planned price setting, the arbitrary system of tariffs, and several other, often "ideological," factors. As Fedorenko notes, "The problem of optimizing the development and siting of production forces cannot be properly solved without first solving questions concerning the economic evaluation of the most important resources used in production, of the production funds, and of natural and labor resources."[16] However, such economic evaluations do not yet exist.

Circumstances have evolved in which the following situation is possible. "In solving questions of siting plants we run into the granting of priority to local interests, departmentalism, opportunism, oversimplification, and other negative aspects that ultimately lead to large national economic losses. Branch ministries and their planning institutes often take a one-sided approach to questions about siting a branch. They fail to adequately consider national economic interests. . . . The resultant siting of plants and even branches of industry is filled with serious shortcomings."[17] Khrushchev once said, "The selection of a building site is frequently made on the basis of 'whose voice is loudest.' "[18] Apparently in mind were interdepartmental examples of solving questions on siting. Other sources point out that plants are often built where the only condition in favor of such construction is that there is a construction organization nearby. No other consideration is taken into account.

This long-time siting practice has led to many serious errors that lower the effectiveness of the USSR's national economy. "Among these errors are the disparity between the rich natural resources of the regions east of the Urals and the extent of their use, when one considers the level of industrial development in the European part of the USSR and the Urals compared to the power and raw materials found there; the inadequate development of the *raions*, and the unsatisfactory use of production funds, labor, and natural resources in the individual *raions*, leading to significantly excessive expenses in the national economy; the extraordinary concentration of industry in the largest cities with a resultant low level of industrial development in medium-sized and small cities."[19]

Either these errors are being corrected very slowly, or errors continue to increase. Thus, for example, "the proportion of industrial output of the eastern zone during the period 1960 to 1965 increased by less than 1 percent."[20] In subsequent years the momentum decreased because plans for new construction were not fulfilled; moreover, the main development of the eastern regions was done at the expense of the mining (extraction) industry. During the Ninth Five-Year Plan, territorial production complexes were created to speed up movement to the east. Five of these complexes were sited in Siberia![21] "However, because of shortcomings in planning, the drafting and financing for the formation of these complexes are proceeding slowly. Very often the makeup must be reexamined, the designs of the overall plans have to be reworked, and individual plants must be added or excluded."[22] This is all understandable given the problems of territorial planning.

It is easy to establish that industry continues to be concentrated in large cities. One need only compare the USSR population censuses of 1959 and 1970.

The problem of siting production forces has long been recognized. There exist special state plans, special decisions, and resolutions whose purpose is to remedy the situation. However, just as in many other aspects, the Soviet system is contradictory. In mid 1973 the great Soviet economist S. Pervushin confirmed that

> the present order of planning and realization of investments does not assist in the accelerated development of new, promising regions. It does not place limitations on the regions in which it has been recognized as inexpedient to expand production capacities at the expense of new construction. Favorable conditions have not been created for industrial production in the small cities. On the contrary, there are definite advantages in having a well-developed production and nonproduction infrastructure in inhabited areas and in the larger cities. Such conditions for the financing of capital construction make it difficult to have a balanced movement [foreseen in plans] of industrial production into the regions that possess promising resources but are located far from communications and industrial centers.[23]

There are many errors, often annoying and foolish, in the manufacturing branches of industry. Here, too, errors in the specialization of plants show up very clearly. Thus, for example, there are several machine-building plants in the Far East manufacturing a product, 90 to 95 percent of which is shipped to other regions of the country. Moreover, the metal is sent there from more than seventy-five hundred kilometers; and the product is then shipped from the plants to users more than eight thousand kilometers away.[24] For the past ten to fifteen years enormous errors have been made in siting the power-consuming industries. It has become laughable.

Several chemical enterprises were built near Volgograd because there was already a hydroelectric station there. Then it was discovered that these enterprises were not only power consuming but heat consuming as well. Therefore, "a central electrical heating system with an output of hundreds of thousands of kilowatts was built. This heating system produced electricity as well as steam. However, it turned out that the chemical plants in that area had no need for the energy of a powerful hydroelectric station."[25] Another example of such errors is that "in Kazakhstan a sugar refinery is being built in a place where there is no work force, no water, and, even more important, no sugar beets!"[26] Hundreds of such examples could be cited.

Some errors in siting are so flagrant and economically unsound that in 1963 Khrushchev felt it wise and "apparently economically advantageous to move several old power-consuming factories to eastern regions."[27] Just what factors are considered in day-to-day decisions concerning where to locate factories?

I have already mentioned several. However, the first deputy of the State Committee of the RSFSR Council of Ministers for the Use of Labor Resources, A. Maikov, provides a more complete answer. He writes: "When choosing a place for a new enterprise, the following things are usually considered: the resources of the construction base, the convenience and economic feasibility of preparing the site for the future plant or factory, the availability of housing and transportation, the engineering and production communications of all types, and the conditions for a water, heat, and electrical power supply. The branch ministries consider these things in selecting a location for a new plant or factory, while trying to spend as little as possible in the process." Obviously the departmental approach prevails, which nearly always contradicts national economic considerations and interests. Maikov notes ironically, "While working on this article I tried to find the document that was confirmed by directive organizations and that spells out who is to choose a site for a new plant or factory, what the requirements are, what organizations examine them, who is brought in for consultation in the event of a disagreement, and who has the final word. I was unable to find such a document. I asked one executive involved in such decisions, 'Where can I read about how one goes about siting new enterprises?' I was given the following answer: 'In a textbook on political economics. . . . The siting of new enterprises is spread out among the ministries, offices, and local authorities. And personal interests serve as their guiding light.' "[28]

Determining Growth Rates and
Means of Comparison

Ever since the 1965 economic reform, the growth rates of an entire industry and its individual branches are determined by the growth of gross product. "In figuring the gross national product among the branches of material production the output is computed in actual prices which are added to other kinds of net income, *including the turnover tax* (italics mine).[29]

There are thus two arbitrary values in the computation of the gross product that do not reflect the actual amount of production. The first are the planned prices, and the second is the turnover tax, which is often varied in order to regulate demand. Moreover, material still in production is included in the total gross output (as it is currently calculated). However, the most relevant factor is that the methodology for determining the amount of gross product as applied in the USSR does not consider the continuous recurrence of computation. By using this methodology, the same product expressed in price is included in the total gross product as many times as it passes through the independent self-supporting organizations (*khozraschet*). For example, based on its value, metal intended for the production of carburetors enters into the gross product of the metallurgical, carburetor, motor, and automobile plants, that is, four times. The recurrence of computation is continually increasing because of the complexity of economic relationships in modern production, but this complexity can be changed as a result of administrative reorganizations. In discussing this last interrelationship, the late Strumilin wrote: "A corrupting procedure occurs regularly: the nation's gross product is a direct result of the number of accountants and independent accounting balances—to surpass the United States quickly, we need only double the number of bookkeeping offices instead of doubling the productivity of labor."[30]

In 1973 and early 1974, in connection with the creation of associations (*ob"edinenie*) the problem of the number of bookkeeping offices was seriously discussed because the gross product of an association will be significantly less than the gross product of the plants making up the association, which are accounted for separately.

Gross product and the productivity of labor are interrelated by the formula: gross product divided by the number of workers equals the productivity of labor, where at a given moment the number of workers is a value that can be fairly precisely established.

Discussing problems concerning the productivity of labor and, through it, the methods of defining the growth of gross product, Strumilin wrote that for individual plants and factories "the errors caused by using the gross product indicator rather than a net indicator can lead to absolutely intolerable values." In individual branches, "systematic errors in drawing conclusions to the point of exaggeration about the growth rates of the productivity of labor [gross product] cannot be excluded."[31] According to Strumilin's calculations, it is only as the result of an increase in recurrence of computation for the period 1950 through 1955 that gross product grew by 185 percent.[32]

To everything that has been said one must add the "ethereal gross product" (that is, having no substance or contrived) or the "ethereal market." When ethereal assignments show up in the beginning of the planning year, they usually remain in the plans. "This is explained by a desire to preserve the projected growth rates of industrial production."[33]

This permits us to conclude that even the highest Soviet economic leaders do not know the actual growth rates of industrial production. The increase of repeated calculations brought about by the complexity and growth of the economy but not taken into consideration by the Central Statistical Director-ate's methodology distorts the picture and makes it impossible to compare the growth rates for individual periods. As a result these figures are only approximate, and it is well known that official figures provide a significantly exaggerated picture. Such statistical methods in relation to questions of the quality of output have led several Soviet economists to conclude that the only economically correct and comparable value is the national economic effect of production. Thus, for example, if a Soviet tractor's serviceability were to be increased from eight to sixteen years (as in the United States), then with the present level of production the output would double, in the sense of the economic effect obtained.

Even more complicated and problematic are the attempts to compare the production level of Soviet industry with that of prerevolutionary Russia (a comparison that Soviet statistics and propaganda particularly like to make) or with those of the advanced market economy nations. The endless comparisons between Soviet and American industrial output are devoid of any economic basis; nonetheless, official and mandatory figures are used. It is easy to convince oneself of the total absence of any scientific or economic bases for making such comparisons after having read the report, "The Scientific Conference on Questions Concerning the Methodology of Comparing the Basic Economic Indicators of the USSR and the United States."[34] The report appeared almost five months after the conference, which is in itself significant, but even in the brief article about the reports one is struck by the lack of methodology for making such comparisons. Soviet economists pointed out in particular the difficulties caused by (1) the different structures of the economies, (2) the different systems of inventorying output, and (3) the incomparability of prices. In addition, calculations are made in different currencies, the parity of which is both unclear and disputable.

Thus, the official figures of comparison published in *National Economy of the USSR* for the corresponding year have an exclusively propagandistic significance. The overall comparisons are unfounded from any point of view. The comparison of the output of individual articles deliberately ignores the ultimate economic effect and the consumer value of what is produced.

Scientific-Technical Progress

The technological level and scientific-technical progress, like nearly everything in Soviet economics, are determined to a great extent by the Party's economic policy. Thus planning, price setting, organization, management, and many other phenomena inherent to the system have determined the actual economic situation. In recent years not only economic but political (ideological) significance as well has been increasingly linked with scientific-technical progress in industry. Nonetheless, it is precisely in science and technology that it becomes clear how the system creates complicated problems that are unsolvable within the framework of the present-day system.

The extensive path of development (that is, building new plants rather than modernizing old ones) has always been a characteristic of the Soviet economic system. At the beginning of industrialization it was justified and natural;

however, it is no longer justified, at least in the postwar years. The longer it is used, the more harmful it becomes to the national economy. It is difficult to list all the negative consequences of this essential error. Today it is a well-established tradition, supported and reinforced by the practice of financing development and by the system of organizing scientific-technical progress, as well as by the price-setting system. The extensive path of development has often played a crucial role in the creation of such phenomena as the interbranch and intrabranch disproportions, the stockpiles of aging machine tools, machines, and equipment and the large number of antiquated technical processes.

Extensive development has taken place under the departmental and local interest approaches to the practical development of individual branches and the intrabranch development of individual production facilities. The main consequences of such an approach have been the poor development of specialization and cooperation, lack of unification, the dispersion and duplication of efforts directed toward the same economic problem, and considerable losses especially in the branches of the mining industry.

Production Spurt System

No Soviet industrial plant has ever worked smoothly. This means that they never put out the same quantity from day to day. Erratic work is so widespread that it earned a special name: the production spurt system (*kampaneishchina* or *shturmovshchina*). In the last ten-day period of the month more output is produced than in the first twenty days of the month. For example, "an investigation made in 1961 of forty-two machine-building plants showed that the majority produced more than half their output as prescribed by the monthly production schedule in the third ten-day period."[35] The production spurt occurs even in plants whose production process is an assembly line. They produce in spurts at the Vladimir and Lipetsk tractor plants[36] and at the Volograd motor plant. It exists in the coal industry[37] and uneven production is characteristic of several other branches."[38] In September of 1973, the Kalinin Electrical Appliance Plant produced 58 percent of its monthly output in the third ten-day period.[39]

There are monthly, quarterly, and annual production spurts, the last being the all-out production spurt. Production spurts generally occur toward the end of each bookkeeping period of an operational plan, a yearly national economic plan, or an individual plan intended to solve a specific problem.

Attempts to eliminate the production spurt have been futile. "A study of the introduction of a planning indicator for realized output shows that no substantial changes have occurred in improving the smooth flow of production." At the same time the economic reform (1965) looked on the new indicator, market output, as a reliable weapon for doing away with the production spurt.

The causes of the production spurt are many, but the "unevenness can be explained not only by the shortcomings in the organization of labor and production but also by the systematic violation of contractual obligations by the plants producing parts for use by others."[40] So-called complacency plays an important part in the production spurt. Complacency appears when a lull in production occurs after a production spurt. "No less is written about lulls that take place at most plants at the start of the month and about the production spurt during the nights and days in the last five days of the month than is written about the flaws of 'gross product.' "[41]

Without ranking them in order of importance, I shall point out the chief negative consequences of the production spurt. First, it leads to overexpenditure and a deficit labor force. "Investigation of several plants, including some of the most progressive, has shown that they have a labor force reserve that allows them to fulfill in the third ten-day period of each month a volume of work from 2 to 2.5 times greater than in the first two ten-day periods."[42]

The production spurt sharply lowers the quality of output. "The uneven operation of some plants is greatly detrimental to the efficiency of machines. . . . It is impossible to discuss raising the quality of output at plants that fulfill most of the month's assignment in the third ten-day period."[43] The following happens in regard to consumer goods. "Many of us even now, when buying something, look to see when it was made. If it was made the twenty-ninth or thirtieth of a month, we do not buy it. If it was made during a production spurt, it is poor quality."[44] There is only one opinion in the USSR concerning the effect of the production spurt on quality. At the *plenum* of a Moscow Party organization "data were introduced from sociological research conducted among workers in the city of Mytishchi. To the question, What prevents you from doing quality work? almost half replied, The production spurt." During the production spurt the quality of output frequently falls so low that the enterprises "work for the warehouse . . . and inflict great harm on the national economy."[45]

The production spurt raises the price of production because early in the month they often have to pay for the enforced idleness of the workers, and then during the production spurt they must pay the workers for overtime.

The production spurt is not the only manifestation of uneven operation in the Soviet economic system. Common, uneven operation creates an atmosphere of tension and uncertainty that destroys work morale. "We are always struggling, conquering, and attacking, always storming something [that is, *shturmovshchina*]; we are standing watch in case something should happen, but when, comrades, are we allowed to work? . . . Harmful, idle talk is verbal militarism in working life."[46] The effects of the production spurt are depicted in figure 10-1.

Fixed Assets

The total of all vehicles, equipment, means of communication, and buildings (plants) which make the production of a given product possible are referred to as

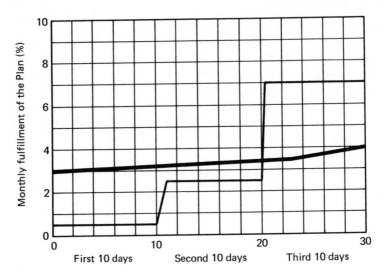

This is what the rhythmic and nonrhythmic work of an enterprise looks like on a graph: time off, stoppages, and forced idleness at the beginning of the month, with rush work and overtime at the end of the month.

Figure 10-1. The Production Spurt

fixed assets. The amount of fixed assets expressed in currency are listed in *The National Economy of the USSR*, which gives a vague notion of the actual amount and structure of fixed assets. In this reference book the USSR's fixed assets are compared only roughly with the fixed assets of leading industrial nations. In all likelihood this is so for the same reasons that any such comparison is dubious. As of 1 January 1971, the fixed assets of industry represented 30.8 percent of the fixed assets of the entire country.

Industrial fixed assets are divided into passive and active assets. Active fixed assets are the most important, for they include the assets that actually create material values. Active fixed assets include machines, equipment, and instruments. Passive fixed assets include everything that makes use of the active fixed assets possible: buildings, installations, and plant communications. The correlation between active and passive fixed assets is one of the most important national economic ratios. In the USSR's industry the active part of fixed assets has stabilized at a ratio of 33 percent.[47] In the United States, even in 1955, this percentage was 48.5.[48] "In other industrially developed nations the percentage is as high as 50 to 55 percent."[49]

The utilization of fixed assets is also important. This means the portion of work time that the active fixed assets actually work. According to this indicator, the USSR also lags behind advanced developed nations, and "the integral load of fixed assets of U.S. manufacturing industry is at least 1.4 to 1.5 times higher than the USSR's."[50] As an example "one might point to the comparatively small amount of the average statistically weighted hours of work of electrical motors in the USSR's industry, equaling about 1,500 hours a year (out of 8,760 calendar hours). At the same time this figure reaches 2,700 in the United States."[51]

Until the 1965 reform inadequate usage of fixed assets was largely explained by their free (no payment) nature. This has caused plants to hoard excess fixed assets and to use fixed assets in an inefficient manner. However, the economic reform's introduction of payment for fixed assets has produced practically no results. The problem is that at the present "in the system of financial payments to the budget by plants, the payments from the unattached remainder of profit dominate. On the average, the amount of unattached remainder exceeds payment for the assets by more than three times, and in individual plants it exceeds payment by ten times or more."[52] The managers of the plant regard the unattached remainder of profit as someone else's money; thus they are not interested in whether this remainder is a little more or a little less. Nor does the absolute figure of 6 percent interest them. However, they are very much interested in having reserves of machine tools and equipment as insurance against the unknown. This interest is created and justified by the planning system in general and by material-technical supply in particular.

The age of fixed assets, particularly the active part, is one of the most important determinants of their effectiveness. The hoarding and aging of fixed assets is one result of extensive development (new construction programs), and thus hopelessly antiquated plants exist on an equal level with new plants. Therefore, one must speak of the average cited age of active fixed assets. "In the USSR the average, normative period of serviceability of equipment is seventeen years. . . . The average age of industrial equipment in the United States is 9.4 years."[53] Nearly a third of machines and equipment in Soviet industry are fifteen to twenty years old and even older.[54] Other sources indicate even longer periods. Moreover, one cannot avoid parallels. Thus, "according to data provided by A. Meddison, the normal period of serviceability of equipment, based on legislation about taxes and amortization, is about ten years in capitalistic nations of Europe, five years in Sweden, and about twenty-seven years in England. *Does this not at least partially explain the low rates of economic development in England?*" (italics mine).[55] Three pages later it is pointed out that "according to data of the Experimental Scientific Research Institute of Machine Tools, the actual average period of serviceability of a machine tool [in the USSR] is twenty-seven to thirty years."[56] Many other examples of old age ("greater than sixty-one years") and high percentages of "physically antiquated equipment" could be cited.[57]

No less important to their effectiveness is the structure of active fixed assets, which determines the methods of production and its technological level. The inner structure of active fixed assets in each branch is different, and therefore I shall examine only the inner structure of the most important branch: machine building. By the end of 1972 the stockpile of machine tools had reached about 3.8 million units.[58]

> However, within the structure of the stockpile of metal working machine tools we have many traditionally poorly producing groups of equipment. For example, the percentage of forge-and-press machines in the USSR is about 17 percent, and in the United States nearly 30 percent (1967); the percentage of lathe and turning machine tools in the structure of metal-cutting equipment in 1958 was 26.9 percent in the USSR and 12.3 percent in the United States. Moreover, in our country [USSR] the percentage of lathe and turning machine tools has increased between 1958 and 1970 from 26.9 percent to 30.4 percent. Specialized and unitized machine tools have increased from 12.6 percent to 15.6 percent, and automatic and semiautomatic machine tools have increased from 2.4 percent to 2.8 percent.[59]

In this way the ratios between "traditional," antiquated groups of machine tools and modern, progressive groups not only lag sharply behind the United States (and even further behind other advanced nations), but their modernization progresses extremely slowly. These ratios, the ratios of yesterday, determine the use of antiquated technology in machine building and metal working. In Soviet machine building, metal working is totally dominated by cutting, which leads to enormous labor losses and to losses of millions of tons of metal: "Losses in the form of metal shavings amount to more than 7 million tons of ferrous metals,"[60] and "nearly three or four times more metal is lost through metal shavings than in other nations."[61] Whereas "every ton of metal lost in shavings costs the national economy some 650 rubles,"[62] net losses due to antiquated technology add up to anywhere from 3 billion to 3.4 billion rubles per year. "Perhaps it would be worthwhile to mention that 24 percent of Russia's stockpile of machine tools, even in 1908, consisted of forge-press machines."[63]

At the required technical level, amortized deductions serve to renew and maintain all fixed assets that are in working condition. In the Soviet Union a differentiation is made between two types of amortization, physical and obsolescence. Physical amortization is the mechanized wear of machines and equipment to the extent that further use becomes physically impossible. Obsolescence amortization occurs when an operating machine becomes economically disadvantageous when compared with a newly introduced machine of the same type, and economic effectiveness of production demands that a switch be made. However, planned prices, which make effectiveness estimates nearly impossible, also make it impossible to determine obsolescence amortization. Therefore, the period of obsolescence amortization might conditionally be considered the amount of time required for new models to make their appearance; this varies from seven to ten years.[64] However, in Soviet economic practice obsolescence amortization is not considered. The planned character of the system has fixed the normative periods for amortization. The amortization periods for active fixed assets vary between twenty and fifty years.[65] However, even these normative periods are not observed, and "in machine building, for example, every year . . . just slightly more than 2 percent of all equipment is written off," although according to the norms "every year about 7 percent of the original pool of machinery should be written off." The reason for this situation is that "the average annual production of machines and equipment does not cover the actual wear and tear of active fixed assets."[66] This in turn is the result of new construction programs, which has led to a gigantic pool of machine tools and equipment, as well as to their poor condition. Although this error would seem obvious, "in recent years of the Eighth Five-Year Plan (1966-1970) 75 to 80 percent of the updating of the USSR's industrial fixed assets has been in adding new plants, and only 20 to 25 percent has been in modernizing old ones."[67]

In recent years overall amortized deductions have accounted for about 7.5 percent of the cost of industry's fixed assets, a little more than half has gone for capital repairs, and the remainder has gone for restoration. "The economic reform has introduced substantial corrective measures in the order of distribution and use of amortization. Before the reform, all amortization totals [for renovation] were sent to the Construction Bank (*Stroibank*) for financing central capital investments; but now up to 45 percent of amortization is at the disposal of the enterprises to form a fund for developing production."[68] "Up to 90 percent of amortization totals designated for capital repairs remain in the hands of the plants."[69] Capital repair of machines and equipment is handled by the individual plant.

Plants modernize their machine tools and equipment, except for capital repairs, through the use of the production development fund. Usually a plant's plan includes a task indicating the number of machine tools, machines, and equipment requiring modernization. "In spite of its great national economic significance, modernization of equipment until quite recently has not been adequate. A tendency to cut back on this kind of work has been noted in recent years."[70] It is also "characteristic that repair of equipment amounted to more than 40 percent of all modernization; in addition, the productivity of 75 percent of machines has increased altogether by 5 percent." In an overall evaluation of modernization progress, this same source feels that "the figures presented by the plants only create the appearance of modernization. However, they do not include the most important data: an economic estimate of the effectiveness of expenditures."[71]

The actual situation can be explained largely by the inertness of the plants' management, for whom the perfection of fixed assets management on their own is an unpleasant and exacting pastime. It is much easier and more comfortable for them simply to obtain centralized capital investments for updating their plant. Then other people, that is, the managers of construction and installation organizations, bear the main burden of work and responsibility.

As a result the updating of fixed assets is inadequate. It moves at a slow pace and usually does not have an adequate economic basis, even within the limits of the Soviet economic system. The domination of the practice of adding new plants, which leads to increasing fixed assets, complicates the problem of updating existing assets.

Capital Investments

Capital investments are state-planned appropriations directed toward creating new fixed assets. Their creation cycle can be divided into construction and assimilation. Assimilation refers to the process that takes place from the completion of construction until the time when the new enterprise attains the projected (planned) production capacity.

The extensive path of development for the Soviet economy determines the large amount of capital investments. In the Eighth Five-Year Plan (1966-1970), overall capital investments amounted to more than 310 billion rubles, including 241 billion rubles for state and cooperative organizations. Less than 30 percent of these investments were aimed at the areas east of the Ural Mountains.[72] Data on percentages for extensive and intensive development are contradictory. I previously presented data showing that in the final years of the Eighth Five-Year Plan only 20 to 25 percent of capital investments went for intensive development; but another source of information states that in 1968, for example, 62 percent of investments were put into intensive development.[73] This figure is somewhat unreliable. The same source states that 55 percent of capital investments went to intensive development in the year 1960, while the other source says 15.6 percent.[74] As a general rule, one must assume that about one-fourth of all capital investments go for replacing existing fixed assets.

Prior to the 1965 reform capital investments, like fixed assets, were free (without cost), that is, they represented state, nonreturnable financing. The reform envisaged that a significant part of capital investments slated for replacement and reconstruction of plants would come from the plants' development fund and long-term bank credits. However, "the decisions of the directive organizations concerning the switch from centralized financing of capital investments in industry to long-term crediting and the plants' own resources (the industrial development fund) have for all intents and purposes not been put into effect."[75]

The standard method is used to estimate the effectiveness of capital investments.[76] However, this method has no economic basis (planned prices) and has several other shortcomings that "lead to errors in many calculations and especially when evaluating the economic effectiveness of new technology."[77] These errors result in enormous flagrant losses and even greater hidden losses that lower the effectiveness of capital investments. In isolated cases the magnitude of errors (particularly in the siting of enterprises) is so great that construction comes to a halt. By 1966 in the RSFSR (Russian Soviet Federated Socialist Republic) alone, 698 industrial construction projects were suspended. These construction sites represented an overall budgeted value of 1.1 billion rubles; 237 million rubles had already been invested in their construction."[78] Characteristically these construction projects were suspended either the year work had begun or in the following year.[79] Throughout the entire economy, such losses amount to anywhere from 200 million to 250 million rubles per year.

The internal structure of capital investments changes very little, and within it "the ratio of construction and installation work to total capital investments . . . is still extremely high and exceeds the corresponding indicators of the most developed capitalist nations."[80] It is not surprising that such a capital investment structure leads to an unsatisfactory fixed-asset structure.

More than two-thirds of capital investments go to create new capacities. For these new capacities, in turn, more than two-thirds of the resources are spent on construction and assembly work, that is, for creating passive fixed assets.

The assimilation of capital investments is a complicated, highly questionable process. I shall discuss only the main features and their results. One of the more significant features is the so-called dissipation of capital investments. For many years, 260,000 to 270,000 industrial construction projects throughout the country were being outfitted at the same time.[81] A vicious circle has been created because when *Gosplan* allocates resources, it must give the greater portion to construction projects begun long before, but it can give only a small portion to construction work just undertaken. Thus, many simultaneous construction projects increase during the allocation process. The chief result of the dissipation of capital investments is long periods of time for construction and growing numbers of uncompleted construction projects which tie up cash and resources for years. "According to Central Statistical Directorate data, total uncompleted construction in our nation had grown to 52.5 billion rubles at the beginning of 1971."[82] After taking into consideration several factors omitted in the Central Statistical Directorate's data, however, the author of the cited article feels that the actual amount equals 62 million rubles.

A second, very important feature of assimilation is that the "ever-increasing estimates have become a real whip in the hands of industrial construction; these estimates disorganize the production collectives and undermine the main principles of planning."[83] The reasons that actual construction costs exceed planned costs lie in the system of awarding bonuses to the planners for an effective decision and in the system of confirming planned projects, whereby a "cheap" construction project can more quickly and easily be included in a plan.

According to Five-Year Plan estimates for 1973, the cost of the Ust-Ilimskaia hydroelectric station was to be 690.3 million rubles, but it was confirmed in the 1973 plan at 1,025 million rubles. The Kuibyshev-Tikhoretskaia oil pipeline was estimated at 143.5 million rubles, and the confirmed cost was 267 million rubles. The construction of the Kostroma cartridge cases and pistons plant, where the construction estimate was set at 52.9 million rubles and the confirmed cost of construction was 236.4 million rubles, broke all records.[84] At the same time planning estimates are being made in *Gosplan, Gossnab,* and at the governmental level for construction materials. These organizations base their estimates on a "million norm," which indicates the materials needed per million rubles of construction work on a specific type of installation. As a consequence, in a long-term plan the sum exceeding the estimated cost does not pass through the planning process and does not receive a material payment. Because of this the material-technical supply for construction suffers.

The overall handling of capital investments has been aptly characterized by T. Khachaturov: "The average period of time for construction is now five years, and for the largest construction projects this period can be as much as twelve years. If one considers that from one to two years are needed for the drafting and confirmation of plans, and three to four years for assimilating rated capacities, then by the time such a plant is ready to operate, the technical parameters included in the plan are often outdated."[85]

The basic reasons for this problem are the dissipation of capital investments, the inadequate financing of building sites, the lack of construction materials and installed equipment, the inadequacy of construction machinery and work force due to an incompatibility between the volume of work and the capacities of the construction organization, and several other shortcomings that could be eliminated.

One need only add that other sources believe even longer periods of time are needed for the assimilation of capital investments. The age of "shortcomings that could be eliminated" is approaching half a century.

Production Specialization

A great number of plants, especially machine-building plants, have been built as complex installations operating as a closed cycle, that is, they are self-sufficient. The concept is that a finished product should be made whenever possible by a single plant. Theoretically, this erroneous principle might have had some justification in the early stages of industrialization, but later the economic insolvency of such a system became clear.

The creation of complex plants, originally based on serious reasons and circumstances, has become a tradition. In 1962 at the November plenum of the Central Committee of the CPSU, Khrushchev noted: "The inclination of our management people toward the old organization of complex works is still so strong that in spite of all directives and appeals to organize specialized production, the number of universal plants continues to grow."[86] This "inclination" was still around much later.[87]

The country's main construction project in 1974, the *KamAZ* (Kama automobile plant), is an excellent example of the creation of a complex giant whose technical rationale, economic effectiveness, and perspective for technological progress are questionable.

Tradition has once again proved stronger in practice than the directives and appeals of central management. For a long time, even the plans calling for the construction of specialized plants have regularly not been met.[88]

This situation has developed for several reasons. Basic reasons can be found in branch planning, where each *Gosplan* department is concerned only with itself and gives no thought to the overall use of the manufactured articles it is planning. *Gosplan* and *Gossnab* make errors in distributing the manufacture of articles among the plants and ministries. "On the average, nearly 120 different types of manufactured articles appear at each machine-building plant. This includes forty mass-produced articles."[89] The price system also has an influence when, contrary to all logic or the existing situation, the delivery of parts produced on a cooperative basis by specialized plants costs more than the actual production.

Another obstacle to specialization is departmentalism, which leads to the production of the same article by a number of factories subordinate to different departments. "In the machine-building industry, 400 plants make metal-cutting lathes, more than 360 make instruments, 11 make blast furnace and steel furnace equipment, 47 plants make tower cranes, 260 produce pumps, 2,000 make gear wheels, 200 make sleeve joints for driver gears, 500 make flanges, and 1,000 enterprises make pulleys."[90] An analogous situation exists in the production of semifinished products and spare parts,[91] and a significant number of instruments are produced in some 4,200 instrument making shops.[92] The most important reason, however, is the disruption of material-technical supply, which is frequently caused by suppliers' violating conditions agreed upon for deliveries. These breakdowns in the delivery system threaten the fulfillment of the plan by the plant, the trust, the chief directorate, and perhaps even the ministry. It is for this reason that all practical economic managers, when deciding questions about specialization and the expansion of contacts, are governed by the simple, tried-and-true logic: "The fewer contacts, the less red tape. I can always get what I want from my own shop [or, on a higher level, my own plant, trust, or chief directorate], but when I have contact with another plant, I can't get past the arbitration stage. The main question is, Why take the risk? Aren't all excess expenditures taken into consideration and written into the plan?"[93] It turns out that everyone is his own boss. This can be seen not just in the level of specialization but in several other phenomena as well.

The level of specialization is very low, and "the low level of specialization for production, for assembly line production, and for the unification and standardization of parts slows down the introduction of the latest technology and of highly productive equipment. The nonspecialized production of an instrument, a prop, spare parts, pumps, and other machinery leads to an increase in labor of anywhere from two to ten times or more."[94] These developments cause enormous losses to the economy. "Just rectifying the problem of manufacturing a rigging could save a billion rubles a year and free two hundred thousand skilled workers and seventy thousand designers."[95] Unification and standardization, "according to rough estimates, [could cut] the number of model sizes of various kinds of output . . . ten to fifteen times, and as much as twenty times for gear wheels."[96]

The specialization problem can be made somewhat clearer by a comparison between Soviet and American machine building. In the United States, less than 1 percent of all machine-building factories have their own forging shops and sections, nearly 1.5 percent have their own casting shops, and about 4 percent have shops that make pit prop hardware.[97] In Soviet machine building, 84 percent of the plants have their own forging shops and sections, 57 to 71 percent produce a different casting, and 65 percent produce pit prop hardware.[98]

The overall importance of specialization has been recognized in the Soviet Union for some time. As early as 1962 the *Ekonomicheskaia gazeta* wrote about specialization in machine building. *"The absence of specialization in machine building is very negatively reflected in the technical-economic indicators of production, and it complicates its planning and material-technical supply, slows down the introduction of the most progressive and inexpensive part-specializing production line and conveyor line production. These types of production are the highest form of technical progress"* (italics in original).[99] Nevertheless, specialization is moving very slowly and, at times, even loses ground. During the Ninth Five-Year Plan, parts and technological specialization was slated to be raised "by less than 1 percent."[100] Regarding the amount of casting being supplied by cooperative effort, "the total volume of their production went from 7.5 percent in 1965 to 6.2 percent in 1970."[101] "With each passing year the products listing for machine-building plants grows larger."[102]

A harmful development arising from the complex plant structure, especially in machine building, is the way maintenance is set up. Its present-day organization (or disorganization) is apparently based on the logic that if a plant is universal it should be able to repair its own machinery and equipment. Although this logic is somewhat applicable to machine-building plants, it is also widespread throughout the economy, even where such logic is totally inapplicable. As a result repair work is not specialized or centralized and is done under primitive conditions. It also ties up a large amount of equipment and people. "Of 3,010,000 metal cutting lathes on hand in the national economy, 800,000 are used for repair work, and they are used from 2 to 2½ times less effectively than in machine building. The amount of manual labor in repair jobs is from 2 to 2½ times higher than in basic shops, and the productivity of labor is from 3 to 5 times lower than for machine building on the whole." This situation occurs largely because the plant manufacturer put out too few spare parts and assembled machines. Thus, in the Soviet Union spare parts amount to between 1.5 and 2 percent of the total cost of manufactured articles, while in the United States they amount to 12 percent."[103] Although this discussion has concerned mostly machine building branches, these same problems can be seen in all branches of the national economy.

Inasmuch as the technical level of repair work is generally higher than the technical level of an individual plant's production, the very newest machine tools and the best skilled workers are concentrated in the repair shops. A paradoxical situation evolves: the newest machine tools repair the old ones, and the old machine tools create new machine tools. The conditions that have come about in repair work have led to "yearly expenditures for maintenance of the nation's machine stockpile reaching enormous amounts, in excess of 14 billion rubles."[104] "According to estimates made by specialists, the specialization and centralization of repair work alone could provide a savings of 1.8 to 2 times," that is, could save between 6.8 and 7 billion rubles. A large number of people are engaged in repair work. "Rough estimates have indicated that at the present time there are approximately 6 to 7 million repairmen. . . . One can surmise that the total number of repairmen will exceed 9 million by the end of 1970."[105]

Notes

1. *The National Economy of the USSR 1922-1972* (Moscow: Statistika, 1972), p. 154.

2. *A Course in Political Economics* (Moscow: Ekonomika, 1970), p. 239.

3. *Voprosy ekonomiki*, no. 1 (1973):23.

4. *The National Economy*, p. 125.

5. *Problems of the Political Economics of Socialism* (Moscow: Gospolitizdat, 1960), p. 111.

6. *Planovoe khoziaistvo*, no. 12 (1967):21.

7. *Ekonomicheskaia gazeta*, no. 20 (1971):13.

8. *Voprosy ekonomiki*, no. 1 (1973):23.

9. *Voprosy ekonomiki*, no. (1966):94.

10. Ibid.

11. *Planovoe khoziaistvo*, no. 2 (1971):35.

12. *Voprosy ekonomiki*, no. 8 (1961):21.

13. *Voprosy ekonomiki*, no. 6 (1966):28.

14. *Voprosy ekonomiki*, no. 12 (1962):46.

15. *Voprosy ekonomiki*, no. 8 (1966):141.

16. *Planovoe khoziaistvo*, no. 8 (1968):16.

17. *Planovoe khoziaistvo*, no. 7 (1968):51.

18. *Pravda*, 26 April 1963, p. 4.

19. *Planovoe khoziaistvo*, no. 11 (1961):19.

20. *Ekonomicheskaia gazeta*, no. 44 (1964):10.

21. *Planovoe khoziaistvo*, no. 1 (1972):16.

22. *Voprosy ekonomiki*, no. 8 (1973):133.

23. *Voprosy ekonomiki*, no. 6 (1973):46.

24. *Planovoe khoziaistvo*, no. 8 (1966):81.

25. *Pravda*, 21 November 1964, p. 2.

26. *Ekonomicheskaia gazeta*, no. 36 (1966):16.

27. *Pravda*, 20 September 1963, p. 1.

28. *Sotsialisticheskaia industriia*, 13 May 1970, p. 2.

29. *National Economy of the USSR in 1970* (Moscow: Statistika, 1971), p. 763.

30. *Voprosy ekonomiki*, no. 7 (1963):115.

31. *Voprosy ekonomiki*, no. 5 (1960):27.

32. Ibid., p. 28.

33. *Ekonomicheskaia gazeta*, no. 19 (1962):19.

34. *Voprosy ekonomiki,* no. 10 (1963):123.

35. *Voprosy ekonomiki*, no. 12 (1961):14.

36. *Pravda*, 19 December 1966, p. 2.

37. *Pravda*, 19 December 1965, p. 2.

38. *Voprosy ekonomiki*, no. 6 (1963):22-23.

39. *Sotsialisticheskaia industriia*, 24 November 1973, p. 2.

40. *Planovoe khoziaistvo*, no. 8 (1971):55.

41. *Oktiabr'*, no. 8 (1966):180.

42. *Voprosy ekonomiki*, no. 3 (1970):97.

43. *Pravda*, 13 December 1966, p. 2.

44. *Oktiabr'*, no. 8 (1966):180.

45. *Sotsialisticheskaia industriia*, 20 August 1971, p. 1.

46. *Novyi mir*, no. 10 (1965):33.

47. *Ekonomicheskaia gazeta*, no. 43 (1969):12.

48. *Voprosy ekonomiki*, no. 11 (1965):9.

49. *Voprosy ekonomiki*, no. 12 (1965):22.

50. *Voprosy ekonomiki*, no. 4 (1968):75.

51. *Voprosy ekonomiki*, no. 3 (1971):11.

52. *Voprosy ekonomiki*, no. 11 (1970):69.

53. *Planovoe khoziaistvo,* no. 9 (1970):78.

54. *Planovoe khoziaistvo*, no. 4 (1971):84.

55. *Voprosy ekonomiki*, no. 2 (1970):69.

56. Ibid., p. 72.

57. *Planovoe khoziaistvo*, no. 2 (1967):65.

58. *Voprosy ekonomiki*, no. 11 (1973):53.

59. *Voprosy ekonomiki*, no. 8 (1972):127.

60. *Planovoe khoziaistvo*, no. 11 (1972):9.

61. *Voprosy ekonomiki*, no. 12 (1970):29.

62. *Pravda*, 7 July 1969, p. 2.

63. *National Economy of the USSR in 1959* (Moscow: Statistika, 1960), p. 76.

64. *Voprosy ekonomiki*, no. 9 (1970):97.

65. *Voprosy ekonomiki*, no. 7 (1971):37.

66. *Voprosy ekonomiki*, no. 9 (1970):97.

67. *Sotsialisticheskaia industriia*, 4 August 1972, p. 2.

68. *Planovoe khoziaistvo*, no. 10 (1970):13.

69. Ibid., p. 14.

70. *Voprosy ekonomiki*, no. 6 (1967):120.

71. Ibid., p. 121.

72. *Voprosy ekonomiki*, no. 8 (1967):8.

73. *Voprosy ekonomiki*, no. 3 (1971):44.

74. *Planovoe khoziaistvo*, no. 9 (1968):86.

75. *Planovoe khoziaistvo*, no. 2 (1968):50.

76. *Ekonomisheskaia gazeta*, no. 39 (1969):11-12.

77. *Voprosy ekonomiki*, no. 1 (1967):37; also *Pravda*, 4 May 1972, p. 2.

78. *Planovoe khoziaistvo*, no. 10 (1968):39.

79. Ibid., 40.

80. *Voprosy ekonomiki*, no. 10 (1970):114.

81. *Voprosy ekonomiki*, no. 3 (1973):35.

82. *Voprosy ekonomiki*, no. 9 (1972):15.

83. *Sotsialisticheskaia industriia*, 8 August 1973, p. 2.

84. *Voprosy ekonomiki*, no. 8 (1973):33.

85. *Voprosy ekonomiki*, no. 3 (1973):35.

86. *Krasnaia zvezda*, 20 November 1962, p. 3.

87. *Planovoe khoziaistvo*, no. 12 (1971):17; also *Pravda*, 14 May 1969, p. 2.

88. *Voprosy ekonomiki*, no. 11 (1967):115.

89. *Sotsialisticheskaia industriia*, 28 June 1972, p. 2.

90. *Voprosy ekonomiki*, no. 11 (1967):110.

91. *Planovoe khoziaistvo*, no. 3 (1972):10; also *Voprosy ekonomiki*, no. 8 (1972):125.

92. *Sotsialisticheskaia industriia*, 30 May 1971, p. 2.

93. *Ekonomicheskaia gazeta*, no. 31 (1967):12.

94. *Voprosy ekonomiki*, no. 9 (1969):29-30.

95. *Sotsialisticheskaia industriia*, 30 May 1971, p. 2.

96. *Voprosy ekonomiki*, no. 11 (1967):112.

97. *Voprosy ekonomiki*, no. 8 (1972):124.

98. *Pravda*, 9 February 1970, p. 2.

99. *Ekonomicheskaia gazeta*, no. 23 (1962):9.

100. *Planovoe khoziaistvo*, no. 12 (1971):17.

101. *Planovoe khoziaistvo*, no. 6 (1972):122.

102. *Planovoe khoziaistvo*, no. 1 (1974):115.
103. *Planovoe khoziaistvo*, no. 11 (1968):24.
104. *Pravda*, 17 April 1969, p. 2.
105. *Voprosy ekonomiki*, no. 4 (1967):119.

11 Scientific Research and Experimental Design Work (NIOKR)

Scientific research and experimental design work form the starting point for the scientific-technical progress of any economic system. In the USSR the totality of scientific-technical progress is an interesting and broad topic. A complete discussion of it would require a tremendous amount of work. Here I shall be concerned mainly with the organization and tempo of this process as well as several main factors that define it.

It is self-evident that in a planned system scientific-technical progress is planned, or should be planned, and that individual stages of scientific research and experimental design work must represent a link in a unified chain. It is also self-evident that the planning of scientific-technical progress, as well as its practical implementation in research and design work and production, must have a clear purpose that has been correctly formulated. In the Soviet system these logical requirements are far from satisfactory in practice.

In Soviet economic literature much has been written about the planning of scientific-technical progress. Every source points out serious shortcomings. First, "it is known that the economic result of introducing new technology is not directly included in plans for new technology. This reflects the contribution to raising the effectiveness of public production. Plans for scientific-technical progress are frequently limited by a list of individual technical measures."[1] However, a plan cannot provide information on effectiveness; there is no way for it to do so, and no scientifically founded methodology exists for establishing effectiveness. Therefore, in this case as well there is no economically based, clear objective for planning before the planning process begins. "On the one hand, this leads to a situation in which not all elements of scientific-technical progress are included in planning, at least not all to the same extent. On the other hand the planning of these elements takes place with practically no coordination. As a result, the integrity of planning is violated; disproportions and lack of balance are wittingly created within the subsystem of scientific-technical progress."[2] The violation of planning integrity leads to "plans for new technology and plans for the development of production existing side by side, without being joined or complementing one another."[3]

At the end of the Scientific Research and Experimental Design Work (NIOKR) where implementation begins, planned price fixing for the new technology begins to play an enormous role. Five authors of an article in *Voprosy ekonomiki* are inclined to feel that one of the reasons for the slow introduction of the accomplishments of scientific-technical progress into production is inadequate regulation of price fixing for new technology, particularly for new equipment models. Frequently prices of new equipment models increase more rapidly than their technical parameters, which decreases economic interest in using them. Prices for new technology are set in such a way that they no longer serve as an effective instrument for distributing the economic effect of using this technology between the manufacturers and the users and for creating conditions whereby it would be beneficial for some to manufacture and others to use.[4]

Thus, there are three general problems: planning, coordination, and price fixing. However, the general director of a machine-tool building association in Leningrad, G. Kulagin, one of the best and more thoughtful directors in the USSR, sees a problem of irresponsibility. This is evident in the inflation of estimates on economic effectiveness, in the poor quality of many engineering jobs, in the departmental approach to assimilating new technology on the part of directors, and, finally, in the poor use of existing modern technology. Kulagin attaches more significance to matters of price fixing as well, looking on them from a self-supporting (*khozraschet*) point of view. In general, he feels that "only when a developer and producer are joined by a single economic and legal responsibility will new technology become advantageous to both the producer and user, *and it will become realistic to expect a sharp increase in the effectiveness of scientific-technical programs* [italics mine]. This can be achieved first through a purposeful and strict policy of price fixing along with organized measures based on principle."[5]

It is difficult to judge what Kulagin meant by "organized measures based on principle." After all, Kulagin himself knows that the creation of large-scale associations and even scientific production associations has turned out to be a totally inadequate organized measure.

Science is the first link in NIOKR. Basic applied science is often referred to as scientific-research work. Science in the USSR has developed at an increased rate in the last decade; expenditures for science during the period 1955 to 1965 increased on the average by 15 percent per year. "From 1965 through 1969 appropriations for science increased from 6.9 billion rubles to 10 billion rubles."[6] In 1966 the United States put 23.3 billion dollars into science.[7]

Science, if it can be thus expressed, has been physically torn from production. Less than 2 percent of all the USSR's scientific workers (about eight hundred thousand persons) are engaged in research work in plant laboratories; at the same time, nearly 60 percent of the United States' scientific workers work in plant laboratories.[8] This can be explained primarily by the system of wages and working conditions for scientists. "For many years now a system for artificially dividing scientific research institutes into categories has existed in our country."[9] There are three such categories. For example, a candidate of sciences who works in a category I scientific research institute receives sixty more rubles a month and twelve days more vacation a year than he would in a category II institute. This same candidate from a category II scientific research institute, should he become a senior lecturer in an institution of higher learning, would get seventy rubles a month more, his work day would be shorter, and he would get forty-eight days of vacation instead of twenty-four.[10] "For some reason he must receive a significantly lower salary in a factory laboratory than he would in an institute laboratory."[11] In a factory laboratory the degree of responsibility is greater, as is working time; but vacation, just as for all engineering-technical workers, is only twenty-four days.

Pure science is studied in the USSR Academy of Sciences, in the union-republic academies of science, and in only a few scientific research institutes of high governmental organizations (State Committee for Science and Technology, *Gosplan*, and *Gosstroi*). Applied science (experimental design work) is concentrated in the branch scientific research institutes of the ministries, offices, and design bureaus, right on down to plant-level design bureaus.

All scientific work is planned in the same manner that was described in the section on planning, although scientific planning has its own specific nature. Only some scientific topics included in the plan are moved forward by all-governmental organizations; the basic portion of the draft plan is filled out with topics put forth by scientific institutions. In the planning of science, "selecting subject matter and determining the greatest long-range trends of scientific research are important and complex. Sometimes the planning of the work of scientific research institutions is based on the traditions of the staff specialists. In addition, scientific workers do not always disseminate necessary information. Thus it becomes clear that topics of a false nature or which have already been solved are frequently planned."[12] In applied science the situation is complicated by the fact that "scientific collectives are not permitted to make mistakes." To make it easier to meet the plan (error is not taken into consideration in the plan), the scientific research institutes and design bureaus strive not to include in the plan "truly scientific problems, connected with risk or with possible violations of planned expenditures and periods of time or even failures."[13]

Science suffers a great deal from inadequate laboratory and instruction instruments. There is no single organization in the country that produces them. The production of instruments is parceled out among many ministries and departments; a significant portion is produced by hand on *kolkhozes* and *sovkholzhes*.[14] All science and applied science in particular suffers from the lack of modern laboratories, experimental bases, and testing enterprises. In actuality "branch-level scientific research institutes today are either not supported by experimental bases or for the most part have low-capacity plants which are often overburdened with assembly line production. These plants are incapable of producing a prototype model out of metal for a new piece of equipment,"[15] writes the director of the All-Union Scientific Research Institute of Machine-Building Technology. The number of design organizations having their own testing and experimental bases looks like this: 83.3 percent of all organizations in the automotive industry, 62.1 percent in instrument building, and only 35.2 percent in the chemical and petrochemical machine-building areas.[16] In this manner, having come up with a new machine or a new piece of equipment, the designer or draftsman must wait until the new design is introduced and starts working at full capacity (the period of assimilation is already known). Only then can he check out the quality of the design or draft solution.

In NIOKR, as in the rest of the economy, material-technical supply creates great difficulties. Thus, if a scientist who is working on a planned topic runs into something new or promising, the material support for work on it can be obtained only 1½ to 2 years later.

Only a comparatively small number of scientific designs ever become models. "In many branches of industry the amount of time required for testing models often reaches eight to ten years."[17] Once made, they are often obsolete.

The true situation in NIOKR means that its influence on the growth of the effectiveness of production is much lower than in advanced industrial nations. Thus, according to estimates made by Soviet economists, "the use of scientific-technical achievements in the USSR national economy provides 40 to 45 percent of the annual increase in the national income,"[18] but according to data from the United Nations, "the introduction of new technology in many developed capitalistic nations provides an increase in the fixed net output of 60 to 75 percent."[19] However, the lack of clear estimates on effectiveness leads some sources to say that one ruble invested brings a return "equal to forty-eight to sixty-five copecks"; other sources say one ruble to one ruble, forty-five copecks; a third says one ruble to two rubles, fifteen copecks; and a fourth says one ruble to three to five rubles."[20] I cannot say which of these methods was used in determining an increase of national income of 40 to 45 percent.

In the majority of cases, one of the last links in NIOKR is project design. Along with many successes in this area, project design in the institutes and bureaus has many serious deficiencies. One that slows down scientific-technical progress is the long time required to compile drafts. There are three main causes for these deficiencies: (1) The hopeless backwardness of the technical outfitting of design organizations directly lengthens the period of time needed for design work. (2) Information about materials, designs, equipment, and machine tools is inadequate (The USSR has no such thing as a "unified industrial catalog" giving technical parameters of products produced in the country).[21] (3) The system of obtaining approval for both design tasks and the plans themselves is highly bureaucratized. Time spent directly in preparing a draft "is only 20 to 35 percent of the time required to get the project off the drawing board."[22] This same source cites the story of work done on the second part of a chemical combine; the total time required was forty months, twelve months of which were wasted just to have the design task approved.

In summing all questions on scientific-technical progress in the civil branches of USSR industry, one should consider that its tempo does not slow down but only speeds up the Soviet technological lag behind advanced nations with market economies. Thus, for example, in West Germany for the period 1958-1965 the increase in labor productivity as a result of scientific-technical progress was 48 percent;[23] in the USSR, according to Academician V. Trapenznikov's calculations, the corresponding figure is 2.5 percent.[24] Amazing discoveries and individual outstanding achievements in the field of science do not change the overall picture.

Target Plans

NIOKR takes on a completely different aspect when it comes to making arms. The rapid tempo and scientific-technical successes in this area stand out clearly when compared with the civilian sectors. The basis for the successes of NIOKR in defense is its unique planning, the so-called target planning. This is matched with a special organization for the practical implementation of the target plan.

> Target methods of planning and management presuppose . . . a somewhat different technique of planning, which in this case starts by putting priorities on general goals; passes through a stage of forming mutually coordinated programs and implemented goals; and ends with a plan for the distribution and development of resources, which can then be transformed into an annual economic budget. To accomplish the established goal, the branches and producers of individual products work together with the help of the creation of a special organization [the association], or jointly implemented programs of target significance.[25]

All target plans represent "complex plans of target significance, the basis for which is carefully worked out and enters into the efforts of all participants, including economic and noneconomic organizations."[26]

Practically unlimited material, both financial and otherwise, is made available to achieve the established goal. "The expense aspect takes on a subordinate significance when evaluating the economic process in target planning because expenditures for the various means used to accomplish a goal are determined and compared only after the goal has been defined, rather than the other way around."[27] In this case resources are generously provided. It is not coincidental that the great economist Veger advances the following parallel: "Experience shows that the creation of one of the new types of fighter aircraft in the United States ended up costing 1.7 times more than projected; a bomber 3 times as much; a missile system 4.9 times as much. In recent years the opposite picture has been observed in the USSR. Estimated expenditures for scientific research work are 97 to 98 percent of planned expenditures."[28] If the established goal is declared a governmental task, then the freedom to expend any and all resources is increased even more. Thus, the consolidation of efforts of the most diverse organizations, from science to intelligence, reaches the maximum, as was the case in the creation of nuclear weapons.

In setting the tasks for each of the participating organizations as precisely and fully as possible, the target plan itself determines the direction of all efforts toward a single goal. In addition, all such efforts are strongly reinforced by organizational measures. As a rule, in fulfilling target plans, "the design bureaus emerge as the main coordinating organ which freely manages the resources for solving the established task."[29] In practice, it is the bureau's chief designer rather than the bureau itself who has these rights. In this manner the entire NIOKR system is not only broken up but joined in a single unit, combining NIOKR and production. One of the more important reasons for success is the special form of its organization. The significance of the organizational side was emphasized as early as 1958 by the president of the Azerbaidzhan Academy of Sciences, Yu. Mamedaliev.[30] Here I am speaking not only of the forms of organization but mainly about the fact that the fulfillment of a target plan is managed, not by an economic bureaucrat, but by a scientist-designer who is personally and deeply interested in seeing his idea or design become a reality.

Some idea of the way a target plan of governmental significance is carried out in practice is provided in a speech delivered by A.P. Aleksandrov, director of the Kurchatov Institute for Atomic Energy, at the 1961 All-Union Conference of Scientific Workers. He said: "In this field scientific work-ups are not removed from their technical introduction, as is the case in several other fields of endeavor. The engineering studies begin at the same time that a scientific work-up is started and the first features for practical application are outlined, and when a more or less unanimous opinion emerges that practical development is necessary. By the time that the scientific research has been completed, one can proceed, and often they have already proceeded, to the production of the new products."[31]

This is precisely how the work went "in creating the most important designs of aircraft, including the supersonic 'TU-144,'" in the mastery of space and without doubt in creating all types of modern armaments for the Soviet army.[32]

Available sources of information do not allow the formation of a completely reliable picture of the NIOKR process and the industrial mastery of new armaments. However, the following represents the most likely sequence of events.

1. The conception of an idea or new design in an all-union scientific research institute or special design bureau.
2. The examination and approval of the idea at higher scientific-technical levels (special scientific-technical councils or in the scientific council of one of the defense industrial ministries).

3. Possibly examination by higher governmental organizations, when the goal being established has all-governmental significance.
4. The description and sanctioning, within the appropriate chain of command, by a higher coordinating organization for the entire project (usually a special design bureau).
5. The compilation of the target plan.

   a. The establishment of general goals, on which the primary goal is broken down.

   b. The compilation, coordination, and intercoordination of the program—tasks with the simultaneous establishment of executors in NIOKR itself, just as in industrial production.

   c. A plan for the mobilization and distribution of resources for the task as a whole and for the executors.

   d. A timetable for all work as well as the setting up of timetables for each executor.

   e. The definition and creation of operational resources at the disposal of the main coordinating organization.
6. The inclusion of the target plan in the national economic plan for resource, financial, and production coverage of the target plan. The target plan is not integrated into the national economic plan but remains an independent part of primary importance.

The atmosphere and conditions under which target plans are executed play an important role. There are many such factors, and I shall therefore discuss only the most important ones.

It is not just the development of the entire plan and its execution that are under the control of scientific design powers. These powers occupy a position of total command. Thus, for example, every chief designer in aircraft building has an aviation plant associated with him. The chief designer has the authority to order the plant to produce a new design that he needs. The designer's assignment *has priority over the plant's current state plan* and is performed first, even at the expense of the plan.

The proposal of problems by scientific design powers is altogether different from the proposal of practical problems by the economic bureaucracy. Science and technology stand at the helm.

The high degree of centralization in the Soviet system has made it possible to establish powerful, central scientific research organizations. They are equipped with the latest technology and are staffed with a concentration of experts. These institutes have great influence on decision making, dealing with the most difficult scientific-technical problems. For example, in the aviation and shipbuilding industries, every new model (or improvement) of any designer undergoes research and testing at the Zhukovsky Central Aerohydrodynamics Institute. The purpose of the research and testing is not only to check the design but also to obtain a highly qualified consultation.

In armaments NIOKR an atmosphere of freedom of creativity reigns; when risk is necessary, there is freedom to take the scientific-technical risk. The creators of weapons and the executors of target plans are surrounded by attention and concern (but security restrictions make it life in a gilded cage); they are given a high standard of living; high norms of material incentives are extended to them. For their work on a thermonuclear weapon, twenty-six leading designers, scientists, and engineers received the rank of Hero of Socialist Labor, and 7,000 other people were awarded medals and decorations in 1962.[33]

Two other comments must be added. First, the very high level of security classification, a near mania for secrecy in armaments NIOKR, is so great that its successes have practically no influence on increasing scientific-technical progress in the civil sectors of industry. In other words, there is practically no spin-off. Second, although armaments NIOKR is a government within a government of the country's overall NIOKR, the government as a whole is a Soviet government with all its inherent peculiarities and characteristics. It is precisely for this reason that General I. Pavlovsky writes:

> In order to save manpower and resources for the selection of the most promising models of military technology, the scientific research institutes and design bureaus when developing their ideas must penetrate more deeply into the secrets of the future. They must painstakingly evaluate the trends and norms of military technology. They must correctly analyze its consequences, taking into consideration the technological achievements in related branches of foreign economies as well, and they must develop rational methods for the planning and operational management of technological progress.[34]

This is all expressed in very general terms, but there is nonetheless a hint of insignificant subject matter, of "inventing the bicycle anew," and of wasting resources through the use of irrational methods.

Output Quality

Quality is closely related to technological level. It is a reflection of the technological level of industry, of industry's scientific-technical progress, and of the effectiveness of all production activity.

For the simple reason that it is physically impossible to do so, output quality is not planned. The existing order of things in the USSR presupposes that every product must conform to state standards (GOST) or departmental technical specifications. However, at this point serious problems arise because of the nature of the Soviet system. The chairman of the State Committee of Standards of the USSR Council of Ministers, V. Boitsov, reports that at the beginning of 1971 "nearly fifteen thousand state standards are in effect in the country. Of this number half have been put into effect during the period 1966 to 1970."[35] Consequently, in 1971 half the state standards had been around for five years or more. Boitsov continues that "in the new five-year plan more than seven thousand state standards will be reviewed." If by 1975 half the state standards sanctioned before 1966 have been reviewed, then by 1975 the other half will have been in effect anywhere from five to eleven years. Although the raising of quality (or consumer value) is a never-ending process under normal conditions, the system of state standards and technical specifications determines a spasmodic improvement of the technological level and quality of manufactured goods over long periods of time. In setting the cost price of manufactured goods and many other indicators, the plan actually makes downward deviation from the standard economically possible. This downward deviation is actually done at times. It is economically impossible to raise the standard, as this would worsen the plants' work indicators and jeopardize fulfilling the plan (especially regarding cost price and therefore profit).

The older these standards and technical specifications are, the more they tend to resemble the dimensions and appearance of a manufactured article. For all practical purposes they do not affect the technological aspect of quality or, to put it differently, its consumer value. This serious shortcoming only began to be eliminated in 1968 when "a standard for standards was adopted–GOST-1, a state system of standardization." According to GOST-1, "optimal indicators of quality are to be established when standardizing output. These should include consumer (operating) characteristics, reliability, longevity, technical soundness of construction, and aesthetic characteristics."[36] However, the transition to new principles of standardization has turned out to be more difficult than expected. Many indicators stipulated by GOST-1 simply do not exist, nor has any thought been given to defining them. The formulation of indicators has been extremely difficult because even today most standards are based on old principles. As a result, "it is not possible to tell whether a manufactured article that conforms completely to set standards also conforms to the modern level or meets consumer demands. Moreover, since the development of new state standards requires considerable time, and progress in the field proceeds rapidly, the technical indicators of standards often become a perceptible barrier to the perfection of technology."[37] The nonconformity of many standards to the modern technological level is explained by A. Vasilkovsky, the director of a plant that produces control-system computers. "The developers (or producers) of goods themselves draw up the projects. It is completely understandable that they do not attempt to set high requirements."[38] The drafts for standards are examined and approved by the State Committee of Standards, but this organization does not have the opportunity, the qualifications, or the time to go into the fine points of the enormous number of standards covering a diverse range of industrial branches.

Finally, even when a standard is on the books, the producers of manufactured goods frequently do not observe them, especially when the requirements interfere with fulfilling the plan. During rush periods this practice increases sharply. The nonadherence to standards is widespread. This general disregard for standards was reflected in a resolution issued by the Central Committee of the CPSU and the USSR Council of Ministers "Concerning the Raising of the Role of Standards for the Improvement of Output Quality." The resolution notes in particular that "the state supervision of the introduction and observance of standards and technical specifications is not being implemented actively enough."[39] As an illustration, an audit has shown that 74 out of 195 plants inspected are flagrantly violating standards and technical specifications."[40]

Many important aspects of production activity, including adherence to standards, are not possible without a modern, perfected measuring technique. However, the measurements (metrological) service in the Soviet Union is poorly organized and is completely outdated. A "statute on measures and measuring devices that was introduced in the 1930s is still in effect." The state organizations (attached directly to the State Committee for Standards) are unable to check all measurements and devices; they do, however, check all control measuring models. Therefore, it is "incumbent on the department-level metrological service to oversee and check all other measurements and measuring devices." All this needs to be set up and organized. The overall situation is clearly reflected in the training of metrological personnel. In the entire country there is only one technical college, in Odessa. "There is not a single institution of higher learning that is turning out engineer-metrologists at this time."[41]

Standards and technical specifications are intended to raise the technical level and quality, but many other things are working counter to this end—the production spurt and the inadequate support by a laboratory and testing base. Planned price setting also has an enormous effect on output quality. "The trend of production toward a fundamental improvement of output quality [and the elevation of the technical level as well] is directly tied to questions of price setting. . . . However, the price-setting mechanism frequently does not 'function smoothly' and even slows things down."[42] The problem is that raising the quality and the technical level requires additional expenditures even within the process of preparing a higher-quality manufactured article. These expenditures are not yet included in the plan, but they will raise the cost price of the output as envisaged in the plan, that is, they will lead to the nonfulfillment of the plan according to one of the important "bonus awarding" indicators. The new, higher-cost price and the price of the manufactured article will be included in the plan only when the appropriate levels in the chain of command recognize the new quality (perhaps the manufactured article will receive a mark of quality).

The ponderous bureaucratism of the Soviet system is yet another obstacle in the path of improving quality. The sanctioning of a new manufactured article or the attaining of a mark of quality takes months and is connected with endless red tape. Approval for a new and fashionable tie can at times take as long as six months.[43] The more complicated a manufactured article is, the greater the number of chain-of-command organizations taking part in the examination and approval of the article and thus the longer the period of time required.

In the civilian branches of industry, the totally unsatisfactory checking of finished goods plays an important role.

I have outlined only the fundamental features of the problems of quality. The problem as a whole, particularly in recent years, has become paramount, not just in the economy, but in the entire system. It is for just this reason that a lead article in *Planovoe khoziaistvo* pointed out that "the sharp raising of output quality for all branches of the national economy is one of the most important *economic and political* (italics mine) problems at this stage in the development of Soviet society. Its solution is inevitably linked with the accelerated tempo of scientific-technical progress and with the raising of the effectiveness of social production."[44] However, knowing the true possibilities and attitudes, the chairman of the USSR State Committee of Standards, Boitsov, warns Soviet economists that "the raising of output quality is not a campaign but a logical program of action."[45] Actually it is possible to raise output quality only when the enterprises are materially motivated. To do this, the problem of payment for quality must be solved. In turn this requires a single, economically based methodology for determining the effectiveness of raising quality. However, there is no such methodology.[46] At the same time, "a large number of branch-level methods and instructions have appeared which contain contradictory recommendations for methods of making estimates. Defining the economic effectiveness of output quality through different methods makes it possible to arrive at conclusions and results that differ considerably from one another."[47] Thus, to raise quality, the Soviet leadership has only administrative planning capabilities, which have so far had no effect.

In the USSR there are three categories of quality: output for general, internal consumption, output for export; and defense-related output (arms, outfitting the army, and so forth). Everything discussed so far concerns the quality of output earmarked for internal consumption. Output designated for general internal consumption is checked by the plants' technical control department (OTK). Every plant management must have this mandatory department, which is subordinate to the plant director. "At many plants [more precisely, at all plants] this department is considered a hindrance, a service that interferes with the collective's fulfilling the plan according to quantitative indicators."[48] In other words, the technical control department stands between the collective and its receipt of bonuses and other types of incentives for meeting or exceeding a plan. This determines one's attitude toward both the department and its people. The technical control department workers are the outcasts of production. "The wages of inspectors average one-third less than those of production workers. It is not surprising that qualified personnel do not remain for long in the technical control departments."[49] However, the technical control department itself is interested in seeing a plan fulfilled, and thus the department adopts a "liberal" attitude toward the quality of the articles being checked. At the same time, however, the technical control department is responsible for quality. This duality of interests creates conflicts. As a result, it frequently happens that "after rejecting a certain manufactured article the foreman of the technical control department is pressured by the shop chief, by the chief designer, and at times by the plant director. This pressure is so great that not every person is able to withstand it."[50] Under these conditions, a firm character is a poor guarantee that low-quality output will be rejected. Attempts to introduce an automated quality check have been unsuccessful. Defectoscopes to audit the production of rolled steel were simply removed.

The quality of export output is always higher than that of output for general consumption. First, there are higher standards and technical specifications for the production of export output. Second, the quality control check is done by organizations of the Ministry of Foreign Trade. However, for many years this check was totally inadequate. Only in 1968 was the State Inspectorate for the Quality of Export Goods created within the Ministry of Foreign Trade. Its chairman, Doliakov, reports that "its basic task is to perform a periodic selective check of the quality of goods being exported from the Soviet Union, the purpose being to prevent poor-quality manufactured articles from being shipped abroad. The State Inspectorate sets up an extensive network of local organizations, that is, directorates, sections, and points, which allows strong control over the quality and condition of export goods at all stages of production—the transportation, storage, and indirect transfer abroad."[51] Whether the quality of Soviet goods corresponds to the quality of world market goods after all this is another question.

Defense-related manufactured goods have the highest quality, not only because defense-related branches of production enjoy a privileged position but also to a large extent because of the organization and strictness of quality control. To ensure this quality control, the military representative system (*voennyi predstavitel'*) was created. This is often referred to as the military receiver system (*voennyi priemshchik*). This system is subordinated to army management (probably the Chief Directorate of Rear Services) rather than to the various ministries of defense industry or to the management of the plants. The military representative has no interest in whether an enterprise meets the plan. He has a great degree of responsibility just for the acceptance of poor-quality output. Everything earmarked for military production and for direct use by the armed forces—from metal and tanks down to meat and boots—passes through the military representative system.

Depending on what the plant provides for military production or for use in the armed forces or what kind of armaments it produces, there may be one military representative (such as at a meat combine where there is a single military veterinarian) or an entire organization of military representatives. At defense-related plants, the military representative department is usually headed by a military engineer. Engineers with various specialties connected with the production of a given type of weapon also work in this department. There is also a staff of specialists and testing personnel. The military representative department usually sets up its own laboratory and testing base as well as everything else necessary for a complete quality check. Toward this end, he not only must check the completed manufactured article but also has the right to check whether all technological and technical norms in the production process are observed.

In the case of large manufactured articles, such as aircraft, tanks, cannon, and motors, the military representative department checks and tests each article. In the case of a mass output, such as small arms, munitions and casings, and so forth, a random check is done. Moreover, the articles to be checked are chosen by the military representative. The entire procedure is accompanied by many formalities. The director notifies the military representative in writing when a given number of articles are ready. The military representative, through his staff, conducts the checks and tests. "Formal acceptance documents" are drawn up to this effect. Only after these documents have been signed by the military representative, does the director have the right to include this output toward meeting the plan.

A single consideration governs this entire system: not to allow errors; not to accept output whose low quality will be discovered only when actually used by the armed forces. Such errors are severely punished.

One must not forget, however, that the system of military representatives with its strict quality control exists within the framework of the Soviet system in general and within that economic system in particular.

Notes

1. *Voprosy ekonomiki*, no. 3 (1974):26.
2. Ibid., no. 12 (1972):71.
3. Ibid., no. 4 (1972):151.
4. Ibid., no. 3 (1974):27.
5. *Pravda*, 6 May 1972, p. 2.
6. *Voprosy ekonomiki*, no. 1 (1971):78.
7. Ibid., no. 9 (1968):61.
8. *Novyi mir*, no. 8 (1967):271.
9. Ibid., p. 275.
10. *Pravda*, 9 May 1969, p. 3.
11. *Novyi mir*, no. 8 (1967):271.
12. *Pravda*, 18 May 1971, p. 2.
13. *Voprosy ekonomiki*, no. 2 (1972):55.

14. *Planovoe khoziaistvo*, no. 2 (1970):76.
15. *Sotsialisticheskaia industriia*, 27 July 1971, p. 2.
16. Ibid., p. 18.
17. Ibid., p. 16.
18. *Planovoe khoziaistvo*, no. 6 (1971):4.
19. Ibid., p. 7.
20. *Voprosy ekonomiki*, no. 9 (1971):61.
21. *Ekonomicheskaia gazeta*, no. 44 (1968):21.
22. *Planovoe khoziaistvo*, no. 8 (1969):53.
23. *Voprosy ekonomiki*, no. 2 (1972):21.
24. Ibid., p. 22.
25. Ibid., no. 7 (1971):74.
26. Ibid., p. 73.
27. Ibid., p. 74.
28. Ibid., no. 2 (1972):49.
29. Ibid., p. 73.
30. *Pravda*, 15 August 1958, p. 2.
31. *Pravda*, 14 June 1961, p. 2.
32. *Voprosy ekonomiki*, no. 7 (1971):73.
33. *Pravda*, 27 March 1962, p. 1.
34. *Planovoe khoziaistvo*, no. 2 (1973):29.
35. *Ekonomicheskaia gazeta*, no. 9 (1971):7.
36. Ibid., no. 30 (1968):27.
37. *Sotsialisticheskaia industriia*, 11 June 1972, p. 2.
38. *Sotsialisticheskaia industriia*, 20 March 1972, p. 2.
39. *Pravda*, 5 December 1970, p. 1.
40. *Pravda*, 28 March 1972, p. 2.
41. *Pravda*, 2 October 1969, p. 2.
42. *Pravda*, 20 April 1971, p. 2.
43. *Sotsialisticheskaia industriia*, 30 November 1971, p. 2.
44. *Planovoe khoziaistvo*, no. 10 (1973):3.
45. Ibid., p. 9.
46. *Sotsialisticheskaia industriia*, 15 September 1971, p. 2.
47. *Voprosy ekonomiki*, no. 2 (1971):15.
48. *Pravda*, 29 January 1972, p. 2.
49. *Pravda*, 21 September 1969, p. 2.
50. *Pravda*, 29 January 1972, p. 2.
51. *Ekonomicheskaia gazeta*, no. 52 (1968):19.

12 The Organization of Industry

The underlying principles for the organization of industry were developed during the years of the first two five-year plans. Since that time they have not undergone any significant changes. The branch principle has continued to function. Even the *sovnarkhozes* (councils of the national economy, 1957-1965), while externally resembling a territorial organization, were organized according to the branch principle.

The present-day organization of industry was based on resolutions passed by the September 1965 plenum of the CPSU Central Committee. According to the new organization, three types of branch ministries play a decisive role: the all-union, the union-republic, and the republic ministries. Defense industry ministries, machine-building ministries, the ministries of railway, air, and sea transport are all-union ministries. The union-republic ministries include the remaining branches of heavy industry, light and foodstuffs industries, agriculture, and the procurement of agriculture output. The republic ministries or directorates were given more than three thousand local industrial enterprises as well as river and automotive transport for general use.[1] Their main job is to provide a portion of the requirements of the local population. In 1971 all-union subordinated industry provided 51 percent of all industrial output, while union-republic- and republic-level industry provided the remaining 49 percent.[2]

Besides the ministries, various state committees play a large role in the organization of industry. The most important of these are *Gosplan, Gossnab*, and the State Committee for Science and Technology. The complete organizational diagram is complicated, multistaged, and inefficient (see figure 12-1). For this reason a resolution by the CPSU Central Committee and the USSR Council of Ministers that dealt with the reorganization of the management of industry was released 3 April 1973. The reorganization signifies "a transition to basically a two- and three-level system of management." Although the resolution envisaged that preliminary work (drawing up new general organizational diagrams) would have to be done "within a short period of time for each branch of industry,"[3] a year later "the branches [were] not energetically preparing their general management diagrams in all cases." "Several ministries are still operating by the previously existing management system and are slow in creating large-scale subsections."[4] The future organizational diagram is not yet completely clear, but in principle it will look something like the one shown in figure 12-2.

In broad terms the task of the industrial associations will be determined by "the overall resolution about the all-union and republic level industrial associ-

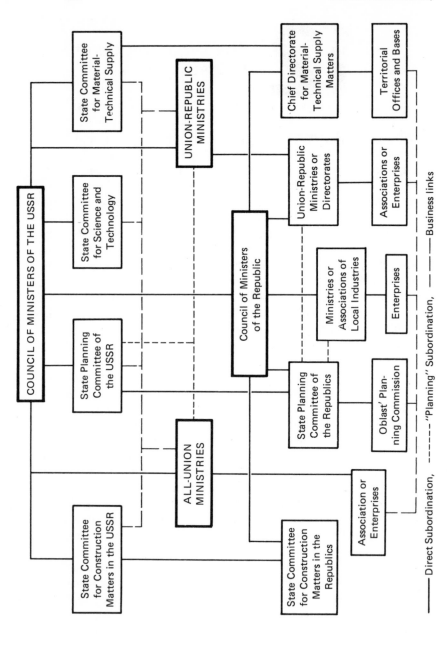

Figure 12-1. A Simplified Diagram for the Management of Industry in the USSR

(According to the resolutions of the September 1965 Plenum of the Central Committee)

——— Direct Subordination,   - - - - - "Planning" Subordination,   ——— Business links

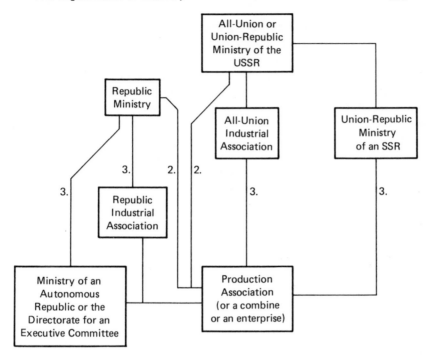

Pravda, 3 March 1973, pp. 1-2.
Figure 12-2. New Diagram of USSR Industry

ations," ratified 2 March 1973.[5] The principles of work for the production associations are defined by "the resolution concerning the production association [combine]," which was passed on 27 March 1974.[6] This document is worked out in considerably more detail than the resolution concerning the industrial associations.

The organization of industry is based on the principle of "economic estimates or self-sufficiency (*khozraschet*)." It is thought that "*khozraschet* is a method for the planned handling of the economy of socialist plants and organizations based on commensurability in a cost [currency] form of expenditures made to produce output and the results of economic activity. It is also based on the use of the organization's own revenues to compensate plants and organizations. The guarantee of production profitability is another basis for *khozraschet*." I have already discussed the feasibility of economically well-founded cost commensurations, but *khozraschet* practice has several other organizational peculiarities. Following the September 1965 plenum of the CPSU Central Committee, a new kind of *khozraschet* came into being, the total *khozraschet*, by which a plant pays for the fixed assets allocated to it by the state. "In contrast to the *khozraschet* system now in effect which, as the *Plenum* pointed out, *in many ways has a formal character* [italics mine], the total *khozraschet* system means that all economic levers are used to the maximum in the interests of developing public production and so that *khozraschet* principles can penetrate all aspects of the economic organism."[7] However, *khozraschet* has not yet actually penetrated "all aspects of the economic organism." Only the lowest levels, the industrial plants, operate on this principle either totally or partially. For them this principle means meeting the financial plan by meeting the production plan. The cost of the production output covers the credit which according to the annual plan was extended to them by *Gosbank*. The plant and its management alone bear the concrete material responsibility for meeting the financial plan. No higher levels of management operate on the *khozraschet* principle, nor do they bear material responsibility for meeting the financial plan. This lack of financial responsibility at higher levels is the source (or one of the sources) of many administrative solutions that have not been thought out and are not economically well founded but are nonetheless mandatory for the plants. This phenomenon is so widespread and significant that the minister of heavy power and transport machine building, V. Zhigalin, considers it absolutely necessary that total *khozraschet* be introduced into the entire industrial organization, right up to the ministerial level. In his opinion this would make it possible "to raise the effectiveness of production and to take advantage more fully of our planned socialist economy."[8]

The new reform for industrial organization presupposes that industrial and production associations will operate on a total *khozraschet* basis. This question has not yet come up in relation to the ministries.

Every *khozraschet* plant or organization has its own property allocated to it by the state. Also, each organization or plant is an independent legal entity which has the right to draw up agreements with other legal entities (plants and organizations). Each also has its own current account in the State Bank system.

The right to make agreements plays an enormous role in fulfilling national economic plans. Agreements represent the final quantitative and nomenclatural elaboration of the national economic plan. To a significant extent, agreements coordinate the work between the plants, the suppliers, and the consumers. In practice this system gives rise to many unpleasant results: there is an enormous amount of paperwork, agreements are frequently not honored, established deadlines are violated, and there are inadequate means for putting pressure on violators. This means that plant managers attempt to keep the number of agreements to a bare minimum. Consequently, this is still another obstacle to industrial specialization.

The material responsibility that a plant management assumes for its own economic activity is largely formal. In practice material responsibility takes the form of material (fiscal) sanctions. Officially "the basic form of responsibility according to law is the complete compensation of losses by the organization incurring them. However, practically speaking, in the majority of cases only forfeitures are recovered. A loss is recovered much less often; and unreceived revenues are recovered even less often. As a general rule, the party incurring losses does not make any property claim on the organization that violated the obligation. Settlement sanctions prove an ineffective means of putting pressure on the violator, as they have no substantial influence on his property situation."[9]

If looked at from the plant's viewpoint, this situation can be explained by the impossibility of coming up with a clear picture of the loss incurred, a lack of desire to spoil relations with suppliers, and the possibility of including forfeitures, fines, and the like in the cost price of the output. If one looks at the system from the point of view of the national economy, then a totally nonsensical picture emerges: the state fines the state. Considerably more effective is individual material responsibility borne by management. The sanctions used on them, especially in cases where a resolution or law speaks directly of the coverage of losses from wages, occasionally have a noticeable effect. In other important instances "established material sanctions against managers for the plant's nonfulfillment of the plan according to basic indicators have no meaning whatsoever because the managers simply receive their bonuses from other sources."[10] This manifests the absence of legal regulation of economic activity, the corporateness of the economic nomenclature, and at times the pure falsification of documents.

Notes

1. A.N. Efimov, *Soviet Industry* (Moscow: Ekonomika, 1967), p. 214.
2. *Ekonomicheskaia gazeta*, no. 9 (1973):11.
3. *Pravda*, 4 April 1973, lead article.
4. *Pravda*, 14 March 1974, lead article.
5. *Ekonomicheskaia gazeta*, no. 14 (1973).
6. Ibid., no. 18 (1974).
7. *Voprosy ekonomiki*, no. 2 (1966):96.
8. *Pravda*, 8 May 1969, p. 2.
9. *Planovoe khoziaistvo*, no. 3 (1972):93.
10. Ibid., no. 5 (1974):58.

13 The Industrial Enterprise

The plant is a first-level, independent, and *khozraschet* production-economic unit within industry. To perform its assigned tasks, the plant is provided with the necessary personnel as well as with fixed and working assets. In principle, the amount of assets (funds) and the number of personnel for a plant is set by higher-level management. Today plants operate on the basis of the "Regulation concerning the Socialist State Plant," which was approved 4 October 1965. This document has somewhat expanded the rights and stabilized the conditions of a plant's economic activity. The recent reform of the industrial organization of a plant envisages that a plant which is part of a production association or combine loses the rights of a legal entity and the "Regulation concerning the Socialist State Plant" no longer applies to it.

At each plant, management is handled by the plant management. A rather typical plant management structure is shown in figure 13-1.

In the organizational and production sense an enterprise is broken down into shops (*tsekh*), and the shops are divided into sectors (*uchastok*) and brigades (*brigada*).

The director is the head of the plant management. He runs the plant on the basis of one-man management (*edinonachalie*) and assumes full responsibility for all the plant's activities, resources, and property. The director is a worker chosen from the economic Party *nomenklatura* (list of Party-sanctioned executives). His appointment as director is made by the personnel section of the appropriate level of the Party (from the Central Committee of the CPSU down to the *oblast'*, *raion*, and city Party committees). A higher-ranking economic management plays only a consultative role when it comes to appointing or removing a director. The director has several deputies. His first deputy always used to be the chief engineer, but in 1965, mostly in large-scale plants, a new position was created: the chief economist. Currently the chief economist is frequently the first deputy to the director. According to the existing regulation "the deputies to a plant's director, the chief accountant [senior accountant having the rights of a chief accountant], and the chief of the technical control department are appointed and dismissed from their positions by a higher-ranking organization according to the director's recommendations."[1] Higher management's confidence in this one-man manager-director cannot be overestimated, it seems. Of the plant management departments, the economic planning department and the supply department play vital roles in the plant's work.

A small amount of the monetary funds found in the plants for bonuses and

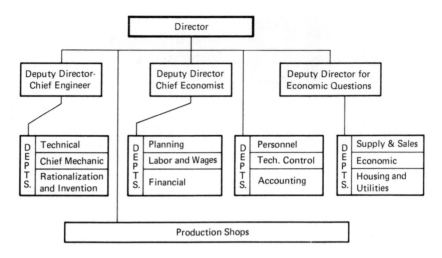

Figure 13-1. Management Structure of a Machine-Building Factory

further development is at the personal disposal of the director. (This was once known as the director's fund.) The director can use this money as he sees fit.

The peculiarities of planning, supply, and management, all requiring the processing of an enormous amount of paper, and the bureaucratic style of management, both from above and within the enterprise, give rise to very large plant management staffs. Based on certain circumstantial information, one can estimate that in all of the USSR's plants there is probably one white-collar worker from the plant management staff for every seven to eight workers. Attempts to automate management work at this level have not yet produced any substantial results.

I have already discussed the inducements that arise among economists faced with the necessity of meeting a plan. Meeting a plan is the law of existence that causes people to resort to tricks and subterfuge. At the plant level, the most common method is to change the listing of articles produced. Thus, for example, one machine tool plant, which according to the plan was to produce 75 machine tools of a given type, produced 6,118 of them. The plan also called for 12,217 machine tools of another type, but only 6,370 of these were turned out. The point is that the planned profitability of the first machine tool was double that of the second. As a result, the overall plan was exceeded by 11.2 percent, "which led to a considerable increase in deductions from the material incentives fund."[2]

Notes

1. *Ekonomicheskaia gazeta*, no. 16 (1969):12.
2. *Voprosy ekonomiki*, no. 1 (1972):74.

14 Material-Technical Supply

General Comments

Material-technical supply as a whole is the most important part of the Soviet economy. Taking the place of a market, the material-technical supply system must support the fulfillment of the operational annual national economic plan with all material resources. Therefore, the material-technical supply plan is perhaps the most important part of the national economic plan. It is especially important because under a planned economy the directing of capital into a given branch, particularly within the execution of an operational plan, has no effect until it is supported by the appropriate material-technical supply. At the same time, this material-technical supply due to its content, structure, and dimensions must conform to the targeted direction of fiscal resources and their sum total. In addition, all items of material value are distributed according to the material-technical supply system. There are few reserves, and the item being distributed has already been determined in the national economic plan. As a result, large-scale overdirecting of resources during the time period covered in the operational plan requires that the national economic plan itself be changed.

The importance of the material-technical supply system is underscored by both the rights and the actual power of supply organizations. They clearly stand apart from the economic organizational hierarchy, and "orders issued by the State Committee for Material-Technical Supply, USSR Council of Ministers, concerning questions under their jurisdiction must be fulfilled by the ministries and other organizations."[1]

In spite of the importance of this system, it is one of the weakest and poorest functioning links in the Soviet economy in all aspects, from planning to distribution. Even during the early 1960s, Nemchinov aptly characterized it as "a metabolic disease" of the national economic organism. He felt "that it is now time to switch material supply onto the rails of state trade."[2] Sharp criticism of the system and practice of supply has been dragging on since 1957, and the situation remains unchanged. A lead article in *Pravda* entitled "Supply-Energy" said that "the existing material-technical supply system still suffers from duplication of effort and too many stages. . . . Early in this year [the second month of the year] the work of many plants has already become seriously complicated due to the untimely receipt of assemblies, parts, and raw materials."[3] In actual practice, the more the Soviet economy grows and the more complex it becomes, the greater the pressure and, consequently, the less the

129

supply system is able to meet the needs of the national economy. The problem is not just in the quantity and timeliness of supply. Supply has a direct influence on the quality of output and on the tempo of scientific-technical progress. It is precisely the supply system that has created a situation whereby "the producer essentially dictates terms to the consumer, frequently acting on the principle of 'take what you can get.' "[4] And "to clash with a supplier is much like arguing with the tailor from whom you have ordered a suit."[5]

The Role of the Supply Organizations in Planning

I have already described the general outline of supply planning and the connection between the supply plan and the production plan. Therefore, I shall only expand and clarify this general outline.

Work on the plan-requisition (*plan-zaiavka*) is usually started some three months before work begins on the production draft plan (*plan-proekt*). The requisitions that are compiled "are unreliable for the reason that materials are ordered for a proposed plan for the following year. The actual plan never coincides with the draft." They are also unreliable because "if there are no goods on the open market, the plants try to order resources in reserve. Otherwise they will not be able to get what they need later."[6] The tendency to create reserves permeates all activity connected with supply. As a result, a situation is created whereby "a consumer's plan [that is, a plant's plan] is usually considered unreliable at the territorial supply organ, and it is deemed necessary to scrutinize the plan a second time. A higher-ranking *Glavsnabsbyt* (chief supply and sales organization) takes the same attitude toward the plans coming from the territorial supply organizations." Finally "a comparison with the preceding year, the experience and knowledge of workers, *and personal contacts* [italics mine] play a decisive role when evaluating a plan [plan-requisition]."[7]

An enormous number of people are engaged in compiling requisitions. Some people work at it full-time, and even more are recruited to help out when the plan-requisitions are being drawn up. Thus, "at a comparatively small plant 20 percent of the workers spend almost the entire year working on requisitions." Throughout the entire national economy more than a million people are diverted for this. The majority of these people are specialists and managers. Much labor and hundreds of tons of paper are expended, all to no avail. "Territorial directorate specialists unanimously assert that the union *Glavsnabsbyts* of *Gossnab* do not even look at the requisitions when it is time to allocate funds. They base the need for resources on the preceding year's expenditure, taking into consideration a natural growth of production and consumption. Nevertheless, *Gossnab* (the sole user of requisitions) religiously observes form."[8] Thus, as in production planning, the principle of "from the attained level" dominates here, too. The simultaneous compilation of material balances, even using electronic computers, does not alter the degree of substantiation and reliability and the degree of conformity of the plan-funds to the production plan. This is the source of thousands of disasters. It is also the source of the overall imperfection of supply planning, which is aggravated by the experience of meeting these plans. One of the first problems is the distribution of funds. "In the distribution of resources [funds], there is a lack of coordination and a multitude of stages. Apart from the *Gossnab* designators, twenty-six thousand designators for industrial output are allocated by the ministries. Sixteen thousand designators are allocated by *Gosplan.*"[9] The following picture emerges: the USSR *Gosplan* distributes scarce commodities and the other more important manufactured articles among the ministries and departments; *Gossnab* distributes other manufactured articles (according to some data there are more than thirty-six thousand designators) among the ministries and departments; and the ministries themselves are entrusted with the distribution of twenty-six thousand designators of manufactured articles. Moreover, when trying to comprehend the words *output designators*, one should think not so much of one specific manufactured article but of a specific group of manufactured articles.

Resources distributed by various levels are concentrated in and dispersed by the ministries. "USSR union-republic and all-union ministries are the administrators of material-technical resources," meaning that they are the ones who control the funds and distribute supply plans (*plan snabzheniia*) as resources in which are combined resources received from all three sources of their distribution. The implementation of material-technical supply plans is accomplished "through the system of *Glavsnabsbyt* and the territorial material-technical supply organs."[10]

Gossnab (the State Committee for Material-Technical Supply), which has a union-republic structure, stands at the head of all material-technical supply organizations. In the republic (except for the Russian Federated Republic where *Gossnab* itself performs this role) there are chief directorates for material-technical supply which are subordinate to the USSR *Gossnab* and to the republic-level councils of ministers. The USSR *Gossnab*, in which more than six thousand people work, is structured on the branch principle, as are *Glavsnabsbyt* and *Glavkomplekt* (chief directorates of assemblies). All other supply organizations are structured on the branch principle, as is shown in figure 14-1.

Besides the USSR *Gossnab* system, "the all-union and union-republic ministries have their own material-technical supply subsections, chief directorates, and departments for supply."[11] "Their share of all material-technical resources amounts to approximately one-third; moreover, they perform work requiring considerably greater outlays."[12] Attempts to come up with a unified supply system under *Gossnab*'s control have been unsuccessful because of departmental interests on the part of the ministries.

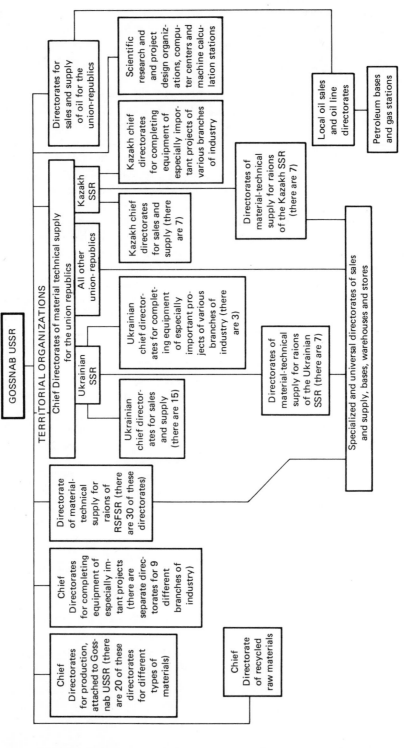

Figure 14-1. Organization of *Gossnab*

The Supply System in Practice

The entire planning process ends with putting together agreements between suppliers and consumers. Such agreements establish direct contacts between suppliers and consumers and determine the monthly volume of deliveries. From 50 to 60 percent of all deliveries, by cost, are based on these direct contacts. According to actual conditions, a delivery is considered fulfilled when the cargo is loaded at the dispatch station on *any day of the month.* At the same time, the bill for loading is a bookkeeping document attesting to the fact that the delivery and thus the plan have been fulfilled. However, the erratic nature of industry work (rush work—*Shturmovshchina*) means that most deliveries are shipped during the last ten days of the month.

A direct delivery (plant to plant) is possible only when the weight or volume is equal to or greater than the transit norm. This norm is equal to the loading capacity of a freight car. If the quantity is any less than this, the delivery must be made through the supply points of the territorial supply directorates. "Random investigations have shown that plants use about two-thirds of the overall products list [designators, not volumes or cost] in quantities less than transit norms. Although all these materials should be logically shipped first to depots and supply points and from there to the consumers, the territorial *Gossnab* organizations do not receive about half the materials they have ordered. Therefore, the enterprises are compelled either to order much more than they need, and thus create over-the-norm reserves, or to resort to multitudinous changes to the detriment of output and production profitability." This all leads to an incorrect allocation of resource reserves which makes them impossible to manipulate. Thus, at the end of 1970, 86 percent of the resource reserves was in the hands of consumers, 5.2 percent was in the hands of producers, and 8.8 percent was in supply depots.[13] The remaining deliveries (nearly one-third of the products being delivered) go through the territorial supply organizations. As a rule, the plants use their own transport and receive and deliver supply items from local depots and supply points. The supply system is far from a smooth operation, especially in providing certain materials.[14]

A positive development has been the creation of stores that sell supply items to the plants and other organizations on a clearing basis, that is, no cash is transferred. "Seven hundred such stores were in operation and were servicing 142,000 customers as of 1 July 1971."[15] The selection of manufactured articles being sold in these stores is still limited, but the selection will be expanded and a mandatory minimum selection will be established. Organizations that suffered the most from the stagnation and sluggishness of the supply planning process will be the first ones switched to a supply system based on wholesale trade. The organizations included are the scientific research, drafting-design, and technological organizations.

Supply has been the object of sharp criticism for some time. Its day-to-day operation is a reflection of yesterday's technology, it has never attempted to adapt itself to the technical peculiarities of capital construction, and the system itself is multistaged, complicated, slow and inflexible and suffers from duplication of effort. These are the inherent defects in the supply system that has been created and exists under the conditions of a planned, directed economy. Other faults and problems are created by the supply system itself. A typical problem is the issuing of orders (documents drawn up for a delivery) to suppliers (plants) that have not yet started operation, although this should be easy to find out beforehand. There is also a situation whereby "individual supply-sales organizations change and nullify more than 40 percent of all orders issued."[16] Incorrect territorial allocation of deliveries occurs, causing cross-transportation.[a] Direct contacts established between plants are frequently changed. To make their lives easier, the supply organizations resort to hoarding manufactured articles that are difficult to obtain; as a result, the deficit increases. This all moves bureaucratically through a paper snowstorm, diverting labor and obscuring the true situation. The top levels of management are convinced that they alone are the keepers of economic life and the infallible captains of the Soviet industrial ship.

As early as 1961 the late N. Kovalev, former chief of the USSR *Gosplan* computer center, wrote: "Today one need not be amazed that there are so many inadequacies and disruptions in material-technical supply."[17] However, generally one is amazed that the system manages somehow to continue functioning.

The defects in the material-technical supply system have led to another system that in principle is faulty but is actually quite necessary. This is the system of fixers (*tolkach*), sometimes called procurers (*dostaval*). One need not look for a job title of fixer or procurer within the staff of a plant or institution. There is no such position. Nevertheless, fixers exist. Their job is to speed up or insure that a delivery is made within the agreed period of time. To do this, the fixer goes to the supplier and appeals daily to the supplier's sense of patriotism and duty, reminds him, cajoles him, takes the necessary people out to dinner, and gives them presents. In other words, he does everything possible to insure the scheduled delivery or to accelerate the receipt of an overdue planned delivery. However, it often becomes necessary to obtain materials that were not foreseen in the supply plan and for which there are no orders. In this case, "ministries, plants, and organizations send out large groups of fixers wherever they are needed. On the last two days of October of last year, there were 118 representatives from various organizations at the Magnitogorsk Metallurgical Combine. Moreover, most of these people had come there to 'extort' nonfunded metal [not already allocated in the plan]. As a rule, the most qualified fixers are sent out to 'extort' nonfunded materials."[18]

The era of scientific-technical progress is reflected in fixing as well. Under modern conditions, supply questions are inseparably linked with the solution of

---

[a]Cross-transportation (*vstrechnaia perevozka,* literally "meeting shipment") is that peculiarly Soviet phenomenon by which lumber, for example, is shipped from the Urals to the Far East by one organization, while at the same time lumber is shipped from the Far East to the Urals by another organization. As a result of this cross-transportation, the lumber shipments pass each other in transit.

complicated, technical questions that are beyond the comprehension of a mere fixer. Therefore, the "engineer-expediter" (*inzhener-uskoritel'*) has come into being. "Special accommodations have been built by the plant suppliers for this contingent of specialists. A staff has been set up to handle these people. Reception days have been established." At the Leningrad association (*ob"edinenie*) "Pozitron" alone, fifty out-of-town engineer-expediters show up on reception day. "How many of these 'expediters' in all the country's enterprises are helping to save their plant's production schedule?"[19] In the final analysis, the fixers and expediters help fulfill the national economic plan by correcting scandalous errors, miscalculations, and disruptions in supply, and therefore it is as if no one notices them.

When it comes to solving a supply problem, and all other means have been exhausted, the Party organizations come into play as the highest coordinator and very often save the day. Because of their power, they can solve and bypass many things. For this reason, economists appeal to them when they do not succeed by normal and fixer methods. The secretary of the Leningrad City Party Committee attests to the fact that many Party committees are compelled to use "the authority of Party organs to 'push through' and 'dislodge' needed replenishing materials and raw materials." He also points out that in 1968 nearly four thousand letters and telegrams were sent to the Leningrad City Party Committee "and that this same amount of 'economic correspondence' had been addressed to the [Leningrad] *oblast'* party committee during the same period of time."[20]

What is happening on a broad scale today in material-technical supply can be generally but accurately characterized as follows: "The 'fixers' [an antiquated method] are functioning at the same time as electronic computers."[21]

Notes

1. A.N. Efimov, *Soviet Industry* (Moscow: Ekonomika, 1967), p. 214.
2. *Pravda*, 21 September 1962, p. 3.
3. *Pravda*, 24 February 1971, p. 1.
4. *Pravda*, 27 February 1974, p. 2.
5. *Pravda*, 20 September 1973, p. 4.
6. *Sotsialisticheskaia industriia*, 27 February 1971, p. 2.
7. *Planovoe khoziaistvo*, no. 7 (1970):4.
8. *Sotsialisticheskaia industriia*, 27 February 1971, p. 2.
9. *Pravda*, 26 March 1971, p. 3.
10. Efimov, *Soviet Industry*, p. 210.
11. *Ekonomicheskaia gazeta*, no. 36 (1971):10.
12. *Pravda*, 24 February 1971, lead article.
13. *Sotsialisticheskaia industriia*, 3 August 1972, p. 2.
14. *Sotsialisticheskaia industriia*, 16 August 1972, p. 2.

15. *Ekonomicheskaia gazeta*, no. 36 (1971):13.
16. *Planovoe khoziaistvo*, no. 1 (1970):53.
17. Ibid., no. 8 (1961):18.
18. *Ekonomicheskaia gazeta*, no. 6 (1974):17.
19. Ibid., no. 3 (1971):10.
20. Ibid., no. 9 (1969):6.
21. *Pravda*, 20 May 1971, p. 3.

15 Labor in the USSR

General Comments

"Labor in the USSR is a *requirement* and a matter of honor for every citizen capable of working. Labor is based on the principle, 'He who does not work, does not eat' " (italics mine).[1] The real situation in the socialist structure of Soviet society gave rise to the bittersweet addendum, "And he who eats, does not work!"

As Article 12 of the constitution also maintains, the socialist principle, "From each according to his ability; to each according to his labor," is put into practice in the USSR. This means that the earnings of the worker, or, more broadly, his material security, depends directly on the degree of his labor contribution to Soviet society.

Every able-bodied citizen of working age *must* work. Exceptions to the rule are made only for women with small children (and for all women of the Soviet elite), students at secondary and advanced educational facilities (although a "working semester" has been instituted for them also), and a few other cases. According to the official definition, an able-bodied citizen without a job is a parasite. Administrative measures are applied to force him to work. On collective farms, economic sanctions are applied to the nonworker which apply almost exclusively to his personal subsidiary farming.

The Soviet government, or more accurately, the Communist Party leadership, is the absolute monopolist-employer. It sets the amount (intensity) of labor, establishes the hours, wages, and working conditions, and even the frequency of "volunteer Saturdays" (*subbotniki*, when the worker works without being paid). In this way, the Communist Party leadership bears full responsibility for labor conditions. This is not merely anti-Soviet reasoning on my part, but a problem recognized by a significant part of the Soviet labor force, particularly the young. The Soviet press never deals with personal questions and opinions but only with problems that have attained a certain proportion and depth. For this reason, the journal *Molodoi kommunist* deemed it necessary to quote parts of a letter written by a young worker, T. Trofimov, and to give him a critical answer. Trofimov writes: "Under capitalism a worker can move from one monopolist to another if he is unhappy. Under socialism, there is just one 'boss,' the greatest of all monopolists; the state. . . . Where can the worker go to look for a better job if wage limits are set once and for all, and if any surplus initiative and energy runs up against a socioeconomic stone wall? What we have is freedom in a society of those who do not care, where the majority of its members have been deprived of incentives (both moral and material). On paper there is a free choice of action open to the individual, action aimed toward the benefit of society, but in reality there is only despair, inflexibility, and stifling conservatism."[2]

Nowhere but within labor itself does it become apparent with such force that the Soviet society is a society of indifference, that the Soviet economy from the standpoint of both the government and the collective is a household without a head. (*Translator's note:* a play on the Russian words *khoziaistvo*, meaning both "economy" and "household," and *khoziain*, meaning "boss" and "head of a household." It is difficult to retain the full flavor of the expression in English translation.)

The Labor Force

The selection and composition of the managerial ranks personify the principle of Party spirit in the economy. All managers come from the Party's so-called list of executives (*nomenklatura*). In selecting these people, the proletarian *idée fixe*, which is active in the Party even today, has created a promotion system whereby a worker joins the Party and quickly moves to a position of leadership. As a result, "the majority of our leaders have formed their careers primarily on the basis of long years of experience. They acquired their knowledge in bits and pieces through the process of self-education. . . . We know of 'captains' of very large 'ships of industry,' who from the time they were shop foremen have never formally studied anything anywhere. Others are aided by natural acuity, outstanding ability, or powers of observation or intuition. However, some are tormented all their lives."[3] Today these people have come to be called "school-of-lifers." Some of them have not even received a secondary education. In 1966, 32 percent of the directors of enterprises were school-of-lifers. In the past few years attempts have been made to promote specialists and Party members to positions of leadership. A typical career follows the following pattern:

Becomes a worker-*Komsomol* member

Finishes technical school while a *Komsomol* member

Starts to work in low-level technical management and joins the Party

Finishes an institute, often through correspondence courses

Occupies an upper-level technical position, and occasionally, though rarely, on the merits of coauthorship, receives the degree of candidate of sciences

Works two to three years in Party work

Becomes a deputy director or director, and sometimes rises even higher

By their training they are poorly qualified specialists. With conditions the way they are in the USSR, both the student, a member of the *Komsomol* or Party, and the faculty training him know that this student must finish school no matter what his ability or level of knowledge may be. It is hoped that the manager will acknowledge that the level of his training is extremely low, and he will allow qualified specialists to work with him.

However, the demands made by the higher Party leadership on the quality of economic leaders are more political than businesslike. "Political qualities and a thorough understanding of Party policy are the most important criteria. One might say that the economic activity of a manager is always Party-oriented in substance. The program of the Party is at the same time a program of economic development."[4] In the last few years this theory and practice has led to conflict between the demands of scientific-technical progress and contemporary methods of management. In this conflict there has not yet appeared the type of "hot-shot manager" who meets the demands of contemporary life. With rare exception management is dominated by a "hard-line bolshevik" who creates, furthers, and practices the theory that "without strong language the plan will not be fulfilled!" Coarseness from above poisons the business atmosphere and human relationships in economic activities.

The number of specialists, that is, the middle link of management, has grown considerably, increasing 94-fold between 1913 and 1971.[5] However, many things have led to the point that specialists are not used effectively. Therefore, there are not enough of them to go around. This is the general situation: in 1966 only 56 percent of all engineers were employed in sectors of physical production, and 22 percent held jobs that did not require an engineering degree.[6] In 1968 more than a third of all engineering-technical positions were occupied by school-of-lifers, while at the same time forty-one thousand graduates of higher educational institutions and technical schools were working as common laborers.[7] One could cite scores of such examples of absolutely irrational utilization of specialists both on a republicwide and on a unionwide level.

There are many complaints about the quality of the specialists currently being turned out. Basically, this can be explained by deficiencies and errors in specialist training. In 1966 a resolution of the CPSU Central Committee and the USSR Council of Ministers concerning improvements in specialist training noted failures in administrating the learning process and a shortage of "useful, standard textbooks."[8] It also cited the weakness of the academic material base and the harm done by the passion for evening and correspondence schools. In the past few years, expenditures on specialist training have risen at a slower rate than the number of specialists and slower than the economy as a whole. This "has led to a decrease in the qualifications of graduates."[9] The system of specialist training still turns out primarily specialists with a very narrow background, and almost half the training time is spent on narrow specialization. At the same time, "realities in the last few years have shown that the need for specialists with narrow qualifications has decreased over the years."[10] The training of most specialists in educational institutions gives the future specialist a certain background but little training in independent study in his field. It does not sufficiently familiarize him with the methodology of acquiring knowledge and information, nor does it give him a good general, scientific background. Because of this, the lag behind the rate of scientific-technical progress reaches massive proportions among the specialists.

The quality of specialists is lowered even more because children of the "new class," by using connections in high places, are scrambling into educational institutions, elbowing aside more worthy high school graduates."[11] In some instances diplomas are simply bought and sold.[12]

Only 12 to 15 percent of those completing specialist training meet all the current demands. These are predominantly graduates of old, prominent major educational institutions located in the most important scientific and cultural centers of the country.

The status and influence of specialists in the economy has decreased mainly as a result of their irregular legal status. The requirements and responsibilities of specialists are established much more precisely than is their certification. Time and again managers from the list of executives assume a specialist's rights, as if to replace the specialists. This phenomenon in particular was cited in a resolution of the CPSU Central Committee entitled "The Work of the Altai Territorial Committee of the CPSU toward Increasing the Role of Specialists in the Development of Collective- and State-Farm Production."[13]

Their incompatibility with the demands of the present day created a system of retraining for specialists and the managers from the list of executives.[14] By mid 1971 "more than thirty institutes for increasing the qualifications of managers and specialists in ministries and departments were operating successfully."[15] However, retraining, particularly in economics and mathematics, turned out to be very unpopular among potential students, and all these measures gradually fell through.

Somewhat more effective was a periodic certification of the specialist corps, by which the weaker specialists were weeded out. Barriers were established so that high posts could not be occupied by insufficiently qualified specialists. Selection of the stronger specialists also acted as a stimulus for the majority to raise their qualifications. The following example illustrates beautifully the situation as it was before the introduction of certification. In the Merchant Fleet's Central Scientific Research Institute, out of one hundred specialists undergoing certification, it was recommended that eleven be fired and forty-eight be demoted.[16] Fifty-nine percent of the staff of the Central Institute did not meet the requirements for certification!

Throughout the years of the five-year plans, the number of blue-collar workers has continually grown (from 8.5 million in 1928 to 62 million in 1970), as has the number of white-collar workers. As a result of this process, "the number of able-bodied workers employed in the USSR in 1970 reached a very high level, 91 to 92 percent, and it is doubtful that further growth is advisable."[17] Thus, the chances of increasing the number of workers today depends entirely on an increase in the population. At the same time, demographic conditions are such that "by the late 1980s, there will be no increase in the labor force in our country."[18] As a consequence, the ever-present problem of the labor force had already led to a severe and increasing shortage of workers in the late 1960s. The official Party press tries to impress on its readers that this is still due to World War II. The impact of the war is actually secondary. For this reason the war is not mentioned in economic literature; a series of other more important reasons are cited. In my opinion, which is shared by a number of Soviet economists as well, the most important reason is long-term neglect. After this comes the inability to calculate the effect of the law of value in the Soviet economy. In the Soviet system, the value of any article, almost without exception, represents the cost of labor expended in production of a given article. This cost varies in time and form. If value is of no interest or cannot be calculated, enormous overexpenditures of labor are inevitable. This explains why about 12 million workers in Soviet industry and about 45 million workers in the economy as a whole [or 50 percent of the labor force] "are engaged, to a considerable degree, in manual or unskilled labor."[19] The Scientific Research Institute of *Gosplan* believes that the basic reason is that "the extensive development factor still plays a major role."[20] T. Khachaturov points to low labor productivity and large losses in worker time.[21] Economic literature points out a whole network of other canals down which wasted labor flows. Among these is labor turnover, which reached 20 percent of the workers in the RSFSR in 1970.[22] Also cited is the creation of a fund for economic stimulation which is proportional to the fund for wages. This acts as an incentive to increase one's labor force.[23] Frequent changes in plans also require a plant to have a reserve labor force on hand. Thus, the increasing shortage in the labor force is a product primarily of the system itself. The system created conditions of extremely low efficiency in the use of labor and brought about demographic changes that curtailed an increase in labor resources.

The lack of skilled laborers has always been severe. The situation has merely grown worse with the passage of time. The rise in the average level of skilled workers has lagged behind the rise in the technical level of production. This can be explained by the system used to train skilled labor. Set up in the beginning of industrialization, the system remains significantly unchanged. Several attempts to change it have not yet shown tangible results. As before, "75 to 80 percent of the workers in the major professions currently acquire their skills directly from the plant. Their training period does not exceed six months." Obviously such training is completely inadequate and "leads to large losses due to defective products, poor use of equipment, and an increase in downtime during shifts."[24] Such training is falling further and further behind the demands of modern day scientific-technical progress.

The higher-skilled workers (the remaining 20 to 25 percent) are trained through a system of professional-technical education. Here, too, as was stated in a resolution of the CPSU Central Committee, "Measures for the Further Improvement in Training Skilled Labor in Educational Institutions of the Professional-Technical Educational System," "the level of training of skilled workers in professional-technical educational institutions is falling behind the growing demands of socialist production." The resolution calls for the reorganization of educational institutions into "professional-technical colleges with a three- to four-year course of study."[25] Three years later the Soviet leadership was once again forced to reexamine the training of skilled labor. A new resolution of the CPSU Central Committee and the USSR Council of Ministers, "Further Improvements in Professional-Technical Education," states that in the new colleges, "changes which are taking place on the job are not always taken into consideration. Scientific problems in professional-technical education are worked out slowly." On the whole, "there are serious shortcomings in the job done by the educational institutions."[26] The bureaucratic inflexibility of the system is also demonstrated here.

Labor Productivity

In the Soviet Union labor productivity is more significant politically than economically. In the words of Lenin, "Labor productivity in the final analysis is the most important and most basic requirement for the victory of a new social order. Capitalism created a level of labor productivity unprecedented under serfdom. Capitalism can be defeated once and for all by the fact that socialism will create a new, significantly higher level of labor productivity."[27] In fact as a product of the synthesis of the organizational, productive, and social sides of economic life, labor productivity represents in one indicator the efficiency, social balance, and progressiveness of any economic system.

Based on these characteristics of the labor productivity indicator, Soviet planning and statistical organizations, who generally display a sleight of hand with figures, use it to full advantage when talking about the level of labor productivity in the USSR. "Practice shows that in most cases planning organizations prefer to base plans on superficially favorable production indicators [labor productivity] rather than on more accurate plans for labor productivity."[28]

Soviet labor productivity is determined by the following formula.

$$\frac{\text{Gross output in rubles}}{\text{Number of workers}} = \text{Share of the gross output per worker per year}$$

The result is used to determine the level of labor productivity and its growth rate as well as to compare Soviet labor productivity and that of other countries based on similar currencies.

To make things look favorable, one has to have as large a numerator and as small a denominator as possible. The former is achieved by using gross output indicators which to a certain degree do not consider the growth of repetitive accounts but do include unfinished products and products for which there is no market. A small denominator is achieved by counting only workers located directly within the sphere of physical production (earlier, even ancillary workers and repairmen were not included). The entire higher economic apparatus is not included in the number of workers. Judging by the classifications of the Central Statistical Directorate, workers of scientific research and design institutes that "are not a structural part of industrial, agricultural or other production enterprises" are not included in the number of workers. Workers in scientific research and design institutes alone number almost 3.4 million. Similar methods distort the "dynamics of labor productivity" and lead to a series of negative results, the chief of which is the tendency to raise the cost of production.[29] For this reason, "the labor productivity indicator presently being used . . . has been subject to heavy criticism for many years."[30] However, "it is impossible to find a labor productivity indicator sufficiently complete and applicable to enterprises of all sectors of industry. In fact, until now such an indicator has not been found."[31] The absolute level of labor productivity, both of the economy as a whole and of its divisions and sectors, is never reported. The Central Statistical Directorate reference book lists only the percentile growth of national labor and the same indicator for each sector of industry. No such information is given for agriculture, transportation, and a whole group of other economic areas. Nevertheless, *it is known for an absolute fact* "that our level of industrial labor productivity is half that of the United States, and in agriculture, one-quarter to one-fifth that of the United States. We also lag behind several other countries according to these indicators."[32] Some very approximate calculations (using active fixed capital, intensity of its utilization, and the number of workers) produce different figures. Labor productivity in industry is four to five times lower than that of the United States, and in agriculture about eight to ten times lower.

Plans for labor productivity are not generally fulfilled. Thus, for the first three years of the Ninth Five-Year Plan (1971-1973), the plans for labor productivity were fulfilled by 83 percent, 80 percent, and 82 percent respectively.[32]

Low labor productivity cannot be explained only by the reasons set forth earlier. There are still many other factors, among which are socialist production relationships and the scientific organization of labor.

Certain human relationships that take shape as a result of economic activity are inherent to every economic system. Humanity's economic progress is characterized by an ever-increasing democratization of production relationships. The more emancipated labor became, the more it was stimulated materially and socially, and the more society was successful in economic activity. From this correct point of view, Soviet production relationships, long thought to be irrefutable, represent an attempt to turn back the wheel of time. In the 1960s, under the pressure of new conditions, it was said "that under socialism, the most important thing is to optimize relationships between management and labor, based on the criterion of convergence of interests, both material and moral."[34] In other words, "the convergence of personal, collective, and social interests . . . is a very important natural law of socialist economic development." In reality, "the production relationships of socialism" are a burning social problem, the results of which are passive indifference, apathy, a "who-gives-a-damn," scornful attitude toward labor, low-quality work, and low labor discipline. Here is part of the social basis for the alcoholism widespread in the Soviet Union.

Lenin attached great significance to the scientific organization of labor, but Stalin disregarded it. In the early 1960s, one sees the beginnings of a call for "the rehabilitation of the science of organization and management of labor"; however, at that time, this science was not "on the list of social disciplines."[35] It was not taught anywhere, and no books or journals were published on the subject. At that point, however, they began to make up for lost time. Everywhere "new scientific and administrative organizations for handling the scientific organization of labor" were established on the principle, The more the merrier. In the mad dash no serious attention was paid "to the qualitative side of research in the scientific organization of labor or in improving the job being done by existing institutions." The majority of the leading factions underestimated the significance of the scientific organization of labor in mobilizing hidden reserves in production and "only a few at the time grasped the fact that better organization, no matter what the cost, in many cases turns out to be much more effective than the most up-to-date equipment."[36] In the meantime, not only was there no scientific organization of labor in industrial production, it was also lacking in engineering-technical and administrative management work.[37] "One of the reasons for poor dissemination of scientific organization of labor is the poor way it is introduced, making it impossible to attain much success."[38] One should also look here for a cause of intrashift downtime, which amounts to 15 to 20 percent of the total time spent on the job.[39] This also explains why "currently about 60 percent of the labor in industry and construction is done by hand."[40] This list can be continued, but the most important fact is that it all leads to an official recognition of "a shortage of laborers" in the economy as a whole.[41]

Socialist Labor Methods

The so-called volunteer Saturdays (*subbotniki*) laid the foundation for socialist methods of labor. A volunteer Saturday means work without pay for the able-bodied populace of the USSR during their normal nonworking hours. The first such volunteer Saturday occurred on 10 May 1919, with Lenin himself taking part. On volunteer Saturday one either does some special task (cleanup work, tree planting, straightening up the factory grounds or the city), or one does his usual job. In the first instance, the work is done without pay; in the second, the earnings are assigned to a special fund. The idea behind the volunteer Saturday is to organize a demonstration of solidarity, enthusiasm, and devotion to the regime, as well as to get some additional free labor. Volunteer Saturdays still take place.

Somewhat later there appeared a second, more widespread socialist method of labor, socialist competition. As is obvious from the name itself, this socialist method of labor is basically a competition between individual workers, groups of workers (plants, factories, offices), and even between republics, to see who can best fulfill requirements set by the higher Party leadership. Generally, but not always, socialist competition means fulfillment or overfulfillment of the plan or fulfillment ahead of schedule.

The Party leadership attaches not only economic but above all political significance to socialist competition. Even more than a volunteer Saturday, socialist competition demonstrates a worker's enthusiasm for the creation of socialism and his desire to complete his task. It also demonstrates with deeds, not just words, full support for Party policy, the Soviet system, and the Soviet government. The economic significance of socialist competition lies in the opportunity (often purely speculative) to accelerate the work of millions of people. However, even more important, since the mid 1930s socialist competition has made it possible to argue for and justify a constant review of the norms. It has also made possible the acceleration of the work of millions not based solely on "enthusiasm" but on wages. The fact is that even before the appearance of the *Stakhanovite* movement, there were "shock workers" (record-setting workers) whose accomplishments can be explained only by their personal attributes. The miner Stakhanov himself maintained that his work records were the result not solely of personal physical qualities but also of new work methods that he devised. It seems logical that every person can learn a new method and can at least work better than he did before, even if not as well as Stakhanov. Since then the records set by Stakhanov and the representatives of other such movements led to a revision and increase of work norms. This explains the feelings of the overwhelming majority of workers toward socialist competitions. In reality, socialist competitions do not represent spontaneous enthusiasm that need only be organized on paper, as the Soviets would like to picture it. Moreover, "making competitions attractive to a greater number of workers is one of the most important tasks of social organizations and management."[42]

The competitions are planned and supervised. "This supervision is provided by higher-level administrative and trade union organizations [departmental supervision]. The activities of management regarding the organization of competitions are supervised by Party organs [Party supervision], and supervision of the competitions is performed by the competitors themselves [reciprocal supervision]." Trade union committees and management are involved in the operational handling of the competitions. They "organize socialist competitions, tally the results, determine the winners, and publicize innovations."[43] Party organizations are involved in ideological-political leadership.

Thus, competitions are held under Party, administrative, trade union, and plan pressure. They are conducted by directive. This is precisely why the Soviets have had to acknowledge displays of formalism, cliches, and red tape in competitions. They are forced to acknowledge the existence of a search for quantity among the competitors. They are also forced to acknowledge that "instances of compiling groundless, inconcrete, and even blatantly lowered conditions still persist."[44] There are reports of "rush jobs and ledger padding" in order to meet the conditions that have been adopted. There are numerous cases of a lack of genuine openness in tallying the results, in determining the winners, and, most important, in the distribution of prize money.

Although participation in competitions, the display of enthusiasm, and devotion to communist ideals has become almost a standard for citizenship, at the same time the Soviets try to force everyone to participate. In 1974, 78 million workers were involved in competitions, or 79.5 percent of the total 98 million strong labor force.[45] If one considers that socialist competitions are also held on collective farms (kolkhozes) where about 17 million people work, involvement drops to 67.8 percent.

A more up-to-date form of competition is the "communist labor movement" under the slogan "Live and work as communists." Of the 78 million competitors, 45 million took part in the communist labor movement. Although this movement has been going on since 1959, "the qualitative changes characterizing competitions have still not reached the level at which a competition among all productive collectives would become a struggle for a communist attitude toward labor." Moreover, "up to now, socialist commitments, the results of a crew's activity, and the activity of the 'shock workers' of communist labor often differ little from the results of those who do not participate in the movement."[46] Nevertheless, in the day-to-day routine it is advantageous to be counted among the shock workers or to be in a communist labor brigade.

In the Ninth Five-Year Plan (1971-1975) new forms of competition appeared, that is, counterplans of collectives and individual worker commitments. Of all the forms that have been in existence up to now, this one seems to be the most effective. Theoretically, competitions contradict the planned nature of the Soviet economy, since they tend to disrupt the plan with the aim of increasing it. However, competitions are significant means of speeding up production by the cheapest and most primitive ways possible.

Setting Norms for Labor

The norm (rate of output) is the number of units or the volume of work that a worker must produce in a certain unit of time (hour, workday, shift). The number of units or volume of work multiplied by the payment made for making one unit or volume of work determines the worker's wages. Theoretically, the norm is inseparably tied to the planned (desired) wage level of a worker. In reality, the planned level of wages is just the starting point for establishing payment by norm. Next a time study of the job establishes how much a worker can do in a unit of time. The planned level of wages for a unit of time (hour, day, month) is divided by the number of units produced in a corresponding amount of time. Thus, one arrives at the amount to be paid for a norm. When paid either by the piece or by the hour, a worker can receive his normal wage only if he meets his norm. A revision and subsequent raising of the norm forces the worker to work faster. This explains his attitude toward norm setting. *Pravda* cites a typical example of this attitude. At a certain plant the quota per shift for the production of bolts was at first 750 units. Then things became somewhat better. A preliminary time study showed that it was possible to produce 1,200-1,250 bolts per shift. Then the plant's wage and labor department entered the scene. "The workers began to produce the very same number of bolts everyday—1,000. No more, no less. What can you call this other than an attempt to 'put the screws' to the norm setters, to force them to set lowered norms? Now the rate in that shop is 950 bolts. . . . Even more important, cases similar to this one are not a rarity," because the management of the enterprise creates a reserve labor force by setting a low norm.[47]

Technically based and empirical-statistical norms differ in the methods by which they are established. The former are set through engineering-technical estimates of the time needed to produce one unit, and the production process is divided into separate phases, types, and elements. Empirical-statistical norms are set by the time-study method. Industrial sector and plant norms differ according to the administrative level at which they are set. Industrial sector norms (in effect for an entire sector of industry) are quite often technically based norms and are theoretically more accurate. Empirical-statistical norms predominate in plant norms and are often set as *Pravda* described.

Given all this, "in recent years only 7.2 percent of the workers in industry are paid according to industrial sector norms, while 92.8 percent are paid according to norms worked out at the enterprise. Of these, only 16.6 percent are paid according to technically based norms. The majority of workers (including piece-rate and hourly-rate workers) are paid according to empirical-statistical norms that do not reflect the socially necessary expenditure of worker time for production on either an industrial or an individual enterprise scale."[48]

Norm setting for labor plays an enormous role in the national economic planning of labor expenditures (plan for labor), which provides planning organs with initial estimates. In other words, the labor plan is formulated on the basis of norms; and if these norms "do not reflect socially necessary expenditures of worker time," then the plan is in no position to reflect the *optimal* expenditures of worker time but merely reflects the situation as it turned out. Expenditures for labor are also involved in determining production cost. Thus, a mistake in one will mean a mistake in the other. Finally, an overfulfillment of lowered norms leads to an excess in actual earnings above the planned level and a rise in wages that outstrips the growth of labor productivity.[49] It also disturbs the balance between the income of the population and the planned volume of goods and services; that is, it leads to what in the USSR has come to be called "the unmet demands of a solvent public." Out of these unmet demands come not only speculation, black marketeering, and problems with the circulation of cash but unpleasant social and political problems as well.

Wages

Socialist political economics officially believes that wages are the personification of the Leninist principle of material incentive as well as a practical manifestation of the socialist principle of distribution in proportion to the quantity and quality of labor performed. The principle of equal pay for equal work finds its expression through material incentives. Particularly strong emphasis is given to wages as the personification of the Leninist principle of material incentive. The assertion "Through wages, material incentive is achieved as a *result of the labor of every worker*" (italics mine) is considered the gospel truth.[50]

"The planning of wages is a necessary prerequisite to basing wages on the principle of distribution according to labor performed."[51] The planned nature of the system demands the planning of wages as well. This is because the national economic allocation for wages, that is, the amount of money paid to the worker, is a piece of vital initial information in planning the production of a whole series of industrial sectors, as well as in planning domestic trade and the country's cash circulation. The allocation for wages on a national scale, subdivided by ministries and departments, is fixed by *Gosplan* and is based on the theoretical principle that the rise in labor productivity will be greater than the rise in wages. The method of planning wages is based on "estimates of the planned average wage made on an established basis, taking into account a rise in labor productivity chiefly as a result of accelerated labor and an increase in worker skill."[52] In other words, planning here is also based on the principle "from a level already attained."

Operational and methodological guidance for wages is in the hands of the State Committee of the USSR Council of Ministers for Labor and Wages. Ministries and departments have their own departmental system of organizations for labor and wages. The local organization is a department at the plant. One of the main tasks of the departmental system is to adjust, within the bounds of wage allocation, the wages of groups or individual workers to the concrete conditions of production and labor.

Gosbank monitors the wage funds by issuing payments proportional to the percentage of the plan fulfilled by the plant.

Wages are made up of separate elements which are connected, but which have a somewhat different economic character. The basic elements of wages are shown in figure 15-1.

In the 1960s one more element appeared in the supplemental wage sector, the awarding of a premium to a plant based on the results of its work for the year. "A considerable amount of money is currently being spent with this in mind. At many plants, these payments make up more than 30 percent of the allocation for material incentives."[53]

Wages are divided formally into hourly and piecework categories with several modifications of each. For example, there is straight piecework, piecework plus bonus, progressive piecework, and lump-sum wage payment. Lump-sum wage payment is finding greater recognition and more widespread use in the 1970s. The hourly wage system is divided into simple hourly and hourly plus bonus. More than 60 percent of the industrial labor force is paid according to various piecework wage systems.

In a planned economy it is theoretically possible to distribute the ever-increasing volume of consumer goods either by raising wages and stabilizing prices or by stabilizing wages and lowering prices. The Soviet leadership, as one might imagine, chose the first course for two basic reasons. The first is propaganda. A rise in wages appears to the world to be a sign of an increase in the well-being of the populace. The second is organization. It is easier to raise earnings by a planned percentage than to reset prices. Therefore, nominal wages (basic and supplementary) have risen continually throughout the years of the Soviet system's existence. However, this seldom meant an increase in real wages or in the worker's standard of living. A particularly sharp rise in nominal wages began in 1965, and in 1972 it amounted to 130 rubles, 20 kopecks.[54]

The realities of the wage system clash with theory and with the principles that the system personifies according to socialist political economics. The system does not implement the Leninist principle of material incentive and in no way personifies the principle of distribution according to labor performed. In theory, a wage system should create a unified body of the interests of workers, the collectives, and society. "However, in reality, we still have not found sufficiently effective forms for distributing income that will promote such a fusing of interests. . . . There is no direct logical interdependence between payment for labor and the results of productive activity. The individual worker does not feel that the productive success of the collective depends directly on his contribution. Planning in practice and the expenditure of wage allocations do not promote a savings in labor and do not create stimuli for technical progress."[55] The supplemental part of the wage system "does not sufficiently induce the productive collective body or individual worker to take on an ambitious plan." In other words, it does not induce one to work. The system of supplementary wages "does not always provide for a degree of reward based on the concrete

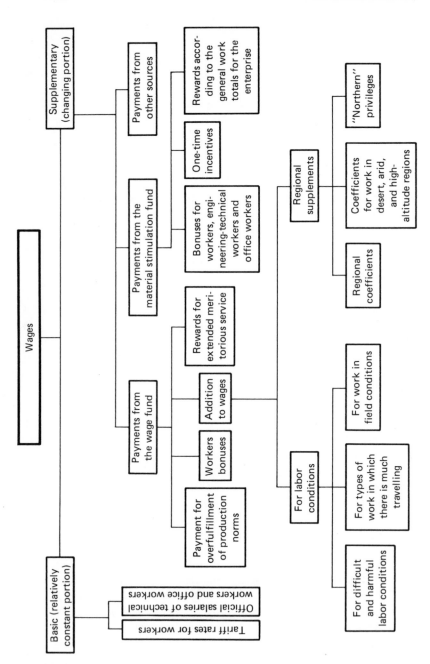

Figure 15-1. Wage Structure

results of each worker's labor."[56] Most Soviet economists believe that the proportion of supplementary wage payments is too low and cannot create a real material incentive for improving labor indicators. In 1969 supplementary wages amounted to the following: 13.1 percent of the wages for a blue-collar worker, 20.1 percent for an engineer-technician, and 18.8 percent for a white-collar worker.[57] Some people feel that "a premium can play a real stimulative role only when its proportion of the total wages is about 20 to 25 percent,"[58] while others quote even higher percentages.

In real life one is seldom able to put into practice the principle of an increase in labor productivity comparable to the increase in wages. "The results of enterprise activities in the first half of 1974 show that in many cases the rate of increase in average wages exceeds the planned rate, and the relationships envisioned by the plan are not being preserved."[59] "The relationships established in the plan are also disrupted, in part, on the national economic scale. For example, in 1968, the deputy chairman of *Gosplan* wrote: 'We cannot allow the average wage in various plants and even sectors of industry to continue to rise faster than labor productivity.' "[60] Despite some improvement, the statement made in the early 1960s still holds: "Although considerable resources are spent on prize money throughout the country, these expenditures do little to contribute to encourage initiative in the laborers and to contribute to the production of the more important products. The shortcomings of the premium system are further aggravated by the lack of any clear or stable connection between the results of each worker's labor and the level of payment for that labor."[61]

The shortcomings of the wage system decrease the efficiency of the economy by lessening the driving force of worker material interests. Of this decreased efficiency is born the politically unfavorable phenomenon of which Marx and Engels wrote: "A concept invariably disgraces itself as soon as it divorces itself from 'interest.' "[62]

The Standard of Living

For the first time, the new program of the CPSU adopted at the Twenty-Second Party Congress (October 1961) defined that Party policy is aimed at creating a high standard of living for the laborer. Up to that time, a high standard of living for the worker was mentioned only in connection with that bright communist "tomorrow," for the sake of which one must work and tighten one's belt today.

A program of the CPSU, however, cannot create well-being by itself. Political tradition requires a demonstration of the effectiveness of a program. For that reason, it is difficult to find reliable Soviet sources concerning living standards and conditions of the Soviet population and its workers. Let me cite an example. *Pravda* mentions "that each of us consumes an average of 470 grams of cereal grains a day," which comes to *172 kilograms per year.*[63] *The National Economy of the USSR in 1970* quotes an official figure for the consumption of grain products, such as cereal grains, flour, groats, legumes, and pasta products, as 149 kilograms per capita per year.[64] The reason for this discrepancy is that a high consumption of cereal grains means a low standard of living.

Many currently unalterable reasons of both an economic and noneconomic nature keep the Soviet worker's standard of living at the minimum level. More important, because of these reasons the standard of living, even with an increase, will always lag sharply behind the living standard in developed nations with free market economies. The significance of this inevitable conclusion is difficult to overestimate in its historical perspective.

Wages make up more than three-quarters of the populace's income.[65] More than 22 percent of the 1972 income came from social welfare funds—pensions, scholarships, and other payments and privileges.[66] A glance at family budgets shows that "on the whole, the average wage of one worker fluctuated at a level of about 50 percent of the average family income. . . . Two members of the family work in 70 to 80 percent of all worker families." By some strange logic, this same source stated that "it would not be correct to interpret this fact as the result of a still insufficiently high standard of living, or, in particular, as the result of insufficient wages."[67] However, how is one to interpret this? This is just how everything is envisaged in the plan. All production is planned, and a certain amount of labor is required to accomplish it. The proportions of accumulation and consumption are planned, and these determine the material benefits that a worker may receive. Thus, the system and the leadership determine the inevitability of work and determine who should not have to work. Insufficient wages are the method used to force people to work.

The largest item in the family budget is food. According to official statistics in 1972 food amounted to 34.8 percent of all family income.[68] The accuracy of this figure is doubtful. Only sixty-two thousand family budgets were surveyed. Items were taken into account that do not easily lend themselves to accounting (outside income and so forth). The difference between 1 percent of "all family income" and 1 percent of just wages is not clear. One can imagine that on the average, expenditures for food come to about 45 percent. Nevertheless, the diet is unsatisfactory. "In all the climatic zones of the country, cereal grains make up the largest proportion of calories in the daily diet of the population. First place in the daily diet (in the Russian Soviet Federsted Socialist Republic, three thousand large calories) is occupied by carbohydrates, that is, on the average 56 percent of the diet, with bread comprising the majority of it. Fats make up only about 30 percent of the caloric intake, and protein 13 to 14 percent. The second most important item is expenditures for fabric, clothing, and footwear (15 percent), and the third is "for education, medical care, and other free [?] benefits from social welfare funds (14 percent).[69]

Although two working members per family is the typical number reported, in reality all able-bodied family members work. Nonetheless, working for the government does not provide for the family sufficiently, and various means of increasing income—legally, quasi-legally, and illegally—are widespread. A very widespread form, if not of raising income, then at least of lowering expenses, is spare-time farming by collective farm workers and blue- and white-collar workers, as well as truck farming by blue- and white-collar workers. Practically all collective farm workers and more than 2 million blue- and white-collar families have their own spare-time gardens. Tens of millions of Soviet families, even in such large cities as Moscow, have their own truck gardens. A quasi-legal and very widespread sideline is performing mutual favors. These are chiefly repairs, on everything from apartments to televisions and automobiles. Repair work is almost always connected with illegal sidelines. Because of the lack of other sources, materials used in making repairs or spare parts are pilfered from the government. Finally, state property is stolen on an unbelievably large scale, not only as a sideline but sometimes as a person's livelihood. This is particularly widespread in commerce, in the processing of agricultural products, and in factories where the products can be used by the populace at large and where the products are scarce commodities (spare auto parts, for example). I could cite dozens of good examples, but perhaps an anecdote from the well-known "This is Radio Erevan" series will more vividly describe the magnitude of this phenomenon.

Comrade Karapetian: "Will there still be stealing under communism?

Radio Erevan: "No! Everything will have already been stolen under socialism!"

According to somewhat outdated information from the sometimes frank Khrushchev, "In the cases turned over to the courts in the first half of 1962 alone, the damage done by stealing amounted to more than 56 million rubles."[70] However, probably much less than 1 percent of the crimes committed and a very small percentage of the crimes uncovered are turned over to the courts. Petty pilferage, of which there are millions of cases, are generally punished administratively. Workers from the Party's list of executives are the ones involved in large-scale robberies. In most cases, Party discipline replaces punishment by the court.

The living standard of the population is inseparably linked to living conditions, above all with communal, commercial, and everyday services. Despite considerable housing construction, the city dweller received eleven square meters of usable living space in 1970.[71] The room principle of occupancy is still widely practiced. This means that a family receives a single room in an apartment. The condition of the quarters is bad, because "rents cover only about a third of all expenditures from the housing fund."[72] The quality of the newly constructed buildings, particularly of the prefabricated structures, is very poor.

The roofs leak, and drafts blow through the joints between panels and windows.[73] The buildings' heating, hot water, and elevators do not meet today's technical standards or the present-day concept of city living.

Commercial services are extremely poor, and not just because many consumer goods are still in short supply. Due to poor organization, items that theoretically should be on hand in sufficient quantities are often not in the stores. The commercial outlet network is poorly developed. In 1971 there were 128 square meters of floor space in commercial outlets for each thousand inhabitants in the USSR, 210 square meters in Czechoslovakia; and 280 square meters in East Germany.[74] In that same year there were 8.51 square meters of floor space per salesperson in the USSR, while in the United States there were 20.5 square meters.[75] Contemporary sales methods are implemented very slowly, and the organization in the older stores is such that "the population today spends a tremendous amount of time shopping, about 30 billion hours a year. This represents the labor of 15 million workers. . . . The shopper spends five to six times as many hours in a store as are needed to make a purchase."[76]

Everyday services such as laundry, tailoring, and repair shops have started to develop quite rapidly only during the Eighth and Ninth Five-Year Plans. Nevertheless, the development plans were not fulfilled (between 1965 and 1970 growth was 220 percent instead of the planned 250 percent). "The level of production of everyday services should be 1½ times greater than it is now."[77] Forced to live with an insufficient supply of low-quality everyday appliances, the people waste billions of hours doing everyday tasks.

The living standard and living conditions of the Soviet people have already led to demographic consequences, the most important of which is a sharp decline in the birth rate.

Notes

1. Article 12, *The Constitution of the USSR.*

2. *Molodi kommunist*, no. 11 (1966):52.

3. *Pravda*, 2 December 1968, p. 2.

4. *Voprosy ekonomiki*, no. 9 (1973):110.

5. Ibid., no. 3 (1973):40.

6. Ibid., no. 12 (1970):110.

7. Ibid., no. 5 (1971):127.

8. *Pravda*, 9 September 1966, p. 1.

9. *Voprosy ekonomiki*, no. 11 (1968):157-158.

10. *Pravda*, 24 May 1970, p. 3.

11. *Pravda*, 26 July 1966, p. 4; 1 August 1966, p. 2; 26 July 1968, p. 3; 23 October 1969, p. 6; 19 May 1970, p. 2.

12. *Pravda*, 19 May 1970, p. 2.

13. *Pravda*, 27 July 1971, p. 1.
14. *Resolution of the USSR Council of Ministers*, 6 June 1967.
15. *Pravda*, 1 August 1971, p. 2.
16. *Pravda*, 18 February 1971, p. 3.
17. *Voprosy ekonomiki*, no. 2 (1974):39.
18. Ibid., no. 9 (1971):135.
19. *Planovoe khoziaistvo*, no. 6 (1974):13.
20. Ibid., no. 4 (1971):43.
21. Ibid., no. 6 (1974):12-13.
22. *Sotsialisticheskaia industriia*, 15 March 1972, p. 2.
23. *Pravda*, 24 June 1970, p. 2.
24. *Voprosy ekonomiki*, no. 6 (1973):11.
25. *Pravda*, 17 April 1969, p. 1.
26. *Pravda*, 29 June 1972, p. 1.
27. V.I. Lenin, "Great Initiative," *Works*, vol. 29, p. 394.
28. *Planovoe khoziaistvo*, no. 1 (1963):54.
29. *Voprosy ekonomiki*, no. 5 (1974):125.
30. Ibid., no. 2 (1969):50.
31. Ibid., p. 52.
32. *Planovoe khoziaistvo*, no. 6 (1974):12.
33. Ibid., no. 7 (1974):7.
34. *Voprosy ekonomiki*, no. 10 (1970):56.
35. A. Berg, *Pravda*, 24 October 1962, p. 4.
36. *Pravda*, 11 May 1970, p. 2.
37. *Planovoe khoziaistvo*, no. 12 (1969):7.
38. *Voprosy ekonomiki*, no. 8 (1971):3.
39. *Ekonomicheskaia gazeta*, no. 43 (1971):4.
40. *Pravda*, 6 December 1971, p. 2.
41. *Planovoe khoziaistvo*, no. 7 (1974):10.
42. *Voprosy ekonomiki*, no. 9 (1974):105.
43. Ibid., p. 106.
44. *Pravda*, 8 May 1968, lead article.
45. *Planovoe khoziaistvo*, no. 7 (1974):4.
46. *Voprosy ekonomiki*, no. 3 (1974):44.
47. *Pravda*, 18 January 1970, p. 2.
48. *Voprosy ekonomiki*, no. 3 (1970):97.
49. *Pravda*, 27 September 1972, lead article.
50. *Labor Questions in the USSR* (Moscow: Gospolitizdat, 1958), p. 275.
51. N.A. Tsagolov, ed., *A Course in Political Economics*, vol. 2 (Moscow: Ekonomika, 1970), p. 567.
52. *Planovoe khoziaistvo*, no. 3 (1968):19.
53. Ibid., no. 9 (1974):131.
54. *National Economy of the USSR in 1972* (Moscow: Statistika, 1973), p. 516.

55. *Sotsialisticheskaia industriia*, 24 August 1973, p. 2.

56. *Pravda*, 30 August 1974, p. 2.

57. *Voprosy ekonomiki*, no. 5 (1971):21.

58. Ibid., no. 4 (1968):135.

59. *Planovoe khoziaistvo*, no. 8 (1974):3.

60. Ibid., no. 9 (1968):17.

61. Ibid., no. 10 (1962):8.

62. Karl Marx and Frederich Engels, *Works*, vol. 2.

63. *Pravda*, 9 July 1970, p. 2.

64. *National Economy of the USSR in 1970* (Moscow: Statistika, 1971), p. 561.

65. *Sotsialisticheskaia industriia*, 24 August 1973, p. 2.

66. *Ekonomicheskaia gazeta*, no. 4 (1974):17.

67. *Planovoe khoziaistvo*, no. 4 (1970):50.

68. *National Economy of the USSR in 1972*, p. 562.

69. *Planovoe khoziaistvo*, no. 3 (1974):76.

70. *Krasnaia zvezda*, 20 November 1962, p. 7.

71. *Voprosy ekonomiki*, no. 8 (1973):56.

72. Ibid., no. 2 (1973):41.

73. *Pravda*, 26 May 1970, p. 2.

74. *Voprosy ekonomiki*, no. 12 (1971):5.

75. Ibid., no. 9 (1973):43.

76. Ibid., no. 4 (1969):52.

77. *Pravda*, 1 September 1971, p. 3.

16 Agriculture

Introduction

The development of agriculture in the USSR since the October Revolution can be divided into three periods: War Communism, NEP (New Economic Policy), and Collectivized Agriculture.

War Communism, continuing the almost 3½ years from the October Revolution until March 1921, was characterized by the expropriation of peasant farming. The state gathered agricultural products without compensation, and each farm was told how much and what it must turn over to the government (*prodzrazverstka*—"appropriation of produce"). The economic results of this period were the collapse of the country's agricultural system, a sharp cutback in agricultural production, starvation, epidemics, and uprisings.

In the NEP period, lasting from 1921 to 1928, agriculture developed along capitalistic `lines. The peasants paid taxes which, with the passage of time, became more and more a monetary tax rather than a tax in kind. The land belonged to the state, but the peasant did what he saw fit with it. In seven years agriculture reached a quantitative and, more important, qualitative level that it had never reached in prerevolutionary Russian history and would never again reach under the Soviet system.

Collectivized agriculture, Stalin's socialist restructuring of agriculture, created economic conditions that transformed agriculture into a most difficult economic, social, political, and even strategic problem. The so-called socialist restructuring created an enormous economic loss in agriculture, decisively squelched all chances for its further development, and created a general disproportion between agriculture and industry.

According to Soviet economists, the general economic disproportion results from insufficient supplies of industrial goods used in agricultural production, as well as a faulty price-setting system and insufficient material interest in the results of their labor by agricultural workers.[1] The general disproportion is the source of economic losses throughout the entire economy.[2] It is especially dangerous during wartime.[3] The agricultural situation applies a powerful brake on any large-scale military adventure and is an influential factor in favor of the policy of peaceful coexistence.

Throughout its existence socialist agriculture has been characterized as follows: "The level and rate of agricultural development still does not meet the growing demands of the nation for produce and agricultural raw materials."[4]

This assertion is true for both the past and the present, and it will obviously remain true in the future.

One point of view is that Stalin and the subsequent Party leaders, although they all spoke of the necessity of developing agriculture, never actually understood the task of developing agriculture to the level necessary to provide all the nation's agricultural products. It is said that they viewed and still view agriculture as an object of expropriation that provides the lion's share of the materials necessary for the CPSU to attain its political goals. Without a doubt, agriculture is expropriated even today, and this is one of the most important reasons for its backwardness. However, it seems to me that today this expropriation is due to inertia. This is another situation for which there is neither the strength nor the conditions to overcome it. Nonetheless, the experiences of World War II and the social-political climate in the country have inspired all the post-Stalinist leaders with a sincere desire to lead agriculture out of its dead end. This explains the constant restructuring of agriculture that began in the mid fifties but has still not been finished in the late seventies.

Price Setting

The law of value is in effect in agriculture as well. Here it takes the form of differential land rent. According to the late Strumilin, even in the poorer sectors, the law of value in agriculture requires reimbursement of material expenditures only, and only the normal equal pay for equal work, that is, on a par with other workers.[5] This situation is possible only when prices tell the producer what products to produce, in what amounts, and of what quality, in a given agricultural environment. In other words, prices must provide information in agriculture as well so that they acquire the three functions of prices.

However, just as in other sectors of the economy, Soviet agriculture operates with planned prices, set and implemented the same way as in other sectors. "The differential land rent from collective farms (*kolkhozes*) and state farms (*sovkhozes*) all goes into one single socialist till, the State Budget, via prices [planned prices]," while "the state receives its rent by means of a special type of tax, the turnover tax."[6] It is also maintained that the level of set prices foresees "that under normal circumstances all production expenses are covered, and there is a net profit that provides for expanded reproduction, labor incentives, and a rise in the living standard of agricultural workers."[7] Planned prices are differentiated according to major zones. Intrazone differentiation is permitted based on minor zones.

In practice, the basic planned prices (procurement prices) are the purchase prices for *kolkhozes* and the delivery prices for *sovkhozes*. Delivery prices are lower than purchase prices, and only *sovkhozes* that have been experimentally converted to a completely self-supporting operational basis receive prices equal to *kolkhoz* prices. Moreover, there is a system of incentive-procurement prices for produce delivered in excess of the plan. All these prices are widely differentiated depending on the quality of the produce delivered. In addition to the state-planned prices, there are prices not controlled by the government, such as prices for commissioned trade carried out by a consumer cooperative and prices at the *kolkhoz* markets. Approximately 10 percent of a *kolkhoz's* produce is sold at these prices.

Actual planned price setting strays far from the theoretical principles on which it is supposed to be based. It is well known to Soviet economists that expanded reproduction at a rate of 5 to 7 percent per year, even in good agricultural regions, requires a profit margin of 45 to 60 percent based on the production cost of produce.[8] In 1966, however, the overall profit margin of *kolkhozes* was 35 percent and that of *sovkhozes*, 25.6 percent, while the profit margin in cattle breeding on *kolkhozes* and *sovkhozes* was only 8 percent.[9] The profit margins for field-crop cultivation and stock breeding, for the cultivation of individual crops, and for various types of stock breeding cannot be explained. These profit margins vary greatly. In 1970 the cultivation of grains produced a profit of 121 percent, and that of sunflowers 220 percent, while sugar beets and potatoes each produced a profit of 11 percent. Cattle and pig breeding produced a 30 percent profit, while milk production yielded an 8 percent profit and eggs a 14 percent profit.[10] These figures reveal defects in planned procurement prices and a general imbalance in the entire pricing system, for agricultural products as well as for industrial goods used in agricultural production (vehicles, fertilizers, and fuel). Prices with no basis in fact lead to many bad consequences. The most important is that it is impossible to specialize in agriculture, since one cannot specialize in the production of unprofitable produce. In particular, *kolkhozes*, which are completely self-supporting operations, cannot operate at a loss. Having barred the way to specialization by using a price-setting system, the Soviet government at the same time barred the way toward its own particular goal, that is, a sharp increase in agricultural efficiency.

The zonal differentiation in prices is totally without reason and does not fulfill its function of adapting prices to the concrete conditions of production. For example, one zone is 4.8 times larger than France, and 8.7 times larger than Italy, but a single price is in effect for soft wheat and rye.[11] Naturally, production conditions in the various parts of the zone vary greatly. By the same token, there are certain products whose production cost varies greatly in different places but which have just one price all over the USSR.

The pricing problem for agricultural products is important because the money received from the government for produce delivered is the greatest portion of the income for agricultural organizations (for example, about 90 percent of all monetary entries into *kolkhoz* accounts). The problem of prices, vitally important for both industry and agriculture, arises again and again in production, planning, and management. The problem is not being resolved at the present time.

Fixed Capital

On 1 January 1972 the fixed capital of agriculture amounted to 12.3 percent of the national economy's fixed capital.[12] Although capital investment in agriculture rose considerably within the past few years (the late 1960s and the early 1970s), the percentage of fixed capital has still not reached anywhere near its optimal level."According to economists, it would be necessary to increase the amount of capital per hectare of land by at least 2.5 times the present level in order to place the nation's agriculture on an industrial footing [to put it on a level with countries with a highly developed, modern agriculture] and to promote economic efficiency of production." "Moreover, one must take into consideration that a significant portion of the fixed capital for cattle breeding needs to be replaced."[13] In the final analysis, "in our country the capital-labor ratio in agriculture is 2.8 times lower than that of industry. If one does not count cattle breeding, the ratio drops to slightly less than a third that of industry.[14]

The composition of fixed capital in agriculture is also far from optimal. "The ratio of the cost of vehicles, machinery and equipment [the active part] to the cost of production-oriented structures [the passive part of production facilities] is presently 0.5:1. In the United States, this ratio is 1.1:1.0."[15] The improper structuring of capital investments aimed "primarily at increasing the 'massive' part of the fixed capital (buildings and structures, particularly for cattle breeding, because of a sharp rise in the number of cattle)" has lowered the effectiveness of investments and preserves an unsatisfactory fixed capital structure in view of current requirements.[16] As a result, between 1956 and 1968 the rise in net production per ruble of capital investment decreased by a third.[17] Between 1970 and 1972 alone, the return on capital decreased by 22 percent.[18]

The microstructure of the active part of fixed capital is also unsatisfactory. The complete absence of some vehicles and machinery and the insufficient quantity and low quality of all of them makes the complex mechanization of many labor-consuming processes impossible. Partial mechanization does not contribute to any significant rise in labor productivity; in fact, it lowers its efficiency by making production more costly. Finally, the effectiveness of fixed capital is lowered because, particularly within the past few years, "the rise in prices for new machinery has started to significantly outstrip the growth in productivity and the economic efficiency gained by using them."[19] For example, the productivity of a new tractor in comparison with an old one rose an average of 200 to 230 percent. At the same time the price rose by 350 percent, and spare parts are 650 percent more expensive than those for the old tractor.[20] In conclusion, it is difficult to even imagine "what an enormous amount of work has to be done so that along with a general increase in the amount of capital available, which will be approximately 200 percent in the near future, there will be drastic changes in the structure of fixed capital and combined production expenditures."[21] For all these years, this gargantuan task has never been correctly directed or coordinated but has gone the tortuous path of some successes and many failures. For the time being, the problem remains unsolved and cannot be solved in the near future.

The Agricultural Labor Force

What has been stated about industrial managers can be broadened to include agricultural managers. A slight difference is that agriculture receives the weaker members of the Party's list of executives when compared to industry. In the post-Khrushchev period staffs have been increased significantly by the addition of specialists having higher or middle special education. By early 1972, 86 percent of the *kolkhoz* chairmen and 96.5 percent of the *sovkhoz* directors belonged to this group.[22] The middle leadership positions were also augmented with specialists. By the end of 1970 they reached 821,000, double the number in 1960.[23] The qualifications of these specialists still leaves much to be desired. This inadequacy is the fault primarily of the special educational institutions that turn out specialists with neither sufficient knowledge nor the habit of studying on their own. A broad survey showed "that only one-sixth of the specialists surveyed felt that their knowledge was sufficient to perform the duties assigned to them."[24] In August 1974 the Central Committee of the CPSU proposed a resolution, "The Work of Agricultural Organizations in Retraining and Raising the Qualifications of Leadership Personnel and Specialists on Collective and State Farms." The resolution noted that "the quality of retraining and raising the qualifications of agricultural personnel still does not meet current demands" and that 934,000 people had already gone through the system.[25]

This persistent shortage of specialists can be explained mainly by a lack of desire to live and work in a rural area. People are particularly alienated by the attitude of the Party-appointed "Comrades in leadership toward them." This was in fact reflected in a resolution of the Central Committee of the CPSU, "The Work of the Altai Territorial Committee of the CPSU to Increase the Role of Specialists in Developing Collective and State Farm Production," published 27 July 1972.

Many other reasons—including some noneconomic ones, the low capital-labor ratio, and the still lower power-worker ratio in agriculture—have led a very large percentage of the working population to be involved in agriculture. In the USSR this amounts to 29 percent of the working population; in England it is 3.5 percent, in the United States 6.5 percent, and in Canada 7.7 percent.[26] There is still a shortage of help during peak seasons, and hundreds of thousands of city dwellers go out and help in the country. At other times the agricultural labor force is greatly underused.

The current structure of the labor force in the rural areas is determined by the constant flow of population into the cities. It is mainly the young people who leave because they are dissatisfied with working conditions and the social atmosphere in the rural areas. "Young people between the ages of fifteen and twenty-four are the ones who most often leave the village."[27] Four to five hundred thousand farm boys and girls, generally between the ages of fifteen and seventeen, enter professional technical schools, for example. Many of them would prefer to remain at home if material and cultural conditions in the village corresponded to those in the city. Therefore, it is necessary to accelerate the implementation of social-economic measures aimed at developing rural areas."[28] "The higher the educational level of the migrants, the quicker they leave the village for the city. . . . The flow of people out of rural areas has intensified in the past few years. . . . The continued increase in the intensity of the migration leaves no hope for a slowing down of this process."[29]

"The departure of the youth leads to an increased percentage of the rural population that is unable to work. . . . The average age of those working in agriculture is about fifty [thirty-three years of age in industry]. The composition of the rural labor force by gender has also deteriorated."[30] It is very important that those age groups in the more educated part of the rural population are leaving the village. Without them it is impossible to conduct a modern program of agricultural industrialization.

The youth problem has something in common with the problem of equipment operators. They leave for the city en masse and go into construction work because they are dissatisfied with wages, living conditions, and social and legal conditions. "Thus, about 10 million equipment operators were trained between 1961 and 1972. During this same period, however, there was an increase of only a little more than a million operators in agriculture."[31] There is simply no one to operate many of the machines. One cannot even imagine an extensive use of equipment in two shifts using agricultural personnel alone. In 1950 there was an average of 147 operators for every hundred tractors and grain combines, but by the beginning of 1972 there was an average of only 92 operators, or 37.4 percent fewer.[32] In the early 1970s, workers and office personnel who had been especially trained at their places of work were being sent to the villages to work as equipment operators at harvest time.

By the end of the 1960s it was finally recognized that "for the subsequent intensification of agriculture, it was not enough merely to have a scientifically calculated quantity of vehicles, electrical energy, and fertilizer. It is important that these means of production are used properly. . . . It is clear that a solution to this problem is possible only after having ensured a massive infusion of young people into agriculture. Currently, one of the most decisive conditions for increasing the number of qualified young people in agriculture is a drastic improvement in living conditions in the village, gradually bringing them up to the level of the city."[33] However, a drastic improvement in the living and cultural conditions of the Soviet village has not yet taken place, and there are no indications of such an improvement.

Planning

Prior to the 9 March 1955 Resolution of the CPSU Central Committee and the USSR Council of Ministers, agricultural planning was done almost exactly as in industry. Planning for the amount of all acreage by crop and yield and the number of head of cattle and its productivity was done centrally for each *kolkhoz* and *sovkhoz*. However, since the 9 March 1965 Resolution, planning is done differently, at least on a national level. *Planovoe khoziaistvo* describes the new planning procedure.

> The state plan for developing agriculture as approved by the USSR Council of Ministers stipulates the volume of state procurements of field crops and livestock products at the union-republic level. The union-republic councils of ministers, in accordance with the state plan, pass these indicators down to the *krai, oblast'*, and autonomous republic level. The *krai* and *oblast'* executive committees and the autonomous republic councils of ministers pass on plans for agricultural development based on these same indicators to the territorial production directorates. These directorates in turn give the state planning tasks for procurements to the *kolkhozes* and *sovkhozes*. They establish the amount of acreage by crop, the amount of livestock and cattle breeding activity, and other production indicators. This is done by starting with the tasks for government procurements of field crops and livestock products and by including the needs of the farm and its workers for these products. This is done at the farm's own discretion but with the participation and help of instructor-organizers from the territorial directorate. The production plans adopted at a general meeting of the *kolkhoz* members or approved by the director must then be reviewed, not by the regional executive committee or by the *sovkhoz* trust (*trest*), but by the territorial production directorate.[34]

The new planning system is undoubtedly better than the old method, since it allows a certain degree of economic freedom. Nonetheless, it does not remove many important shortcomings. As before, planning starts out from the level already achieved and therefore does not stimulate land usage or the development of new land. As before, exceeding an artificially low plan is more desirable than failure to meet a more ambitious plan by 1 percent.[35] "Above all, failures in centralized planning" can be explained by the fact that "currently agricultural organizations are not interested in adopting ambitious plans."[36] Planning is done on the lower level based on a centralized plan for state procurements that comes from the upper levels. These procurement orders are so large that they determine the entire plan for the *kolkhoz* or *sovkhoz*. There still is very little room for initiative at a local level.[37] The fact also remains unchanged that in the state procurement plan "there are fifteen to twenty or more different products purchased" from a single farm.[38] This is the second most insurmountable barrier to specialization after planned procurement prices.

The final plan for each farm is made up by the farm itself. "Equipping the farms with materials and equipment is planned from above. Having now approved the plan . . . the *kolkhoz* or *sovkhoz* does not know how much and what kind of fertilizer it will receive, how much or what kind of equipment it will be furnished, or what kinds of building materials it can expect."[39] The plan is not backed up by materials, and there is no coordinated and complex plan for agricultural economic activity.

The new system of planning was not put into practice immediately. The new system came from *Gosplan* in 1956, but the lower management organs clung to the old method for a long time, passing similar planning decisions to the agricultural enterprises. This was a result of bureaucratic inflexibility and the "prestige" of higher managers; but more important, it was a result of a lack of faith on the part of the lowest links of the management-administrative chain in regard to the managers-executives, that is, the *sovkhoz* directors and the *kolkhoz* chairmen. Finally, in 1964, a resolution was adopted by the CPSU Central Committee and the USSR Council of Ministers, "The Facts of Gross Violations and Misinterpretations in the Practice of Planning *Sovkhoz* and *Kolkhoz* Production." Specifically mentioned in the resolution was the intention "to make those who violate the rights of *kolkhozes* and *sovkhozes* answer directly to the Party and government. Material losses resulting from such violations must be paid for by those who caused the farm to suffer these losses."[40] After this, naturally, one no longer thought about running things at the risk of one's own pocketbook.

Agricultural Management

Current agricultural management is still basically the same as it was before the war. However, the reorganization that began in 1953 and continues to the present has occasionally brought about some significant changes. Many reorganizational changes are no longer in effect. I shall focus on changes in the economic policy of the Soviet leaders and to the elements that have become a part of current management practice.

Before 1953 there were *sovkhozes* and *kolkhozes*, just as there are today; however, the *kolkhozes* did not have their own machinery. The machinery belonged to machine-tractor stations (MTS) which served the *kolkhozes*. Mutual relationships were strictly contractual. The MTS did the basic field work by contract, and the *kolkhoz* paid for the work with money and agricultural products. The MTS did not interfere in or manage the *kolkhoz*'s affairs. The MTS equipment operators were seasonal workers who lived on the *kolkhoz*.

The first reorganization, which lasted from 1953 to 1956, was an attempt to improve agriculture using the MTS. The MTS gained power over the *kolkhozes*. Party leadership in the MTS was increased. The position of regional committee secretary for the MTS zone was created along with positions for regional committee instructors for the MTS zone. Seasonal equipment operators became permanent employees and their numbers reached 1,586,000.[41] Although nothing is written about this, the idea of turning the MTS into an industrial plant was obviously considered. The MTS had to do as much agricultural work as possible, and consequently the *kolkhoz* workers had less influence on the results of agricultural production. The reorganization ran into financial problems. MTS upkeep was exorbitantly expensive. "In the last few years, budget expenditures on tractor work alone have been more than 20 billion rubles a year."[42]

The second reorganization began with a speech by Khrushchev in Leningrad on 22 May 1957. The basic ideas of the second reorganization were directly opposed to the first. The MTSs were done away with, and some of them were converted into technical repair stations (RTS). MTS equipment was purchased by the *kolkhozes*. "Based on its selling price, 21.7 billion rubles worth of equipment was obtained by the *kolkhozes* as a result of the reorganization of the MTS."[43] At the same time, the almost 26 billion rubles spent annually on financing and providing MTS equipment were saved in budgetary financing.[44] Since the use of agricultural products as payment for MTS work was discontinued, the government's procurement system was also restructured. Multiphased and multifaceted commodity deliveries were replaced by single purchases. The need to balance the sharply rising expenses of *kolkhozes* with their income led to an increase in purchase prices. However, to this day it has not been possible to create a satisfactory balance that provides for both increased production and the Leninist principle of material incentive.

"There is already a large disproportion between the profits the farms receive from sales and the costs of equipment and fertilizer delivered to the farms. With the profit they receive, the farms cannot acquire the complement of machinery needed to mechanize production processes in animal husbandry."[45]

The second reorganization also called for some ideological changes. The drastic intensification of *kolkhozes* led to their "ideological rehabilitation." Until this time it was maintained that the road to communism in agriculture would be achieved only through the state farm and the transformation of *kolkhozes* into *sovkhozes*. At the time of the second reorganization, it was discovered that "this in no way comes from the theory and experience of the building of communism."[46] Now it seems that the road to communism lies in the intensification of *kolkhoz* and public property. The intensification of both types of property theoretically means an upgrading of agriculture as a whole. Apparently this results in a second ideological innovation, that is, without an abundance of agricultural products one cannot build communism.

The second period of reorganization lasted until the end of the Khrushchev period (1964). It was also characterized by a series of changes and additions to the organization and management of agriculture. Basically these were decided on at the January 1961 plenum of the Central Committee. One of the most important was the creation of *Soiuzsel'khoztekhnika* (the All-Union Association for the Sale of Agricultural Equipment to Collective and State Farms), which replaced myriad organizations supplying and serving agriculture. At that time, the grandiose program of using chemicals in agriculture began. This has been continued by the post-Khrushchev leadership as well.

The post-Khrushchev leaders introduced their changes to the reorganization, leaving much that had been done during the Khrushchev period. One of the most important changes was the 1 July 1966 introduction of guaranteed wages for *kolkhoz* workers.[47] Since that time wages on collective farms have risen considerably. The March 1965 plenum of the CPSU Central Committee opened broad opportunities for obtaining credit from *Gosbank*. These opportunities were so extensive and so poorly controlled that as early as 1971 many *kolkhozes* had become insolvent debtors of the bank.[48] This financial problem remains unsolved.

Another important measure is the course of the industrialization of agriculture. This was a replacement for the poorly defined concepts of chemical treatment and mechanization. The Brezhnev leadership interprets this concept of industrialization as the creation of production-organizational conditions in agriculture like those that took shape in the early 1950s in U.S. agriculture.[49] According to this concept, "the chief trends of the modern scientific-technical revolution in agriculture are industrialization and chemical treatment based on integrated mechanization and electrification of labor processes in land cultivation and cattle breeding."[50] Agricultural-industrial combines and associations are being created in accordance with this concept. Plans for the construction of large cattle-breeding complexes have been approved.[51]

Reorganization, which has become almost chronic, is accompanied by many features. In the spring of 1950 began the so-called trend toward consolidation of *kolkhozes*. By 1971 the more than 200,000 *kolkhozes* had been reduced to 32,800. Many of them in the northern part of the European section of the USSR were turned into difficult-to-manage farms, uniting dozens of small population centers that have poor roads and communications.[52] V. Ovechkin explained the true motives for this consolidation when he wrote: "I think in some regions they continue to consolidate *kolkhozes* because it is easier for the secretary of the regional committee to deal with twenty chairmen than forty. It is done for the personal convenience of the regional leaders."[53] While the number of collective farms was being reduced, the number of state farms rose from four thousand to sixteen thousand.

A second important side effect is that at the beginning of each reorganizational change, the Soviet leadership has tried to improve the mood in the countryside and to make peace with the peasantry. Before the first reorganization, this was manifested by the law concerning agricultural taxes (1953) which lowered taxes on the *kolkhoz* workers' private production and canceled all debts due to these taxes. When beginning the radical change that led to the liquidation of the MTS and the transfer of equipment to the *kolkhozes*, Khrushchev exempted the *kolkhoz* workers' private production entirely from taxes in kind and drastically reduced the monetary portion of these taxes. Khrushchev considered this measure important "because we shall create a better political atmosphere in the rural areas" and "this will be very well received politically by our people."[54]

For the very same reasons, the Brezhnev leadership has introduced the guaranteed wage, set up pensions for *kolkhoz* workers, and promised to issue them passports.

This period of reorganizations coincides with two prominent measures of a national scale and significance, the development of the virgin lands (beginning in 1954) and the start of the extensive plan for land reclamation (1966).[55] These measures changed the geography and economic conditions of production but did not change the principles of organization and management.

Management Structure

During the reorganizations, the structure of agricultural management underwent significant changes. I have already mentioned the reorganization of the procurement system and the creation of the new organization *Soiuzsel'khoztekhnika*. Many important functions of the Ministry of Agriculture were transferred to other organizations. Planning was transferred to *Gosplan*, and supply was transferred to *Soiuzsel'khoztekhnika*. In February 1961 a complete reorganization of the ministry took place. After this the chief task of the ministry "was to further increase the efficiency of land cultivation, to promote technical progress in all sectors of agricultural production based on the development of agricultural science, to improve the work of scientific research organizations, and to disseminate and introduce more practical knowledge into the production process."[56]

Strange as it may seem, it was discovered at this time that "until recently no organization in the country has really been able to manage agriculture, to study the needs of *kolkhozes* and *sovkhozes* and to achieve more efficient use of land, equipment, and other means of production."[57]

Finally, on the basis of decisions by the March 1962 plenum of the CPSU Central Committee, a resolution was drawn up by the CPSU Central Committee and the USSR Council of Ministers concerning the "Reorganization of Agricultural Management." As a result of this resolution, it has been maintained that a "well-balanced system of agricultural management was created."[58] In late 1969 the Third All-Union Congress of *Kolkhoz* Workers passed a resolution concerning the "Formation of *Kolkhoz* Worker Councils" set up along territorial lines, that is, *raion, oblast'*, and republic, and one in Moscow.[59] These supplemented the general scheme of management organizations; however, their place in the overall structure is not certain, and knowledge of their activities is highly limited. The general administrative diagram, shown in figure 16-1, is complicated even in its simplified version.

Republic ministries for production and procurement of agricultural products became the organizations that really administrate agricultural production. The specialized association subordinate to the republic council of ministers also plays an important role in procurement.

Territorial production directorates, encompassing an area that depends not on any administrative boundary but on the number of *kolkhozes* or *sovkhozes* within its boundaries, became the basic link in the day-to-day direct management of agricultural production. They are called either *kolkhoz-sovkhoz* or *sovkhoz-kolkhoz* production directorates, depending on which type of farm predominates within the boundaries of a given directorate.

"Production directorates manage the organization of production and procurement of agricultural products; carry out planning, accounting, and accountability; examine financial production plans and annual reports for collective and state farms; study the problems of efficient land use; introduce more progressive systems of land use; develop measures for the improvement of the structure of sown areas; deal with the organization of purebred livestock breeding; and work with the organizational-economic consolidation of *kolkhozes* and *sovkhozes*."[60] In addition, they keep an eye on the correct wage payments for *kolkhozes* and *sovkhozes*, handle negotiations for agreements for the delivery of produce above and beyond the plan, and are the guardians of the *kolkhozes* and *sovkhozes* in a number of other cases.

However, in practice they have not even succeeded in creating this "orderly system of management for agriculture," which is predicted by a resolution of the CPSU Central Committee and the USSR Council of Ministers. By the mid seventies "the structure of agricultural management which has developed . . . is too complicated, thus revealing its effectiveness. . . . The *kolkhozes* are managed by *raion* and *oblast'* agricultural directorates, as well as by *kolkhoz* councils, whose functions are basically consultative and advisory. *Sovkhozes* are not subordinate to *raion* and *oblast'* agricultural directorates. As a rule, *sovkhozes* are managed by specialized economic organizations—trust and associations. Special ministries for *sovkhozes* have been created in the majority of union republics. The trusts and associations are subordinate to these ministries."[61] This article expresses the view that the imminent perfection of agricultural management must lead to the creation of "a unified organizational system." The reorganization is still not finished.

Agricultural Production

Agricultural production is based on the principle that all arable land and other agricultural land is government property. This is the source of the ideological

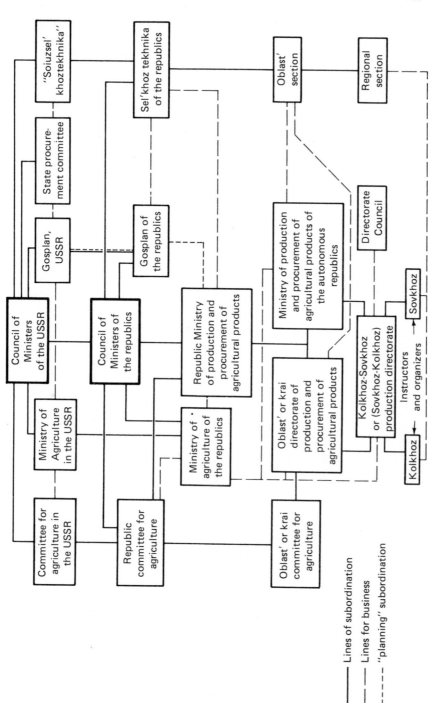

Figure 16-1. Simplified Diagram of USSR Agriculture

basis of the government's right to land rent via the turnover tax on agricultural products.

There are two sectors in Soviet agriculture: the private sector, which is represented by the private plots belonging to *kolkhoz* workers, white-collar workers, and blue-collar workers, and the socialist sector.

Activity in the socialist sector is performed by four types of organizations: *kolkhozes*, inter-*kolkhoz* associations, *sovkhozes*, and *soiuzsel'khoztekhnika*. The main producers of agricultural products are the *kolkhozes* and *sovkhozes*. The other two organizations play an auxiliary service role.

The *kolkhozes* are the basic and most widespread Soviet agricultural production organizations. In 1972 there were 32,100, in 1940 there were 236,900, and in 1960 there were 44,900. The reasons for their sharp decrease have already been given. Officially a *kolkhoz* is also called an agricultural *artel'*. Based on the meaning of the old Russian word *artel'*, they should be independent agricultural cooperatives. In reality they are completely controlled by the government. They were created by force and terror, and the members of the *artel'* are masters of neither the farm itself nor its products, no matter how strongly the official Soviet version maintains the opposite. In 1967 *kolkhozes* produced 40.4 percent of the gross agricultural production, and their proportion of commodity production was 50 percent.[62] Consequently, their marketability coefficient was 1.23.[a] As a whole *kolkhozes* are multisectored farms in both crop growing and cattle breeding. This presents a great barrier to increasing efficiency. A large share of the crops grown by collective farms is in the production of labor-consuming crops (cotton, sugar beets, sunflowers, flax). *Kolkhozes* form their fixed capital out of their own pocket. They buy all their necessities from the government, including machinery, fertilizers, and so forth, all so-called goods for production. In this sense the relationships between the government and the *kolkhozes* represent a broad spectrum of domestic trade with its widespread practice of a compulsory assortment of goods.

In the early 1960s a new form of *kolkhoz* production activity appeared, the inter*kolkhoz* association. A very small number of them deal directly with agricultural activity; their chief job is auxiliary activity. Of the five thousand inter*kolkhoz* associations in existence at the end of 1972, thirty-six hundred were involved in construction or construction-related activity.[63] In second place are poultry-raising and cattle-feeding organizations (more than nine hundred). Inter*kolkhoz* associations function like a *kolkhoz* joint-stock company, but they are still government-controlled enterprises, and their entire administrative staff is appointed by the local production directorate.

The *sovkhozes* are the second basic producer of agricultural products. In 1972 there were 15,700 *sovkhozes* (4,200 in 1940 and 7,400 in 1960). The significant increase is explained by the conversion of many weak collective farms

---

[a]Marketability coefficient = $\dfrac{\text{Commodity Production (\%)}}{\text{Gross agricultural production (\%)}}$

into state farms and by the campaign for the development of virgin and long-fallow lands. Aside from this, and probably more important, the Soviet leadership views the *sovkhoz* as a more reliable source of agricultural products and as a backbone of socialist agriculture given the actual conditions in the USSR. In 1967 *sovkhozes* produced 29.6 percent of the gross agricultural production, and their share of commodity production was 37 percent.[64] Thus their marketability coefficient was 1.25. A comparison of the marketability coefficients of *kolkhozes* and *sovkhozes* completely refutes the current assertion in Soviet literature and theory concerning the significantly higher marketability of *sovkhozes*. The contribution of state farms is higher in the production of grains (about 50 percent), wool, eggs, and vegetables.

The *sovkhoz* is a purely governmental organization headed by a director, just as any industrial organization. His assistants are chief specialists, one of whom is the deputy director. *Sovkhoz* departments and farms are headed by managers. Together they form the *sovkhoz* management. An organizational diagram of a typical *sovkhoz* is given in figure 16-2.

Like an industrial enterprise, a *sovkhoz* has a permanent labor force and fixed capital allotted to it by the government. Replacement of fixed capital (buildings, machinery, equipment) is done through the plan system. This means that the *sovkhoz* receives fixed capital at no cost. For this reason a *sovkhoz* is much better equipped than a *kolkhoz* (about twice as well equipped). Although the state buys *sovkhoz* products at lower prices, "the *sovkhozes* net 15 to 20 percent less than the *kolkhozes* for the very same product, since their prices are different for many products. At the same time, through a redistribution of the national income throughout the state budget, the *sovkhozes* receive a considerably larger sum of money for expanded reproduction than that lost by the difference in prices. By adding this sum to the *sovkhozes'* earnings for produce sold to the state, it turns out that *sovkhoz* produce costs the government approximately 1½ times more than *kolkhoz* produce."[65] Such relationships to actual prices are already accounted for in the plan, but failure to fulfill the plan increases the unprofitability of the *sovkhoz* even more. Thus, "out of 10,753 *sovkhozes* in the USSR Ministry of Agriculture, 5,480 finished 1965 with a profit of 903 million rubles, while 5,273 *sovkhozes* sustained a loss of 2 billion, 4 million rubles."[66] In the late 1960s and early 1970s *sovkhoz* efficiency rose at a slower rate than that of the *kolkhoz*. *Sovkhoz* land use was also not as good, and "if one takes into account total expenditures and all resources, *sovkhozes* have no advantages over *kolkhozes*."[67] Probably for this reason "since 1 July 1967, 410 *sovkhozes* were experimentally put on a self-supporting basis (*khozraschet*)."[68] The goal was to increase the production and the initiative of *sovkhoz* leaders. By 1971, 8,200 *sovkhozes* had already been put on a completely self-supporting basis.[69] However, the new operational conditions "still do not provide the incentives for *sovkhoz* collectives to develop ambitious plans" and "in reality, what is most decisive is the influence of factors that do

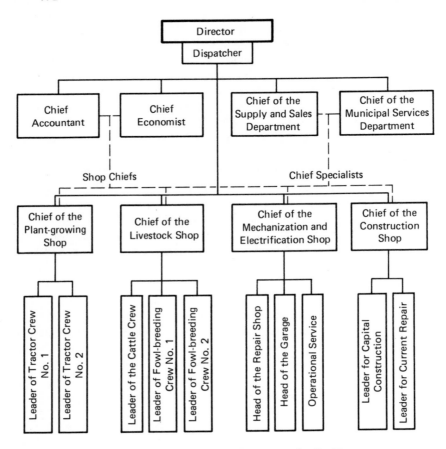

Figure 16-2. Management Structure of a *Sovkhoz*

not promote the disclosure of available reserves during planning."[70] As a result, Minister of Finances Garbuzov reported, "In 1973, *sovkhozes* in the Ministry of Agriculture had profits of 3 billion rubles compared to a planned profit of 4.2 billion rubles. Many *sovkhozes* had losses. This was the result of increases in production costs of agricultural products and non-production-related expenditures and losses."[71] It is not merely a matter of management but of unbalanced prices as well. In 1971 the profitability of potato production on the *sovkhoz* was minus 2 percent, and milk plus 2.6 percent. The profitability of total *sovkhoz* production was only 25.8 percent as opposed to an optimally necessary profitability of 40 to 45 percent.[72]

Soiuzsel'khoztekhnika (the All-Union Association for the Sale of Agricultural Equipment to *kolkhozes* and *sovkhozes*) was created in early 1960 at the same time that the USSR Ministry of Agriculture was reorganized. The new organization was created on a union-republic, territorial basis, and its basic role was to form a tie between agriculture and industry. Its functions are

1. To make more complicated and major equipment repairs
2. To sell new equipment to *kolkhozes* and *sovkhozes*
3. To sell spare parts, tools, and similar industrial items necessary for agricultural production
4. To perform special jobs on *kolkhozes* and *sovkhozes*, using its own labor force

Soiuzsel'khoztekhnika plays the same role in agriculture that *Gossnab* plays in industry; it has the same problems and difficulties. These are magnified even more by the fact that *Soiuzzel'khoztekhnika* supplies spare parts not only for *kolkhozes* and *sovkhozes* but for its own equipment repair plan as well. Many conflicts arise.

The Kolkhoz

By law the highest management organization for *kolkhoz* affairs is the general meeting of *kolkhoz* workers, or a meeting of duly authorized representatives on *kolkhozes* with a large number of *kolkhoz* workers or *kolkhozes* spread over a wide area. The general meeting must decide all principal questions concerning the *kolkhoz*'s activities. This includes approving its annual production plan. According to regulations, the general meeting must elect a *kolkhoz* chairman, a board of directors, and an auditing commission. In practice, however, and it has always been this way, recommendations for a *kolkhoz* chairman are made by management organizations. This was formerly done by the regional committees of the CPSU and the regional production administrations. The "recommendation" always comes from the Party's list of executives and is accompanied by a dummy democratic election. The *kolkhoz* workers long ago became accustomed to having a chairman thrust on them. A good description of this procedure appeared in *Ekonomicheskaia gazeta*.[73] This article is about the chairman of the Tolstikove *kolkhoz* who subsequently turned out to be a successful manager. Very few recommended chairmen, however, do a good job. Nonetheless, as long as he is on the Party's list of executives, even if he makes a mistake on one *kolkhoz*, he will be recommended for another. Khrushchev notes this logic in a speech published in *Pravda*: "Ivan Ivanovich has been in management for twenty years. Sure, he made some mistakes on twenty *kolkhozes* but let's send him to number 21. Maybe he'll amount to something this time."[74]

In reality the chairman is a confidential agent of the Party and a one-man boss, the ruler of a *kolkhoz*'s destiny. The life of any *kolkhoz* worker depends very much on the will of the chairman. Because of the absolute power of the chairman, a specialist working on a *kolkhoz* as a rule "does not take an active part in production management but more often plays the role of an advisor or counselor."[75] The chairman sometimes adheres to but more often discards even token *kolkhoz* democracy while trampling on the regulations; he appoints and removes all lower *kolkhoz* managers, crew chiefs, and farm managers. He often displays willfulness and petty tyranny. A satirical article, "The Outlaw Goose," tells of a chairman who hated geese.[76] After he was recommended for his next *kolkhoz*, he had three thousand geese belonging to the *kolkhoz* workers destroyed. The story came to light only because the village intellectuals (teachers and doctors) not only did not butcher their geese but described the incident in the newspaper. Another chairman borrowed a bulldozer and tore down the home of a pensioner who had worked for many years in the village post office. What degree of willfulness and impunity in illegal actions, what degree of megalomania and complete contempt for *kolkhoz* workers must one have to allow such actions, even to contemplate such deeds?

For land cultivation a *kolkhoz*'s labor organizations are production crews, and for cattle breeding they are farms. A typical *kolkhoz* organizational diagram is quite simple, as can be seen in figure 16-3.

Every *kolkhoz* has its Party and *Komsomol* (Young Communist League) organization, whose leaders do not participate in the production effort. In addition every *kolkhoz* has a large group of people involved in auxiliary activity and service to the leadership but not in the production effort.

The *kolkhoz*'s main obligation to the state is to meet the plan for delivery of agricultural products, in the largest quantities possible of course. Here, as in many other instances, official Soviet statistics differ sharply from real life. For example, the gross harvest of grains was 181.2 million tons in 1971 and 168.2 million tons in 1972,[77] while state grain purchases equaled 64.1 and 60 million tons for the respective years.[78] In other words, 35.4 percent of the gross harvest was purchased in 1971, and 35.6 percent in 1972. But for some reason Kazakhstan sold 61.6 percent of its gross harvest to the state in 1973,[79] Saratov *Oblast'* sold 62.6 percent,[80] and the entire Russian Federated Republic (RSFSR) sold 40.8 percent.[81] Inasmuch as the marketability coefficients of *kolkhozes* and *sovkhozes* are almost identical, these general figures are correct for both types of farm. One can assume that the state received roughly 50 percent of the actual grain harvest. Since the state purchase figure is the more reliable, one can usually calculate that the actual gross harvest is equal to two times the volume of state purchases.

A second important *kolkhoz* obligation to the state is to fulfill the production plan for all indicators. This should ensure expanded reproduction, guaranteeing deliveries to the state in the coming years.

As for monetary obligations, the *kolkhoz* pays income taxes to the state at a rate of 12 percent of actual net income, not planned income as used to be the case. A *kolkhoz* is also required to insure all its property and crops with state

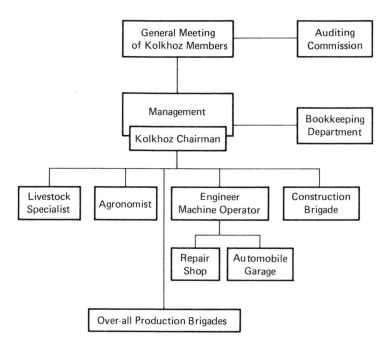

Note: Diagram for the management of the economy of the kolkhoz "Put' k Kommunizmu" (The Path to Communism) (Located in the Rubtsevskij region of the Altai krai).

Figure 16-3. Management Structure of a *Kolkhoz*

insurance organizations (*Gosstrakh*). Before 1 January 1968, insurance policies were arranged so that only a small part of the losses on insured property were reimbursed by insurance organizations. For example, a *kolkhoz* that had losses of 51,000 rubles due to natural disaster was reimbursed no more than 10,000 rubles.[82] Since January 1968 new, improved, and expanded insurance terms have been introduced, and it is obvious that "the reforms in insurance are an important measure toward assuring the continuity of the *kolkhoz* production process. However, this is only a beginning."[83] Obviously this reform is also only a halfway measure.

Indivisible *kolkhoz* funds, that is, monetary resources that are not divided among the workers, represent *kolkhoz* accumulation used for financing the growth of fixed capital. In other words, indivisible funds are the source for financing expanded reproduction. The establishment of guaranteed wages, under which the first appropriation of funds goes for wages, was reflected in the allotments for indivisible funds. "At the October Plenum of the CPSU Central Committee, it was emphasized that on certain *kolkhozes* there was not enough concern over a rise in production. Allotments for indivisible funds were decreasing."[84] Some *kolkhozes* stopped making allotments for indivisible funds. Their numbers "were particularly large in [Soviet] Georgia, Azerbaidzhan, and Armenia. On a national average, this amounts to about one-quarter of all *kolkhozes*."[85] The article "Methodological Instructions for Distributing *Kolkhoz* Income" points out "the necessity of increasing fixed capital" but does not venture to establish a standard for allocations.[86] Since expanded reproduction is inevitable, some of the *kolkhozes* accomplish expanded reproduction through government loans.

On the *kolkhoz*, just as in industry, there are output norms and calculations for wages. Prior to 1966 these calculations for the *kolkhoz* were figured in labor-day units and not in monetary terms. The labor day was paid for both in cash and in kind, but neither was planned. The labor day had the connotation of being "leftovers," as it has been called in Soviet economic literature, that is, at the end of a fiscal year the remaining products and money were divided according to the number of labor days for each *kolkhoz*. The result of this division was multiplied, according to type, by the number of labor days logged in the account book of each worker. This was how they determined the quantity the worker was to receive. This operation was repeated for each type of product being distributed, and the sum of these amounts made up his total yearly wage. Thus the *kolkhoz* worker was doing a job, but he did not know how much he would receive for that job. Before the final distribution, the *kolkhozes* gave out advances during the year, primarily in kind but sometimes in cash. These were based on the previous year's levels. Obviously, the labor day never had anything in common with the Leninist principle of material incentive.

The guaranteed wage meant, above all, that wages were now a planned indicator and were included in the *kolkhoz* plan. In other words, a nebulous figure was replaced by the ruble, a wage established in the plan for a certain amount of work. Although the transition to a guaranteed wage represented a positive measure of enormous importance, it was not easy or simple, even though the State Bank made *kolkhoz* loans readily available. *Kolkhoz* worker wages began to rise sharply, (3 rubles, 50 kopecks a day in 1968, which was more than double the wages of 1957-1958).[87] The new wage system is a great economic lever for improving conditions in agriculture, even though the system is excessively complicated and that "it is not always clear to the worker on what his wages are calculated, how rapidly he is supposed to work, and which work indices he has to attain in order to receive a certain wage."[88]

The annual earnings of various professions within the *kolkhozes* vary a great deal. "On some *kolkhozes* an unusually high wage has been established for administrative-management personnel."[89] On all *kolkhozes* the administrative-management personnel look out for themselves. The equipment operators come after this group by wage level, followed by cattle raisers, and finally the field hands doing general farm work. The field hands, who are in the majority, never have work to do the whole year round. Their work load is between 150 and 190 days a year. The *kolkhozes* have at their disposal considerable labor resources during a large part of the year (they are rife with concealed unemployment). "According to the calculations of serious economists, the value of the gross production of *kolkhozes* alone could be raised by a minimum of 8 billion rubles [or by 25 to 27 percent] through the better use of labor resources, and in a very short period of time! This constitutes a flood of goods for which the market is longing, for the *kolkhoz*, unlike the factory, will never produce anything that the market does not need."[90]

The Kolkhoz Farmstead

Despite some success in the development of *kolkhoz* production and the rise in wages, the basis of existence for the *kolkhoz* family is private subsidiary farms. According to the new *kolkhoz* regulations, private plots consist of one-half hectare of land containing a house, farm buildings, and a garden.[91] Together this is called a *kolkhoz* farmstead. The new regulations state that the farmstead "may have one cow with calf up to one year of age and one heifer up to two years of age, one sow with litter up to two months of age or two feed hogs, up to ten sheep or goats (total), a beehive, fowl, and rabbits."[92] The *kolkhoz* family does what it sees fit with its garden. Former limitations on growing certain crops have been lifted. The *kolkhoz* family gets almost all the vegetables and potatoes, dairy and meat products, as well as fats, that it needs from its private plot. Of the total volume of agricultural products obtained by *kolkhoz* families in the Russian Federated Republic, the private sector provided about 90 percent of the potatoes, 80 percent of the vegetables and melons, almost 100 percent of the milk, meat, and eggs, about 52 percent of the hay, but only 3 percent of the raw livestock feed.[93] In 1964 retail prices, products obtained from private plots amounted to an income of 1,300 rubles a year.[94] Besides this, private plots bring in monetary income as well. Based on this very fact, "the private plot is characteristic of day-to-day family life on the farm. With very rare exceptions, the entire family works these plots."[95]

The *kolkhoz* farmstead remains the subject of controversy and differences of opinion among Soviet leaders and economists. Some feel that private plots distract the *kolkhoz* worker from *kolkhoz* production and should therefore be eliminated as soon as possible. The problem of competition between the results of labor on the *kolkhoz* and in the private sector plays no small role. The private sector clearly demonstrates its advantages.

Others come to the defense of the *kolkhoz* farmsteads and advance many important considerations in their defense. The entire private sector, half of which consists of *kolkhoz* farmsteads, produces 20 percent of the agricultural products and 40 percent of the livestock production.[94]

"Private plots to a certain extent serve as compensation for the noncreative nature of labor, particularly for those engaged in physical labor."[97] Private plots react more quickly to the demands of the people, and they produce "precisely the crops and products that the public sector of the *kolkhozes* and the state do not produce."[98] Even more important, private plots "teach the people an economic grasp for work and industriousness, and they also give people a responsible regard for their work as well as other similar qualities necessary in public production."[99] Obviously these qualities are insufficiently taught or are not taught at all in public production. Finally, private plots of *kolkhoz* workers and blue- and white-collar workers perform an enormous amount of selective work in developing new strains of fruits and vegetables, many of which have industrial significance.

Since 1 January 1958, the *kolkhoz* farmstead pays the government only a relatively small monetary tax. The post-Khrushchev leadership has carried out an almost protectionist policy with regard to the *kolkhoz* farmstead. Nevertheless, many unsolved problems (most important, the problem of the feed base for individual livestock raisers) have weakened the *kolkhoz* farmstead economy and reduced the number of cattle.[100] These problems affect the provisions available to the urban population. It is hard to judge the true strength of this influence.

Official statistics show the rather large share of many important products that are produced by private plots. Other data, however, differ sharply from the official figures and place them under suspicion. According to official statistics, private plots produced 42.6 percent of the meat between 1960 and 1964, 45.2 percent of the milk, and 76.5 percent of the eggs.[101] However, for some reason the figures in the Orlovskaia *Oblast'* for that period were 66 percent, 55 percent, and 90 percent respectively.[102] With ideological consistency, official statistics give the productivity of private cows in 1970 as 1,890 kilograms per year,[103] while a different source says that productivity is 3,000 kilograms per year for Kalinin *Oblast'*.[104]

Social Problems in Rural Areas

Despite the ideological position concerning the gradual elimination of the differences between urban and rural areas, until very recently the gap was widening. This is particularly true when speaking of the *kolkhoz* portion of the rural areas.

Funds for public works are allocated to the general rural population, and to the *kolkhoz* workers in particular, in disproportionately small amounts in some cases and not allocated at all in other cases. Thus, in 1965 a little more than 1 million rural children, including 150,000 children of *kolkhoz* workers, were in permanent children's institutions, while in urban areas more than 6 million children were in such institutions. At this time, the number of urban children under seven years of age was approximately 15.7 million, while in the villages it was 18.4 million. The situation is no better when it comes to medical services for the rural populace. "In 1964 there were about nine times more doctors and three times more hospital beds per ten thousand urban inhabitants than there were for rural inhabitants. Each rural inhabitant paid half as many visits to medical institutions as his urban counterpart did."[105]

Kolkhoz workers have had a pension plan only since 1965. The minimum pension based on age is set at 12 rubles per month, while the maximum is 102 rubles, just as it is for *sovkhoz* workers.[106] However, half the pension comes from *kolkhoz* resources. In 1968 a *kolkhoz* worker's monthly pension averaged 18 rubles, 50 kopecks.[107]

Kolkhozes build with their own funds what the state builds for the urban population. Between 1950 and 1969 the following were built at *kolkhoz* expense: 46,000 schools for 6.6 million students, children's institutions to accommodate 92,000 children, 6,200 beds in hospitals and outpatient clinics, and cultural houses and club facilities for 55,000 persons.[108] Aside from this, "funds for public use such as paid vacations and governmental subsidies for the maintenance of housing, almost always go to the blue- and white-collar workers."[109]

Day-to-day service facilities for the rural population are several times worse than for the urban population. In 1964 expenditures for day-to-day services amounted to 12 percent of the family budgets of industrial workers 3 percent of the budgets of *kolkhoz* families. Considering the difference in their budgets, this is from six to eight times less. "The number of public food service establish-ments in rural areas is one-third to one-half that in cities and towns.[110] Commercial services for the rural areas are no better.

The job done by preschool institutions, schools, and clubs is not satisfac-tory, chiefly because of difficulties in recruiting or a lack of qualified person-nel.[111] This is explained by the lack of desire among the intelligentsia to live and work in a rural environment. Because schools are poor, the chances for the rural youth to go on to higher education are one-third to one-half those of urban youths.

Finally there are "judicial complications to rural life."[112] The adult *kolkhoz* worker is limited in his freedom of movement, since most of them do not yet have an internal passport. Those who do obtain passports, at times through complicated and strange means, flee the *kolkhoz*. Every *kolkhoz* worker is the recipient of arbitrary treatment. The *kolkhoz* chairman and even the manager of the local store can taunt him. In recent years serious attempts have been made to combat this. "Before, for example, I could take away their [private] plots, forbid them to make hay, cut off their electricity—in other words, I could do just about anything. But now, everything is forbidden."[113] This was the complaint of a *kolkhoz* chairman to a newspaper correspondent. Nevertheless, he still has his hands on many levers and still has many opportunities to show a disagreeable *kolkhoz* worker who's boss.

The educated youth are not running from low wages but from the judicial complications of rural life, from dirty and hard manual labor, from the lack of culture, from the vulgarity and petty tyranny of the rural leaders, and from the cultural isolation. They are fleeing in such numbers that "the problem of a concerted effort to replenish *kolkhozes* and *sovkhozes* with qualified young people has attained governmentwide significance."[114]

Notes

1. *Voprosy ekonomiki*, no. 6 (1962):6.

2. *Planovoe khoziaistvo*, no. 2 (1968):66.

3. *Military-Economic Problems in a Political Economics Course* (Moscow: Voenizdat, 1968), p. 222.

4. *Planovoe khoziaistvo*, no. 10 (1969):10.

5. *Voprosy ekonomiki*, no. 7 (1960):87.

6. *The Economics of Socialist Agriculture* (Moscow: Ekonomika, 1970), p. 247.

7. Ibid., p. 249.

8. *Planovoe khoziaistvo*, no. 11 (1966):15.

9. *Voprosy ekonomiki*, no. 5 (1968):53.

10. Ibid., no. 1 (1973):57.

11. Ibid., no. 1 (1970):68.

12. *National Economy of the USSR, 1922-1972* (Moscow: Statistika, 1973), p. 60.

13. *Voprosy ekonomiki*, no. 3 (1972):60.

14. Ibid., no. 7 (1968):37.

15. Ibid., p. 38.

16. Ibid., no. 3 (1970):111.

17. Ibid., p. 117.

18. Ibid., no. 8 (1974):26-27.

19. Ibid., no. 12 (1969):68.

20. Ibid., no. 11 (1970):57.

21. Ibid., no. 9 (1966):44.

22. *National Economy of the USSR, 1922-1972*, pp. 286-288.

23. Ibid., p. 284.

24. *Voprosy ekonomiki*, no. 10 (1967):78.

25. *Pravda*, 10 August 1974, p. 1.

26. *Voprosy ekonomiki*, no. 4 (1971):66.

27. Ibid., no. 5 (1973):129.

28. *Planovoe khoziaistvo*, no. 12 (1972):125.

29. *Voprosy ekonomiki*, no. 5 (1973):129.

30. *Planovoe khoziaistvo*, no. 8 (1969):73.

31. Ibid., no. 7 (1974):75.

32. *Voprosy ekonomiki*, no. 7 (1973):43.

33. Ibid., no. 7 (1968):43.

34. *Planovoe khoziastvo*, no. 5 (1962):59.

35. *Pravda*, 7 March 1964, p. 5.

36. *Voprosy ekonomiki*, no. 8 (1970):45.

37. Ibid., no. 5 (1966):141-142.

38. Ibid., no. 3 (1966):56.

39. *Pravda*, 27 November 1967, p. 2.

40. *Pravda*, 24 March 1964, p. 1.

41. *Voprosy ekonomiki*, no. 10 (1957):103.

42. Ibid., no. 6 (1958):102.

43. Ibid., no. 9 (1960):28.

44. *Planovoe khoziaistvo*, no. 1 (1959):5.

45. *Voprosy ekonomiki*, no. 5 (1968):55.

46. Ibid., no. 3 (1958):10.

47. *Pravda*, 18 May 1966, p. 2.

48. *Pravda*, 19 May 1971, p. 2.

49. See *Voprosy ekonomiki*, no. 8 (1970):44; also *Voprosy ekonomiki*, no. 4 (1971):65.

50. *Voprosy ekonomiki*, no. 12 (1969):59.

51. *Ekonomicheskaia gazeta*, no. 38 (1971):12.

52. *The Economics of Socialist Agriculture*, 1970, p. 51.

53. *Novyi mir*, no. 9 (1956):126.

54. *Pravda*, 24 May 1957, pp. 1-2.

55. *Pravda*, 6 May 1966, p. 2.

56. M.M. Sokolov, *The Economics of Socialist Agriculture* (Moscow: Gospolitizdat, 1962), p. 65.

57. *The Economics of Agricultural Organizations, Political Academy of the Central Committee of the CPSU* (Moscow: Gospolitizdat, 1962), p. 82.

58. G.G. Badirian, ed., *Economics, Organization, and Planning of Rural Economic Production* (Moscow: Ekonomizdat, 1963), p. 47.

59. *Pravda*, 29 November 1969, pp. 1-2.

60. Badirian, *Economics, Organization, and Planning of Rural Economic Production*, p. 49.

61. *Voprosy ekonomiki*, no. 3 (1975):33.

62. *The Economics of Socialist Agriculture*, 1970, p. 52.

63. *National Economy of the USSR in 1972* (Moscow: Statistika, 1973), p. 396.

64. *The Economics of Socialist Agriculture*, 1970, p. 30.

65. *Voprosy ekonomiki*, no. 7 (1966):59.

66. Ibid., no. 11 (1966):39.

67. Ibid., no. 5 (1968):49.

68. Ibid., pp. 47-48.
69. *Pravda*, 26 July 1971, lead article.
70. *Planovoe khoziaistvo*, no. 5 (1972):60.
71. Ibid., no. 8 (1974):16.
72. *Voprosy ekonomiki*, no. 7 (1973):46-47.
73. *Ekonomicheskaia gazeta*, no. 8 (1966):39.
74. *Pravda*, 7 March 1962, p. 2.
75. *Pravda*, 11 May 1971, p. 2.
76. *Pravda*, 27 July 1969, p. 3.
77. *National Economy of the USSR in 1972*, p. 292.
78. Ibid., p. 299.
79. *Ekonomicheskaia gazeta*, no. 44 (1973):9.
80. *Pravda*, 11 October 1973, p. 2.
81. *Pravda*, 30 October 1973, p. 2.
82. *Ekonomicheskaia gazeta*, no. 47 (1966):32.
83. *Voprosy ekonomiki*, no. 5 (1971):131.
84. *Pravda*, 20 November 1968, p. 1.
85. *Voprosy ekonomiki*, no. 11 (1968):41.
86. *Ekonomicheskaia gazeta*, no. 28 (1974):17.
87. *Voprosy ekonomiki*, no. 11 (1968):41.
88. Ibid., no. 10 (1968):134.
89. *Pravda*, 5 February 1970, p. 1.
90. *Novyi mir*, no. 8 (1966):164.
91. *Pravda*, 30 November 1969, pp. 1-2.
92. *Voprosy ekonomiki*, no. 1 (1970):37.
93. Ibid., no. 10 (1966):60.
94. Ibid., p. 67.
95. Ibid., no. 11 (1973):159.
96. Ibid., no. 44 (1966):27.
97. Ibid., no. 11 (1973):159.
98. Ibid., no. 11 (1968):54.
99. Ibid., p. 55.
100. *Pravda*, 18 February 1970, p. 2.
101. *National Economy of the USSR in 1972*, p. 370.
102. *Planovoe khoziaistvo*, no. 1 (1966):79.
103. *National Economy of the USSR in 1972*, pp. 370 and 382.
104. *Pravda*, 18 February 1970, p. 2.
105. *Voprosy ekonomiki*, no. 6 (1966):76.
106. Ibid., no. 8 (1964):8.
107. Ibid., no. 8 (1968):21.
108. Ibid., no. 5 (1971):87.
109. Ibid., no. 6 (1966):76.
110. Ibid., p. 80.

111. Ibid., no. 5 (1971):92.
112. *Novyi mir*, no. 8 (1966):148.
113. *Pravda*, 27 June 1967, p. 2.
114. *Ekonomicheskaia gazeta*, no. 33 (1966):18.

17 Finances in the USSR

Money and Currency

The dual attitude of the Bolsheviks toward money immediately following their seizure of power was based on Marxist ideology, which still existed at that time. According to theory, money was considered a remnant of capitalism, but being revolutionarily practical, they understood very well the strength and significance of money. For this very reason, troops seized the State Bank on 20 November 1917, and all Russia's banks were nationalized on 27 December 1917.

Lenin was quick to reject unfounded Marxist assertions about the feasibility of eliminating money and trade under the dictatorship of the proletariat. Thus, Soviet money has survived several reforms within the past sixty years.

According to the decree of 11 October 1922, *Gosbank,* which had come into being a year earlier, started issuing the *chervonets,* a paper note worth ten rubles. By 1924 the *chervonets* was completely replaced by the *sovznak,* an inflated form of currency in use during War Communism and the Civil War.

The next important currency reform took place in 1947, when the old currency was exchanged for new at a ratio of ten to one. The reform was said to be necessary to liquidate the consequences of wartime inflation, when the amount of money in circulation increased some four times.

On 1 March 1950 the ruble was converted to a gold standard, with one ruble being worth 0.222168 grams of gold. This step was considered necessary because of requirements for foreign trade within the Socialist Bloc. Since then, the ruble has replaced the dollar in their mutual calculations, and the so-called convertible ruble has appeared.

On 1 January 1961 there was yet one more exchange of money in which ten old rubles were exchanged for one new ruble. At the same time, prices were lowered by the same factor, that is, by ten times. The value of the ruble is 0.987412 grams of gold, and the exchange rate or parity of the ruble and dollar was set at one dollar to ninety kopecks. The official explanations for the reform sound somewhat strange. The chairman of the *Gosbank* board stated that in calculating goods and currency circulation "certain difficulties arise in the use of calculating machines due to the inadequate number of digits displayed."[1] Lavrov came up with a psychological reason: the use of astronomical figures "has weakened attention to the prime unit of calculation, the ruble and the kopeck,"[2] which has weakened the struggle to save. However, the most interesting peculiarity, and probably the main reason for the change, was entirely different. The free exchange of money held by an individual, as indicated in the resolution "Concerning the Sequence of Converting Currency, Payments, and Calculations in Conjunction with the 1 January 1961 Change to the New Rate," was restricted to ten thousand old rubles of money on hand. The exchange of invested amounts took place automatically in the savings banks (*sberegatel'naia kassa-sberkassa*). A citizen wishing to exchange more than ten thousand rubles was required to explain how he managed to save such a large sum of money. This restriction logically coincides with many legal proceedings that took place at this time. There were trials of "Soviet millionaires," kings not only of the black market, but of black market production of goods as well. The reason for the 1961 currency change was the need to administratively immobilize the large sums of money that had slipped from state control into the private sector of trade and underground business dealings.

There are three official types of currency (based on the 1961 change).

1. USSR *Gosbank* notes (*bilet*), issued in denominations of one hundred, fifty, twenty-five, and ten rubles.
2. State treasury notes (*Kaznacheiskii bilet*), in denominations of five, three, and one ruble.
3. Copper-nickel alloy coins in denominations of one ruble, fifty, twenty, fifteen, and ten kopecks, as well as, copper-zinc alloy coins worth five, three, two, and one kopeck.

The division of paper currency into *Gosbank* notes and state treasury notes developed historically (from 1922 to 1924) and has no practical significance. Just as in other countries, one comes across counterfeit money in the USSR; Krushehev, at least, attested to the existence of counterfeit coins.[3]

The ruble is not rated in the international currency market. "There was no need for this (and this is still true today) inasmuch as under conditions of the foreign trade monopoly and the currency monopoly, foreign trade and other international calculations of the socialist nations are able to develop without having their currencies circulate within the currency market of capitalist nations." "However, this does not mean that the ruble and the currencies of other socialist nations may not one day be put into the world currency market, while retaining their currency monopoly," asserts this same source.[4] However, such a thing would never happen, for two reasons: (1) The exchange rate for any currency unit on the world currency market is an impartial estimate of the health of the represented economic system. (2) If the countrys' money is free to fluctuate, then it will not be protected by any agreements at a high level, and therefore individuals or countries that have accumulated a sufficient amount of this money can have an influence (which can be very strong) on the economy of a given nation. The Soviets consider this to be interference in the internal affairs of a country.

There are different black-market exchange rates for the ruble within the USSR and abroad. They are far from precise and somewhat distort the situation to the detriment of the ruble since it is dictated by the prices for consumer goods. Nonetheless, the black-market exchange rate outside the country generally ranges between 3½ and 4 rubles to the dollar, and inside the country, it ranges between five and 6 rubles to the dollar, while the official rate of exchange is 75 kopecks to the dollar. A reason for the higher rate of exchange inside the country is that higher-quality consumer goods can be purchased in the foreign currency store (*berezka*) for dollars. The illegal exchange rate is tolerable precisely because it is illegal and occurs on a small scale, but the official exchange rate is absolutely intolerable.

The fact that politics plays a dominant role in economics excludes the possibility of the ruble's entering the world currency market; the COSU leadership would never permit foreign economic pressure to bear on its political line. Even today they have made the principle of noninterference in internal affairs the cornerstone of their foreign policy.

As things stand today, it appears that one can simply forget about the ruble entering the world currency market. The phrase stating that the ruble might one day enter the world currency market belongs with other old saws like "Keeping up with the Jones" and "Our currency is no worse than yours."

The political economy of socialism has always stated that Soviet money is different from capitalistic money and even has an advantage over it. In recent times the explanation for this advantage has changed drastically. In early Stalinist times the advantage lay in that Soviet money did not require a gold standard. Since 1950, a comparatively short time after the start of the ideological disorder surrounding this question, it has been stated that the advantage lies in the fact that Soviet money is truly backed by gold. The current explanation, which is broader, vague, and extremely questionable, goes something like this: although money under socialism, just as under capitalism, is an overall equivalent for commodities, "it [money] has ceased to be an overall form of public wealth ... since the work force, plants, factories, land, and its mineral resources, and certain other public resources are not commodities." Moreover, "under socialism the role of gold and the nature of its relationship to currency has basically changed. Out of its blind strength, which subjugates the movement of commodity prices, gold has become an instrument for deliberately setting and changing commodity prices."[5]

It is true that plants, factories, land, and mineral resources are not commodities on the domestic market, but it is not true that money has ceased to be an expression of public resources in these cases. After all, the country's fixed assets are estimated in rubles. In the name of ideology one can be like an ostrich about land and its mineral resources. However, how often has it been written that land and its mineral resources are a form of public resource requiring a fiscal evaluation and a conversion into commodities? (This has been written not so much from a theoretical point of view as from a need for a purely economic practicality.) Since they are not yet commodities, land is being squandered, soil is being eroded, and all mineral resources are being used more and more injuriously. This harmful exploitation of natural resources is becoming more dangerous.

Labor is considered a commodity in the USSR, both theoretically and in practice. Wages are paid in rubles having a gold equivalent. Consequently, labor has a value expressed in gold and according to Marx must therefore be categorized as a commodity. The employer-monopolist establishes the value of this commodity according to his own considerations. Like prices in agriculture, this value can be called the procurement price of labor. The theoretical ostrich in this matter as well only makes it more difficult to resolve many important questions in economic practice, such as how to encourage economizing the labor effort, the growth of labor productivity, and optimal use of labor resources in siting industry. Soviet economists have already written a great deal about these questions.

Nor has gold "become an instrument ... for deliberately setting and changing prices," and planned prices for goods on the domestic market are in no way dependent on or connected to the amount of gold reserves or gold mining in the USSR. However, gold, precisely because of its role as a blind force (if it is now convenient to call it such), does influence the establishment of export prices through market prices. This is true not only of trade with market economy nations but of trade within the Socialist Bloc as well.

This is the actual situation, and money in the Soviet economy plays the same role and performs the same functions as in any other economic system. Soviet money provides a measure of value, a means of circulation, a means of saving, and a means of payment. Moreover, as the Soviets assert, Soviet money has now attained the status of a world currency because of increased foreign trade.[6] However, such an assertion has no basis in fact. In foreign trade within the Socialist Bloc "the nation-members of the Council for Economic Mutual Assistance (*Comecon*) have given inestimable significance to the creation of a collective monetary unit [the convertible ruble] within a system of multilateral calculations." "On its economic base, as a collective monetary unit, the convertible ruble differs from the national currency of any of the nation-members of *Comecon,* including the Soviet ruble, which resembles the convertible ruble only in name and gold content."[7] "On the capitalistic market, gold performs the function of a world currency for the socialist nations in trading with the market economy nations."[8]

The Spheres of Currency Circulation

Currency circulation in the USSR can be divided into three spheres.

The first sphere is currency circulation for noncash transactions between state institutions (intragovernmental sphere). In this sphere money itself does not participate directly but remains in the *Gosbank*. Currency circulation for noncash transactions refers to the transfer of specified amounts of money from the account of one state institution to the account of another. All mutual calculations or transactions between state institutions, enterprises, and services are handled in this manner. The sphere of noncash transactions appears to be so cashless that the prevalent opinion is that the transfer of sums from one account to another involves no real money. This opinion is erroneous, however, for the simple reason that at any moment money can move from the intragovernmental sphere of circulation to the second sphere, the state-citizen-state sphere. A sum entered into the account of an enterprise on a noncash basis today may tomorrow be given to the enterprise in the form of cash for paying wages.

The second sphere of currency circulation is in the realm of state-citizen-state. The state gives money to citizens in the form of wages and other payments (pensions, awards, bonuses), and it is returned to the state through trade (which accounts for more than 80 percent), direct taxes, and insurance. This is the primary sphere of currency circulation; it links the entire country and makes it possible for the nation as a whole to function. It has a decisive influence on all planning, in particular, on the planning of currency circulation, trade, and the production of goods.

The third and final sphere of currency circulation is the citizen to citizen circulation, whereby a portion of the money received by citizens from the state remains in the private sector. This sphere is tied to the state-citizen-state sphere of circulation by the transfer of monies from one to the other. A part of this money, however, is always in the hands of the citizens. Thus is no longer under state control and therefore ceases to be an object of planning. Roughly speaking, one might say that about 7 to 9 percent of all money in circulation remains in private hands. This sphere of currency circulation is used for trade in the *kolkhoz* market, for individually established services, and of course for speculation on the black market. The state is interested in minimizing the amount of money in private hands, as well as in stabilizing this amount because any noticeable fluctuation severely complicates financial planning.

The amount of money in circulation is planned, the fundamental object of planning being the state-citizen-state sphere of currency circulation. On this basis the necessary amount of currency in circulation depends directly on the requirements of goods circulation. Conversely, the conditions of goods circulation determine the necessary amount of money in circulation. These conditions are determined in turn by three basic factors: the amount of goods, the price of goods, and the period of time that the goods remain in circulation, that is, how long the goods are serviceable. The difficulty in planning arises from the fact that the basic planning data can change and thereby lead to a noncorrespondence between the amounts of money and goods in circulation. Thus, the nonfulfillment of a plan for goods production or deviations in plans, or perhaps both together, can cause "demand to exceed supply in retail trade, lead to an increase in prices on the *kolkhoz* market, and lead to other inflationary phenomena."[9] When demand exceeds supply, we have the so-called uncovered effective demand of the public (in other words, the public cannot get what it needs or wants), which arises in the USSR because of the poor quality of goods as well as inadequacies in their production. This means that the public does not acquire them. As a result, the period of time for goods circulation as well as for currency circulation can lengthen (which has happened before). These are all chronic problems, but the planning system can handle difficulties that have developed or are stabilized. It is almost helpless, however, when faced with unexpected difficulties. The tradition of planning from the attained level can account for all shortcomings and can eliminate their influence (a different question is, How much will it cost?). When planning runs into a new phenomenon, however, it is forced to wait until this phenomenon becomes an attained level.

In practice the amount of currency in circulation is determined by the following formula.

$$(AG \times PG)/TUG = 0.8\,AC$$

AG = amount of goods

PG = price for goods

TUG = period of time goods are in circulation

AC = amount of currency in circulation

The coefficient of 0.8 is reached by the fact that 80 percent of all money put into the hands of citizens by the state returns through trade to the state bank (*Gosbank*). All remaining money necessary for circulation can easily be accounted for from the attained level based on previous experience. The goods circulation period is always more or less known from previous experience. When it changed sharply from twenty-eight days (during the last Stalinist years when there was an extreme paucity of goods) to ninety days in recent years (to overcome disruptions in currency circulation), it became necessary to create multibillion-ruble reserves in the USSR *Gosbank*. This reflected the country's state budget at that time.

> Due to the balanced production and distribution of goods, objective conditions develop for planning currency circulation. The planning of currency circulation and its regulation by the bank that puts the currency into circulation is done in such a way that the *amount of money produced and put into circulation corresponds to the actual needs of circulation* [Italics in original]. The planned regulation of currency circulation, while an integral part of the money system under socialism, promotes the creation of necessary proportions and rates of expanded reproduction."[10]

I am convinced that the balanced nature of production, although desirable, is in no way a fact. How currency circulation promotes the creation of necessary proportions in the Soviet economy will have to be handled in the dialectical fantasizing of the previous quotation's authors. Apparently understanding the groundlessness of their assertions, the authors selected the expression *planned regulation* in place of the common word *planning*. In truth, *Gosbank* controls the issuing of money and issues it to the enterprises in proportion to the amount of the production plan they fulfill. If this control (issuing) activity of *Gosbank* can be called regulation, then I have no further objections.

The planned regulation of currency circulation is accomplished in practice "with the help of credit plans and a balance of fiscal profits and expenses for the public and for the USSR *Gosbank* cash plan. The sources and amounts of ready cash put into *Gosbank* banking facilities are reflected in the cash plan, and their issue for specific purposes is determined by the volume of currency either entered into or removed from circulation."[11] The *Gosbank* cash plan, which is confirmed by the government, is the most complete workable document for controlling (regulating) currency circulation. At the same time, "a substantial inadequacy in the present system of planning currency circulation is that the change provided for by the cash plan regarding the amount of currency in circulation is not based on scientifically founded estimates necessary for the circulation of currency in the planning period. The serious shortcomings of these estimates are the approximate nature of the estimates, the conditional character and estimated (expert) nature of many values, and the inadequate use of statistical data."[12]

The shortcomings of financial planning have been discussed for many years; however, the situation has still not changed for the better, nor can it change. As before, "the forms and methods of financial planning still have little effect on eliminating nonproductive losses and expenditures in the national economy. Nor do they fully promote the most rapid use of enormous internal production reserves. The use of such categories as profit, payment for production funds and standardized working capital, fixed payments, credit, and interest must be further perfected."[13]

The State Budget

"The state budget is the basic instrument for redistributing the gross public income."[14] The redistribution is caused by the need to maintain the nonproductive sphere of the state (the governmental apparatus, the army, public education); it is caused by the noncoincidence of the value of a surplus product created by individual branches of production and that created in individual territories (republics, large economic regions, and *oblast's*). "In the USSR ... about half of the national income is distributed and redistributed through the state budget."[15] "The state budget, being a state financial plan, plays an important role in planning the national economy."[16] "One of the most important tasks of budget planning is to determine the amount and types of governmentwide expenditures for the individual branches of the economy taking into account the most effective use of monetary assets."[17] The budget is therefore an integral part of a national economic plan, but the plants usually receive the budgeted financing of a plan based, not on the general plan, but on the plant's actual fulfillment of the plan. This makes it possible to maintain complete financial control over the activities of the plants, which are state self-supporting organizations. However, the financing of industry is only partially based on budgeted resources. Thus, in 1968 budgeted financing accounted for only 46.2 percent of the resources directed toward industry; the other 53.8 percent came from other sources, primarily from the assets held by the plants and branches themselves as well as from bank credits. It is difficult to find a logical explanation for this division of resources, which in the final analysis come from the same source. It is presumably designated to conceal actual expenditures. As a result, even though the state budget is supposedly the basic state financial plan confirmed by the Soviet government, it is inadequate for practical purposes. Therefore, we have the so-called synthetic plan. "An annual financial plan compiled by USSR *Gosplan* for the national economy comes out as the synthetic plan, which ties together the entire system of financial planning. The goal of the consolidated national economic financial plan is to assist in the mutual coordination and agreement of all financial plans with the production plans of the national economic branches. . . . The consolidated financial plan differs from other plans in that it is not confirmed by the USSR Council of Ministers and has no operational significance."[18] Nonetheless, during the execution of the annual operational plan, the consolidated financial plan is a most important working document for financial activity.

The USSR state budget consists of the all-union budget, the republic-level budgets, and the local budgets. Budget unity is ensured by the fact that the union council (*sovet soiuza*) determines both the all-union budget and the republic-level portions of the budget when examining and confirming the overall state budget. Each republic specifies its own budget in further detail and determines its own central republic budget as well as the *oblast'*-level budgets. Each of these budgets is confirmed by the corresponding level of the council of workers' deputies. "The budget revenues of the socialist government can be subdivided into three basic groups: (1) revenues from state plants and organizations, (2) payments from *kolkhozes* and other cooperative organizations, and (3) resources coming from the populace."[19]

Revenues from state enterprises consist of turnover tax and payments from the profit of plants and other organizations. The share of revenues from the turnover tax is continually decreasing (from 40.7 percent in 1960 to 31.7 percent in 1972).[20] All this data is far from factual and does not convey the true picture. Payments from the profit of state plants consist of charges for fixed assets, the so-called financed payments, and deductions from the net surplus of profit. According to the plan, the payment for production assets is 32 percent of all payments into the budget from profit, the financed payments amount to 8.4 percent and net surplus from profit comes to 59.6 percent.[21] The net surplus from profit is a relatively new kind of payment into the budget; "it represents the sum by which financial resources exceed the planned requirements for them."[22] To put it simply and clearly, *profit is deliberately preplanned for the plants so that the profit will significantly exceed the requirement*; this excess is then transferred into the budget by *Gosplan*. Such a measure only obscures what is already an unclear picture in industry. "Some economists feel that the increase between 1960 and 1966 of the profitability norm, calculated on profit, can be explained 'only by the transfusion of a portion of the entire surplus product [the turnover tax] into the profit structure,' and if such transfusions had not been done, then for this period the profitability of industry would have decreased from 13.6 percent to 9.8 percent."[23] Such a trick in financial planning immediately accomplishes two things: (1) The profitability of socialist industry increases, (2) The truth about the actual size of the deeply antisocial turnover tax is concealed. This deception is used to both parade and propagandize the advantages of socialism.

Apart from the fact of disguising, "one should keep in mind that in heavy industry branches only a very few *goods* are subject to the turnover tax [italics mine]. Essentially only consumer goods (automobiles, motorcycles, bicycles, refrigerators, washing machines, televisions, and radios) and goods used both by consumers and as means of production (such as electric energy, petroleum products, and gas) are so taxed. Thus, it is basically consumer goods that are subject to the turnover tax."[24]

To summarize, one might state that official data on these items of revenues for the budget do not correspond to reality. The turnover tax is the key source of assets for the budget; the turnover tax is obtained exclusively from commerce, which uses its monopolistic position for the most antisocial exploitation of the public. Only in this manner has it been possible to conceal the losses and expenses of this system, the least effective system in the history of mankind.

Previously the turnover tax was paid by retail trade; that is, payment occurred when the goods were received for sale. This practice was later changed, with the turnover tax being transferred to the wholesale price of industry. Now the plant pays the turnover tax before the retailer receives the goods to be sold. This has had a negative effect on the variety and quality of goods. However, "a suggestion that they transfer the payment of the turnover tax to the retail network [that is, actually to reestablish and improve the previous situation] would entail unsolvable technical difficulties both for finance organs and for the credit system."[25] Moreover, "finance organs frequently insist on the production of an output that has no market but is subject to a high turnover tax. Budget revenues are increasing formally, but actually the plants' working capital or money in the bank which was received as loans is going into the budget."[26] The following picture emerges: *All means are good that ensure that Gosbank regularly receives the maximum amount of turnover tax.*

Before the revolution, all leftist political parties and groups, particularly the bolsheviks and Lenin himself, scoffed at Russia's budget. They called it drunken, because the state held a monopoly on alcoholic beverages. However, in its pursuit of a regularly paid, maximum turnover tax, the world's first socialist state of workers long ago surpassed not only the now defunct czarist regime but also the advanced capitalist countries in the regular drunkenness of its workers. This is the only unquestionably successful example of the Soviets having "caught up and surpassed." Many people in the USSR understand this (the late Strumilin, for example), and they write with pain and indignation of the habitual drunkenness of the populace. Risking disfavor, they note that "even before the revolution, vodka was considerably more expensive than bread, and today it is some thirty-six times more expensive. However, can we consider this poison of the mind, this source of all excesses, this bitter grief of wives and small children, to be publicly useful just because we know that everyone guilty of using it today is fined without due process by billions of tax markups in the price of this narcotic? While these billions of rubles in markups are also included in the total revenue in unchanged prices, this itself violates their comparability to a certain extent."[27] The dimensions of this phenomenon are enormous, as the billions of fines and the violation of revenue comparability bear witness. If one can call prerevolutionary Russia's budget drunken, then the budget of the world's first socialist state must be called the most drunken, or, to use Strumilin's terminology, narcotic.

The main expenditures in the budget are for the national economy, for social-cultural events, and for defense. At the beginning of the 1970s, these expenditures were, respectively, 49, 36, and 11 to 12 percent. Once again one must consider, however, that the budget covers only about half the investments in the national economy. One must also closely examine the question of actual investments for defense.

Appropriations from the state budget for defense needs represent funds with which the state credits the armed forces during the planning year. A large portion of these funds (probably around 70 to 75 percent) are spent by the armed forces to purchase arms and munitions from industry. However, there is a policy of planned price setting, "by which consumer items are valued a bit higher than cost, and prices for the means of production are correspondingly lower."[28] This "bit," expressed by a definite coefficient, extends to a group of branches (arms), or to a single branch (aircraft), or to a group of articles (armored transports). The coefficients for various kinds of arms are unknown; however, it is well documented that when the armed forces buy arms (or pay in accordance with planned procedure), they do not pay the full production cost.

The difference between cost and price is covered by the plants' own assets, including not just defense industry plants, but also, for example, plants that deliver metal for arms production. This situation is explained very simply because all ministries which produce arms are included in the USSR's heavy industry, which enjoys all priorities.

Other expenditures directly connected to raising the nation's defensive capability come from widely diverse sections and subsections of the state budget and are channeled through the budgets of nearly all (perhaps without exception) USSR ministries and departments. Thus, it is primarily the machine-building industries who pay for the maintenance and production of several hundred thousand overly large and complicated lathes, which are used for military needs. School construction, which is made more expensive by including the features of a hospital, is financed through the Ministry of Education. The Ministry of Health pays to transform health resorts normally open during warm seasons into year-round establishments. Nuclear and missile designs are financed under science; the training of pilots, parachutists, snipers, and frogmen falls under physical training. All additional expenditures connected with defense requirements and the adapting of plants and other building projects under construction to these requirements are covered under capital construction by the funds for financing the national economy. At the expense of the financing of the national economy, defense-related measures in transportation, including the construction of purely strategic railways, highways, and waterways, are financed through the budgets of the Ministry of Transportation and other transportation ministries. The construction of the Baikal-Amur Railroad (BAM) has become the top-priority all-union construction project and has almost entirely eclipsed the construction of the Kama Automobile Plant (KamAZ). This construction is generally being done for strategic reasons, especially because of its accelerated tempo. Moreover, every planning decision made by *Gosplan* is evaluated from the standpoint of raising defense capability. These evaluations plan the decisive role; costs plays only a secondary role.

The sum total, or the percentage of the budget represented by additional expenditures for raising defense capability, is impossible to determine. In a few cases, the economic organizations (who have much more information than is reported in official statistics) might establish the amounts of expenditures with an adequate degree of precision. In most cases it is simply impossible to make estimates for two chief reasons: (1) In practice, two versions of a solution are never presented, one taking into account and the other disregarding defense considerations. (2) In many cases it is impossible to separate production expenditures into individual items.

As a result, I can state with conviction that even the Soviet leadership itself has only an approximate idea of the true amounts spent for defense. In my opinion, the hidden and additional expenditures considerably exceed the basic military budget. All together (and this figure is purely an estimate) they amount to about 32 to 35 percent of the USSR's state budget.

Several comments need to be made about the entire financial side of defense capability. First, a portion of the defense expenditures not included in the military budget is by nature more stable than the military budget itself, since the military budget can easily be altered simply by changing the number of people in the armed forces. The stability of this portion of expenditures stems from the greater stability of the development of the entire economy where changes are difficult and slow. Second, and this is not just Soviet tradition, defense expenditures are generously provided for. Therefore one need not regard the occasional prevalence of profits over expenses in the USSR state budget as reserves for defense-related expenditures, which are set differently and are usually connected with delays in currency circulation. Third, the planned nature of the Soviet economy determines that only money that has gone through the planning process can provide for the production of material goods; for it is only in the planning process that fiscal resources are covered by physical material resources, whose material structure is organically tied to the nature and trend of the use of fiscal resources. Therefore, the sudden and rapid growth of arms production within the planning period (within the annual operational plan and, for the long term, even within the five-year plan) is possible only at the expense of the mobilization reserves of the defense industry plants. However, as is quite plain, the expenditure of mobilization reserves is an extremely risky undertaking.

Credit in the USSR

Along with the planned financing of the entire economy is bank crediting, which amounts to the concentration, accumulation, and balanced distribution of resources that are not tied up in a yearly financial plan. However, in essence, the planned provision of resources for the entire national economy has much in common with crediting. As a result, both forms of financing frequently conflict with each other in practice. The long tradition of financing leads to conditions that hinder the successful incorporation of credit relations.

"The largest and most stable source of credit reserves are state budget funds accumulated over the years from yearly excess profits over expenses."[29] The second most important source of credit reserves is profit received from credit, that is, the interest paid for credit. This fluctuates from 1 to 8 percent. Eight percent interest is exacted only for overdue credit.

There are two kinds of credit: short-term, which is usually granted for one year and serves mainly to stimulate the working capital of enterprises, *kolkhozes,* and so forth; and long-term, which serves chiefly the noncentralized capital investments in the national economy.

The credit process is based on specific principles emerging from the very essence of credit.

The first principle of credit is the time period. The time period is based on the period of time that the loan will be used. This also gives the credit institution the right to demand payment based on the established period. Violating established time periods demonstrates that the borrower's operation has definite shortcomings. In such cases the bank takes strong measures, demanding that the borrower improve his operation.

Another principle of credit is conformity to the plan. This means that all bank loans extended to economic organizations should be reflected in the bank's credit plans and should be interconnected with the plants' plans. Credit is extended for planned expenses. Moreover, loans are granted to the same degree that planned tasks are met and in the amount that is actually needed by the plant at a given time.

An important feature of credit is its material security. This presupposes that the amount of credit is covered by actual expenditures or by the plants' reserves of material goods. Credit is extended not just to cover an abstract requirement for additional money but for concrete economic needs.

An integral principle of credit is differentiation, meaning that the bank takes different attitudes toward different plants and organizations when extending credit.[30]

As can be plainly seen from the credit stipulations themselves, economic managers resort to credit services only in extreme cases. They avoid the active pressure of the bank, one more bank control over the execution of the plan, the strict control over directing credit spending, and any sort of arbitrary differentiation.

The economic reform placed new requirements before credit, and in theory, it should have become a meaningful lever for increasing the national economy's effectiveness by strengthening the feeling of responsibility for the expenditure of assets. However, the actual effects are far from smooth, not because the reform is new or unusual, but because contradictory interests immediately come into play, as often happens in Soviet practice. Thus, in attempting to expand the use of credit, the economic reform made it easier to receive short-term credit. The plant managers immediately took advantage of this for their own interests.

The main shortcoming is that credit has developed more intensively in recent years than the "yield" has grown.

And what is the reason for this? Primarily, it is plain that plants do not take a responsible attitude toward resources borrowed from a state loan fund. Some economic managers have started to take a consumer attitude toward credit: the bank will pay for all goods, and the loan can be completely repaid with personal working capital.

And what does such practice lead to? Inasmuch as credit is "cheap" and easy to get, one need not economize or look for reserves or be concerned about increasing one's own working capital.[31]

Thus, practice has distorted the concept of credit as one of the tools for increasing the effectiveness of the Soviet economy.

Things are no better with long-term credit designated to augment the plants' fixed assets. Bureaucracy is the main problem here. "The rigid limits 'from' and 'up to,' created by various instructions, have made credit a very mobile form for financing the national economy. Long-term credit is very inflexible, unmaneuverable, and difficult to obtain on a large scale in practice." There is confusion and duplication of effort in organizing credit for these needs. *Gosbank* is involved with 90 percent of this and *Stroibank* (Construction Bank) is involved with the other 10 percent. "Thus, the borrower often finds himself in a dilemma: if you go to *Stroibank,* they will turn you down, if you go to *Gosbank,* you still do not know what their attitude might be. There are many such examples."[32] Due to all these problems, "the plants continue not to use *Gosbank* loans to expand their fixed assets" in the meantime. "The proportion of such credit ... amounts to about 3 percent of the total amount of capital investments."[33]

In summing up all credit activity and its consequences, we shall simply quote the famous Soviet economist D. Alakhverdian: "The rate of growth of nonpayments is substantially outstripping the rate of growth of credit investments in the national economy."[34] This tells us everything about the effectiveness of credit and the effectiveness of the economy as well.

Banks in the USSR

The USSR's banking system and its organization and role in the functioning of the entire Soviet system almost completely complies with Lenin's views on this problem. "Socialism would be unattainable without large banks. Large banks are the 'state apparatus' that we need to achieve socialism and which we take directly from capitalism. The largest of the large banks is the State Bank with divisions in every *volost* [smallest administrative division in czarist Russia] and at every factory. This is about nine-tenths of the socialist apparatus. It is statewide bookkeeping and statewide computation of production and distribution; it is, so to speak, the backbone of socialist society."[35]

Gosbank has become this "largest of the large" banks and began operation on 16 November 1921.[36] From its creation to the present, *Gosbank*'s significance and role in the Soviet economy has continually increased. According to its new charter of 1949 (the old charter dated from 1929),

> *Gosbank* is the only currency issue bank, the only bank for short-term credit, and the only calculating center of the USSR. Based on the state plan for the development of the USSR's national economy, *Gosbank* regulates currency circulation in the country, conducts short-term crediting, and performs calculations in the national economy. It also

takes in unattached fiscal resources from the enterprises and economic organizations of industry, agriculture, trade, transport, and other branches of the economy; it performs cash transactions of the USSR state budget and performs calculations on foreign trade and other payments from abroad.[37]

A 21 August 1954 resolution of the USSR Council of Ministers and the CPSU Central Committee "extended additional powers to *Gosbank* for exerting influence on the economy."[38] For the most part, this amounted to a strengthening of *Gosbank*'s control over the activities of economic organizations. The decision of the July 1955 Plenum of the CPSU Central Committee expanded *Gosbank*'s powers to the granting of credit for new technology and for technological improvements in production. At the same time, significant work was done to perfect and make technological improvements in *Gosbank* itself.

The economic reform and the change of the wage system in the *kolkhozes* increased *Gosbank*'s role even more and expanded *Gosbank*'s credit powers. Local divisions received the right to extend credit, as did the *oblast'* and republic-level *Gosbank* offices.[39]

As a result, during the last twenty years, even more than the previous period, *Gosbank* has developed into the most important organization in the entire Soviet system and especially in the Soviet economy. Its strength, power, and influence on the economy are enormous. It is enough to recall its role in levying the turnover tax; here *Gosbank*'s position directly and clearly contradicts the general line for raising output quality, but *Gosbank* emerges victorious in the dispute. *Gosbank* is actually the only bank in the country; in practice, all other banks are only functional branches of *Gosbank*. *Gosbank* is subordinate to the USSR Council of Ministers and in theory has the rights of a ministry; in practice, however, it has greater rights than a ministry. This clearly places it outside the organizational hierarchy and the purview of legal statutes.

Gosbank is organized on the all-union principle (similar to the all-union ministries) and has its offices and divisions throughout the USSR. The *Gosbank* system is shown in the diagram in figure 17-1.

A *Gosbank* board (*pravlenie*) performs the role of a republic office for the RSFSR. In 1971 the USSR *Gosbank* had "more than four thousand institutions in large and small cities, in villages and settlements. More than seventy-eight thousand savings banks are part of its system."[40]

The extent of its work is enormous, and "*Gosbank* carries on business operations with 570,000 plants, factories, *kolkhozes, sovkhozes,* schools, hospitals, scientific-research institutes, and institutions of higher learning. More than 4.2 million accounts are open for these organizations and there are some 83 million accounts for those who save in the savings banks."[41] There is already a chief computer center within *Gosbank;* the Ninth Five-Year Plan created thirty local computer centers and expanded the network of machine calculating

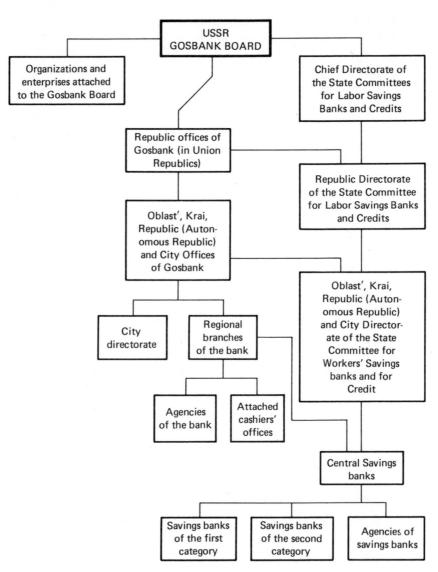

Figure 17-1. Organization of *Gosbank*

stations. The diversity and size of *Gosbank*'s functions require a complicated structure for its central apparatus, as is shown in the diagram in figure 17-2. The diagram draws attention to the fact that credit for defense-related industry is handled separately from credit for the rest of industry. The diagram does not show the chief directorate of savings banks, which has the rights of a directorate. It is included in the structure of *Gosbank* and has its own territorial network.

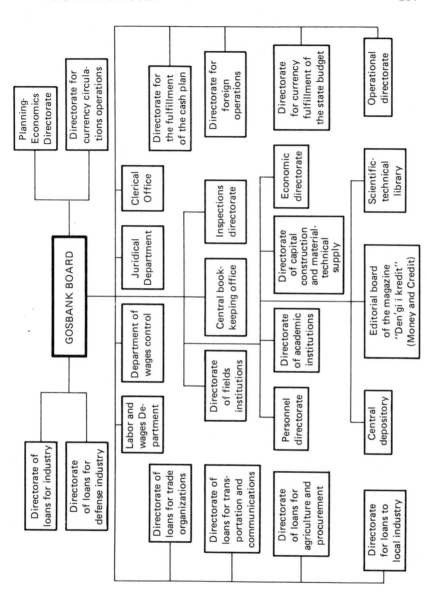

Figure 17-2. Structure of the Central Apparatus of *Gosbank*

Besides the *Gosbank,* there are *Stroibank* and *Vneshtorgbank* (Foreign Trade Bank). *Stroibank* is engaged primarily in financing centralized (planned) capital investments. It is partially involved in extending credit for centralized capital investments being done by the *khozraschet* (self-supporting) organizations. The very existence of *Stroibank* is defined and explained by the specific nature of its work; the monetary assets at its disposal, however, come from *Gosbank* which controls the activity of *Stroibank* as well.

The existence of the *Vneshtorgbank,* through which pass all foreign trade transactions as well as other financial operations being handled in currency or in gold, is explained by the specific nature of its work. However, both the currency and gold assets of the USSR are stored by and are under the control of *Gosbank.* Therefore, all *Vneshtorgbank* operations are also controlled by *Gosbank.*

To a certain extent the *Comecon* bank can be included among the USSR's banks. The USSR is the chief depositor; the bank itself is physically located in Moscow, and its transactions are carried out in convertible rubles. Its task is to serve foreign trade within the Socialist Bloc (between the member-nations of *Comecon*).

The work of every Soviet organization is evaluated by itself as well as by higher-ranking organizations according to various systems of indicators. Thus, for all *khozraschet* organizations such estimating indicators are the primary indicators of the national economic plan. The indicators for evaluating the work of a bank and for awarding premiums to its workers for fulfilling these indicators are handled in the following manner: "It so happens that the workers are not motivated to apply credit funds more effectively.... *Gosbank* institutions are not eager to use their own basic weapon in the struggle to attain good economic indicators from the economic organizations that they serve.... The use ... of sanctions is attended by a complicated system of drawing up documents.... This is why there is a need to find an expedient and economically justified indicator for *Gosbank*'s operation, an indicator that is more suitable for this institution."[42]

Notes

1. *Pravda,* 13 May 1960, p. 3.
2. *Planovoe khoziaistvo,* no. 5 (1960):9.
3. *Pravda,* 11 May 1962, p. 3
4. N.A. Tsagolov, ed., *Course in Political Economics,* vol. 2 (Moscow: Ekonomika, 1970), p. 291.
5. Ibid., pp. 282-283.
6. Ibid., pp. 286-287.
7. *Voprosy ekonomiki,* no. 4 (1974):76.
8. Tsagolov, *Course in Political Economics,* p. 287.

9. Ibid., p. 289.
10. Ibid., p. 538.
11. *Ekonomicheskaia gazeta*, no. 43 (1966):7.
12. *Planovoe khoziaistvo*, no. 9 (1961):29.
13. Ibid., no. 8 (1974):3.
14. Tsagolov, *Course in Political Economics*, p. 518.
15. Ibid., p. 520.
16. Ibid., p. 526.
17. Ibid., p. 527.
18. *Finances of the USSR* (Moscow: Gosfinizdat, 1962), p. 51.
19. Tsagolov, *Course in Political Economics*, pp. 520-521.
20. *National Economy of the USSR in 1972*, (Moscow: Statistika, 1973), p. 725.
21. *Voprosy ekonomiki*, no. 6 (1970):31.
22. *Pravda*, 30 May 1968, p. 2.
23. *Voprosy ekonomiki*, no. 8 (1974):75.
24. *Planovoe khoziaistvo*, no. 8 (1970):65.
25. *Voprosy ekonomiki*, no. 8 (1971):51.
26. *Pravda*, 21 October 1966, p. 2.
27. *Voprosy ekonomiki*, no. 11 (1969):66.
28. *Planovoe khoziaistvo*, no. 10 (1969):31.
29. Tsagolov, *Course in Political Economics*, p. 530.
30. *Ekonomicheskaia gazeta*, no. 17 (1969):12.
31. *Pravda*, 23 November 1968, p. 2.
32. *Ekonomicheskaia gazeta*, no. 11 (1968):35.
33. *Pravda*, 28 December 1967, p. 2.
34. *Voprosy ekonomiki*, no. 11 (1970):71.
35. V.E. Lenin, *Complete Works*, vol. 34, p. 307.
36. V.V. Ikonnokov, ed., *Gosbank USSR* (Moscow: Gosfinizdat, 1957) p. 15.
37. Ibid., p. 37.
38. Ibid., p. 38.
39. *Pravda*, 28 December 1967, p. 2.
40. *Pravda*, 4 October 1971, p. 2.
41. Ibid.
42. *Voprosy ekonomiki*, no. 2 (1967):122-123.

18

Domestic Trade

Soviet domestic trade passed through several stages in its development and finally took the form of state monopoly trade. Although a distinction is officially made between state and cooperative trade, both are under the control of the state, both are subject to economic planning, and both are monitored by the planning and financial organizations of the state. In 1972 these two types of state-controlled trade accounted for 97.6 percent of all internal trade turnover (*tovarooborot*), whereas only 2.4 percent was accounted for by the *kolkhoz* market, which is not directly controlled by the state but is strongly dependent on the situation in the state sector of trade.

The CPSU leadership makes wide use of its monopoly position in trade for its own goals. Large segments of the Party and Party leadership look on trade as something secondary and almost hostile, left over as a legacy and vestige of capitalism. The question, Will there be trade under communism? is still being discussed. It is probably for just this reason that "little attention is being devoted to consumption (as an independent phase of production) and to the closely related problems of sales, market forces, and the study of demand in the political economy of socialism and in economics in general."[1] These views have determined the tempo and character of trade development during the entire postrevolutionary period. They have determined the principles on which Soviet trade actually operated. They also determine the selection, qualifications, and general composition of the list of executives who control trade; and naturally they determine the general composition of lower-level cadres.

Until 1956 the basic ideological principle in trade was Stalin's theory that the law of socialist development in trade is the predominance of demand over supply. It was in this manner that the dearth of commodities in the USSR and the policy of belt tightening were theoretically substantiated. The new Khrushchevian viewpoint of abundance, written into the Party program and adopted in toto by the post-Khrushchev leadership, states just the opposite. The new viewpoint contends that in the interests of creating a genuine abundance, the predominance of supply over demand should be basic to socialism. Such a contention has little in common with logic, but it does reflect the swing of the pendulum in so-called ideology. Only at the very end of the 1960s and the beginning of the 1970s has a normal viewpoint been voiced, that is, the necessity of balancing supply and demand in quantity as well as in assortment, quality, and price. The drive for abundance led to considerable growth in trade turnover (almost 2¼ times between 1960 and 1972, and almost 7 times since (1950), which meant a growth in both the quantity and selection of goods offered to the populace. As a result, Soviet domestic trade found itself in a new, unaccustomed position. New and complicated problems arose both for it and for the industries producing the goods. Clearly the two most important problems are (1) the quality of consumer goods and (2) the study and determination of consumer demand, without which a balance of consumption and production is impossible, as is any optimum planning of commodity production.

The problem of correspondence in supply and demand does not require only a study of demand and the creation of a clear picture of it. Conditioned by the specific nature of the Soviet economic system, the problem is unsolvable without creating businesslike and effective relations between trade and industry. This need, in turn, demands an organizational restructuring of contacts within industry that would provide for fulfilling all requirements of trade organizations in the entire technological chain of production, as reflected by a variety of indicators.

The Planning of Trade

The official theory attributes a multifaceted role to trade in the production and reproduction cycle. It is contended that a planned socialist market "promotes the attainment of the final goal of socialist social production, the guarantee of the fullest possible satisfaction of worker needs."[2] Trade, it is further contended, expresses the socialist principle of distribution according to labor in material terms and brings about close ties among branches of the national economy, between urban and rural areas, and among various regions of the country. Practically speaking, the main role of trade is usually no different from most real and ephemeral trade functions. The chief role of domestic trade in socialist social production is to provide the Soviet state with the money necessary for the system as a whole to function. Monopoly of domestic trade makes it possible to exact a huge turnover tax. Thus, in the eyes of the Soviet leadership, the most important practical role of domestic trade is to ensure currency circulation within the state-citizen-state sphere with as little interruption as possible. The procedure and practice of planning domestic trade support this position.

"Compiling the trade turnover plan is linked to working out indicators for many other branches of the economy: the consumer goods production plan; the plans for the wage funds and amount of wages for blue- and white-collar workers; the plans for purchasing agricultural products; plans for currency circulation, for the state budget, and for the development of culture." It follows logically that "the goods turnover plan must be closely coordinated with the *Gosbank* cash plan."[3]

"The consolidated plan of trade development for the USSR as a whole and for the union-republics is worked out by *Gosplan* in conjunction with the Ministry of Trade, which is a union-republic organization."[4] "The overall control of rural trade planning for the country is provided by *Tsentrosoiuz* of the USSR. . . . The drafts of plans worked out by the consumer cooperative system are included as part of the plan for trade development for a given union republic."[5]

"During this work, the goods turnover plans are coordinated with the purchasing capabilities of the populace on the one hand and with commodity resources of both the USSR as a whole and the union republics, on the other. Balancing retail goods turnover with the purchasing capabilities of the populace and with commodity resources is one of the main requirements of scientific, economically based planning and is a deciding factor in the successful fulfillment of the plan."[6] Consequently, the balance method for coordinating parts of the plan is used in planning trade as well. However, *Gosplan*'s balances include only a limited number of commodity groups (twenty-three in all); and the balances of *Gosplan*, if taken together with those of the Ministry of Trade, are clearly insufficient, even though these are far more numerous (four hundred in all) and encompass the most important commodities. This insufficiency has become especially obvious under the conditions in which trade found itself after the theory of abundance appeared. In a practical sense, planning has always viewed "the purchasing capabilities of the populace" as a planned quantity, without internal variety or content. Orthodox economists even today consider that "in the planned socialist economy, it goes without saying that there is no place for a market element. The volume of production and supply of goods, the level of prices, *social needs, and demand are determined beforehand* in a planned manner. . . . In doing this, the state proceeds from an interest in satisfying to the greatest possible degree the growing needs of the members of socialist society" (italics mine).[7]

However, trade practices regarding the growth in supply of goods, that is, regarding the increased choices for the purchaser, have shown that frequently it is not so much quantity as the available goods structure that determines the trade organizations' fulfillment of economic plans. Thus, a component of the market element has arisen in planned trade: demand that is alive, changing, at times capricious, unamenable to planning, and at the same time a determinant of success. As a result, any realistic planning done in the usual way from the attained level, that is, from yesterday's demands on a specific structure of supply, has become impossible.

When goods were scarce, it could easily and irresponsibly be contended, as Mikoyan once did, that "thanks to the fact that our economy is planned, we can consider demand directly without any roundabout methods and develop production in accordance with this demand. This is the great advantage of our system."[8] Now circumstances make it necessary to study demand using these very roundabout methods.

Industry makes absolutely no attempt to study demand.

> The task of studying the market is entrusted to trade organizations. . . .
> However, we do not yet have satisfactory economic and mathematical
> instruments for solving this task. This is explained by the fact that the
> research conducted in the field has been uncoordinated. There was no
> single center which could coordinate this work and which could work
> out the basic scientific trends to be followed. For example, more than
> ten scientific collectives are working to forecast popular demand for
> goods, but their work is uncoordinated, and many of them have widely
> varying methodological positions. . . . Procedures for collecting and
> analyzing necessary information have not yet been adjusted, a step
> which would ensure a good statistical base for these computations and
> research.[9]

However, the fault lies not only in the fact that statistical information is not
forthcoming. "The lack of complete compatibility in nomenclature of the goods
which are considered by trade and budgetary statistics makes it impossible, for
all practical purposes, to forecast popular demand based on combining these two
sources of information and on checking the authenticity of the data by
comparing them."[10]

In the final analysis, all attempts to organize a centralized study of demand
have failed to produce results.[11] The creation in 1972 of the Interagency
Council for the Study of Popular Demand for Consumer Goods, attached to the
Ministry of Trade, has met the same fate. It is useless to look in the council's
publication, *Kommercheskii vestnik,* for an article on the methodology and
organization of calculating existing demand.

Calculating and forecasting short-term popular demand are for practical
purposes handled by requisition orders (*zaiavka*) from trade organizations. These
requisition orders are the basis of industry plans for goods production. "The
entire, colossal assortment of goods is produced in response to the requisition
orders of trade organizations. It turns out that the trade organizations guess
demand correctly only 50 percent of the time."[12]

The universal economic indicator for domestic trade planning is the yearly
goods turnover, expressed in rubles. *Gosplan* sets its volume on the unionwide
scale, sets its distribution by republic, and sets the distribution to the republics
of goods covered by the *Gosplan* goods balance. *Gosplan,* together with the
Ministry of Trade, distributes goods to the republics, whose balances they draw
up together. "According to the accounting data of the Ministry of Trade, goods
distributed in a centralized manner in 1967 made up 69.8 percent of all market
stocks."[13]

The goods turnover plan reaches every trade organization and serves as the
main index for measuring the success of work. Therefore, it is also the chief
assessment on which material incentives (bonuses) for trade enterprise employees are based.

In planning the circulation of the mass of goods, that is, actual physical goods and not just their value, the main role, for practical purposes, is played by the Ministry of Trade (approximately 70 percent of all goods) and *Tsentrosoiuz*, which carries out the same functions in trade with the rural populace. The other trade organizations of ministries and departments play an insignificant role in planning.

The price system in domestic trade has undergone a number of changes in recent years and has been significantly simplified. In principle, there now exist the industry selling price, which includes the turnover tax; the wholesale price, which is set by wholesale trade organs and which differs from the industry selling price by a minimal surcharge (about 1.25 percent) to cover the costs of distribution at the wholesale level; and the retail price, which differs from the wholesale price by a surcharge covering the costs of distribution at the retail level (about 6.5 percent). The costs of distribution in retail trade, as a percentage of the goods turnover for a particular year, have remained practically unchanged from 1940 through 1972.[14] The low distribution costs are a subject of theoretical pride and are proof of the advantages of socialist trade in comparison with capitalist trade, where the costs make up 25 to 30 percent.[15] In practice, the low costs of distribution are a source of the inadequate development of the trade network and of the technical backwardness and neglect of Soviet trade, both wholesale and retail.

Obviously, industry prices are the basis of trade prices. However, prices in the trade system, fulfilling the role of planned regulators of supply and demand, can change significantly, basically because of changes in the size of the turnover tax, which is hidden in the price of consumer goods. "A socialist state, taking into account the correlation which actually exists between supply and demand for certain goods, systematically changes the level of prices on those goods for which there is a substantial disproportion between supply and demand. In the process of such a change in prices, the price level of a particular type of goods can systematically increase and decrease in relation to cost."[16] I am talking here about accounting for long-term disproportions, but planned trade is simply not able to take into account market-determined variations. At the same time, "market conditions exist in a socialist economy as well, particularly if we consider the fact that numerous rapidly changing factors influence the purchase of consumer goods." Therefore, "under socialism, the market is also subject to rapid market-determined changes."[17] Thus, difficulties and problems are created in planning the production of goods and their circulation, leading to the accumulation of huge reserves of nondisposable goods, goods that will never find a buyer.

Contacts between Industry and Trade

Before 1960 there were no contacts between industry and trade for determining the structure of the entire assortment of goods. The task of the trade organs was to sell what industry produced. Later contacts between trade organs and various industry groups were formed. Mutual contacts with heavy industry factories, which turn out consumer goods as directed by the plan, in principle remained the same as before 1960. "Now the consumer goods market seems to be formed on the principle of passing the hat. Heavy industry factories bestow gifts on the consumer in a most haphazard manner; they turn out whatever they can, planned value being the only consideration."[18] They offer their production to trade organizations but are not required to accept orders from them.

Contacts between the light industrial ministries and the trade organizations are closer. Officially, all products turned out by them are supposed to be produced according to the orders of the trade organizations. "Today the Ministry of Trade sends requisition orders for production of the overwhelming majority of goods to the union and union-republic industrial ministries, but the ministry takes no responsibility for marketing since the republic organizations handle wholesaling operations. This lowers responsibility for ordering goods and leads to an intolerable mix-up in the relations between the trade system and industry."[19]

All-union trade fairs are organized primarily according to goods category to familiarize the trade organizations with possibilities for orders. In 1972 the trade fairs, which usually took place in the fall (when the production plan for the next year is already finalized and cannot be changed) were moved back to spring or summer. At the fairs factories display their products for examination and familiarization, especially new products being readied for production. However, the fairs have not yet been able to create conditions guaranteeing a valid order for specific products. "Instances are common where factories display models of new products which they are not ready to produce in the next year or perhaps will not produce at all, or which they produce in meager quantities. . . . This game is widespread. Regarding the business sector, that is, concluding agreements for delivery of specific articles, some plant managers consider that this can be done later with each wholesale buyer individually. By the end of the year, you see, the client will be far more compliant and will take anything that is offered."[20] Thus, the bulk of goods offered to buyers is influenced by two factors: the orders given to industry by the trade organizations and industry's foisting of their goods onto the trade organizations. Thus, for example, only 70 percent of an order for jackets made of "Bologne" (a water-repellent synthetic) material was filled, but raincoats from the same material (which were no longer in style and were almost unsellable) were produced at a rate of 2.3 times the number of orders for them because the raincoats were more profitable for industry.[21] However, even when an order is implemented completely, its effect is limited. A trade organization sends an order to the producer of a finished product, let us say an order for shoes to a shoe factory. However, neither the trade organization nor the shoe factory is able to influence the producers of the raw materials (for example, leather) and the semifinished products necessary for producing the finished product.

Officially the trade organizations have the right to influence the quality of the goods produced. They cannot check quality at the place of production, but they can check the quality of goods shipped to them. They can reject and return obviously defective goods to the producer, and they can lower the quality rating of the goods. This correct and sensible treatment of the question has another side, however, which reduces quality control to almost zero. The factories that carry out production plans are not concerned about marketing the goods and have no material responsibility for it. This takes place because "under the existing accounting system, factories receive money for finished production immediately after it enters the trade system, whether into a wholesale depot or directly into the retail trade network. . . . It is possible for producers to begin a new production cycle regardless of whether their product will be accepted by the public, that is to say, whether or not it will be sold to the consumer."[22] At the same time, "stores are unable to check the quality of all items received. The incidence of random checking at wholesale depots is 5 to 15 percent [of the goods received] ." It is apparent that the chance of detecting low quality is minimal, and if it is detected, it is so late that nothing can be done. However, even if low quality, which is a direct violation of contracts or state standards, is detected in time, then "violators of delivery contract conditions can be assessed a penalty of not more than 1 to 3 percent of the losses incurred. In addition, these penalties are taken from the factory's general profit and affect the incentive funds [bonuses] only indirectly. For this reason, some factories pay their fines scrupulously and . . . continue to turn out mediocre products. They themselves live comfortably; they 'cope with' the sales and profit targets; they generate incentive funds; and they give out bonuses. In a word, the effect of fines on those responsible for shoddy work is insignificantly small. This is the basis for saying that the trade system has not yet become an equal partner of production."[23] This inequality is rooted in the planned management of the economy, specifically in the fact that production of goods and their sales are based on different indicators. "The orders of the trade organizations are based on natural indicators, while sales plans for the producers are approved in monetary terms."[24] As a result, varying, antagonistic economic (and personal) interests arise in production and in trade. This specific circumstance, along with reasons applicable to the system as a whole, creates what may be the most important problem, the problem of quality. This problem is a double-edged sword; with one edge it strikes the consumer, and with the other it strikes the planned economy and the whole Soviet system. In view of the growing saturation of the Soviet domestic market and the appearance of greater choice for the consumer, it seems to be striking harder and harder at the Soviet system. The planning process assumes that goods planned for production will be sold. Corrections based on long-term effect can be introduced into these assumptions with no trouble; however, it is impossible to take into account rapid changes in market-determined conditions. The whole system of planned assumptions functions in a time framework as well; it is necessary not only to sell but to sell within a specific time period. All this is directly connected to currency circulation and to financing the work of the whole system.

The scale of difficulties created for the system by the shortcomings of domestic trade affects, if only indirectly, the quantity of nondisposable commodity stocks. Thus, "reserves of clothing, linens, and knitwear in the wholesale and retail trade network as of 1 October 1972 were valued at an astronomical sum; only slightly less than 5 billion rubles."[25] For certain types of goods, the growth in commodity reserves significantly surpasses the growth in their sales.[26]

The Organization of Domestic Trade

Many organizations enter into the state sector of trade. Public food service, apparently because of similarities in economic functions, is also regarded as part of trade.

A decisive role in trade is played by the union-republic Ministry of Trade and by the Union of Consumers' Societies of the USSR, which also has a union-republic structure. In addition, many ministries and departments have their own departmental trade network which for the most part duplicates the activities of the stores subordinate to the Ministry of Trade. Trade in some types of goods is almost completely in the hands of nontrade ministries and departments. That is why pharmacies are part of the Ministry of Health; trade in books is handled, strangely enough, by the Council of Ministers Committee for the Press (the censorship organ); newspapers and magazines are sold by the Ministry of Communications, since it handles their delivery. One Soviet source, *Iuridicheskaia literatura,* lists sixteen ministries and agencies that have their own trade organizations and mentions that there are "several others as well."[27] Among the others are the closed distribution points and closed dining facilities which are never mentioned in Soviet literature. These trade organizations serve the elite of the Party managers and the police organs. Entrance into and use of these institutions is accomplished by special passes; their prices are so symbolic [low] that they deserve their basic name, distribution points, places where earthly blessings are not so much sold as distributed among those more equal than others.

Almost every Soviet ministry has as part of its structure a workers' supply administration (*Upravlenie rabochego snabzheniia,* URS), and its organizations repeat the structural chart of the ministry itself. At the factory level, their departments are called workers' supply departments (*Otdel rabochego snab-zheniia,* ORS); and all the activities of the worker supply system are basically connected with trade.

The simplified trade organizational chart in figure 18-1, shows only the most important organizations. However, these organizations account for over 90 percent of the internal turnover of goods in the state sector of trade.

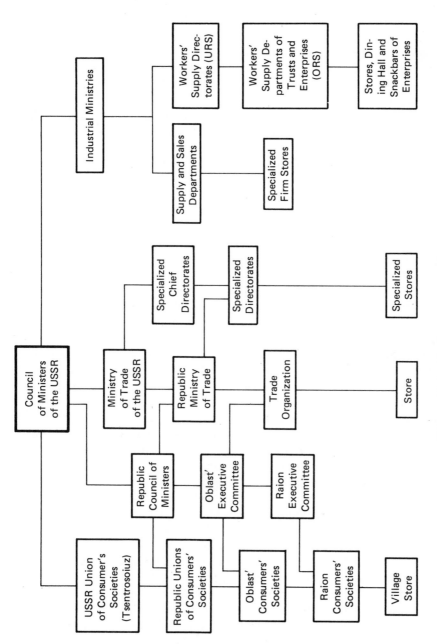

Figure 18-1. The Organization of Trade

Four million people were working in these organizations in 1972, and if those people working in public food services are added, the total becomes 6.2 million. This figure "does not include those employees working in the *oblast'* and *krai* trade administrations, in subsidiary enterprises, in transport, and in other types of activities undertaken by trade organizations."[28] There is no information for determining the number of workers employed in "other types of activities undertaken by trade organizations," but we are talking about many hundreds of thousands of people. "In the state sector of retail trade in the Russian Federated Republic, for every 100 sales persons, there are 110 other employees, including 24 supervisory personnel and 8 performing accounting functions."[29]

In 1972 the entire trade network of the country totalled 686,000 enterprises, which means an increase of almost 1.7 times when compared to 1940. Characteristic of the retail trade network is a high percentage of so-called booths, that is, kiosks in which usually only one person works. In 1972 kiosks accounted for almost 26 percent of the trade network as opposed to only 9 percent in 1927 under NEP. The high percentage of booths is explained by insufficient attention to developing the trade network; a booth is the simplest and least expensive way of increasing the number of trade points. The large number of booths is combined with a predominance of small, crowded shops in the rest of the trade network. In 1971, for example, there were 8.51 square meters of shop space for each salesperson in the Soviet Union; in Bulgaria this figure was 18.0 square meters in 1969.[30] Over 60 percent of all stores in the state sector of trade consist of stores with one or two sales positions.[31] Naturally, in large cities there are large stores [supermarkets and department stores]; however, even "in those Moscow stores dealing in consumer goods, there are now the same number of total sales positions as there were in 1910-1913, even though the population has increased several times over. On the average, up to 150 people per sales position pass through these stores every day, and in large department stores the figure reaches 250 people."[32]

Every small store is specialized to a certain degree, and one must visit several of them to purchase everything that is needed. It is for this reason that "all the stores of the country together receive roughly 850 million shoppers per day."[33] In other words, every inhabitant of the country, from infants to the very elderly, would have to visit more than three stores every day. Practically speaking, those who do the shopping must visit seven to eight stores daily.

The internal organization of sales (requesting an article from the salesperson, paying for the purchase at the cash register, and standing in line to receive the purchased article) creates artificial lines and wastes time. Overall figures for these losses are enormous, and the extent of these losses varies according to different estimates. "However, the lowest estimate is three hundred to four hundred hours per year. For the country as a whole, this is 20 billion man-hours."[34] Other sources indicate a loss of 30 billion man-hours, "which corresponds to the yearly labor of 15 million workers."[35] In other words, every year a Soviet citizen spends 7 1/2 to 10 forty-hour work weeks in lines.

This is the situation in state trade, which is primarily trade in the cities. The situation is even more complex in the rural consumer cooperatives. Although much has been done over the last few years (and significantly more written) to improve trade services for the rural populace, direct data only confirm the failure of the actions and the emptiness of the words. "In 1966, 78.5 percent of all rural families and in 1970, 84.6 percent, went to the cities"[36] to make necessary purchases, thus wasting about 160 hours per year per rural family.[37] This waste is primarily the result of the small selection of goods available in rural stores. It is also partly a result of the poor quality of goods in rural stores when compared to those in city stores. This difference in the quality of goods, in turn, is a consequence of a specific practice in Soviet trade for marketing low-quality goods.

Modern methods of trade are introduced slowly and in insufficient quantity. "Over the last fifteen years, only about 7 percent of the grocery stores and an even lower percentage of stores selling industrial goods have been changed to this form of trade [self-service stores]."[38] There are several reasons for this: the lack of necessary equipment, as well as the low quality of existing equipment;[39] the insufficient packaging of goods by factories and trade organizations;[40] and the demeaning practice of checking the bags, briefcases, and handbags of customers.[41] As a result, many customers refuse to use such trade services.

Trade organizations use very little labor mechanization and equipment. "The level of mechanization in retail trade organizations is at present only about 7 percent." Over a ton of goods passes through the hands of a salesperson in a grocery store every day. "And the goods are cut, poured, and weighed primarily by hand."[42] The Minister of Trade of the RSFSR confirms this by stating: "The lack of necessary equipment slows technical progress in trade, restrains the development of new techniques, and causes many people to be drawn into trade operations."[43] To characterize the rate of technical progress in trade, I shall cite only one example, but one that is not an exception. "The trade system needs automatic scales equipped with an electronic device making it possible to determine not only the weight but the price of the goods as well. The first batch of such scales (eight of them) was produced in 1970. For the current year, the RSFSR [where a little more than 50 percent of the trade organizations of the USSR are located] has been allotted only fifteen electronic scales."[44] An analogous situation exists with refrigeration and transport equipment, with machines for slicing sausage products (up to 500,000 tons of sausage are sliced by hand every year), and with many other areas; however, sales from automated equipment are declining sharply.[45] It is for this reason that "many people are being drawn into trade operations. Today 7 million persons work in this area. Tomorrow, if equipment is not used, every fourth worker [that is, one-fourth of all the workers of the country] will have to get behind the counters."[46] Such is the organizational perspective in this area of the economy.

Domestic Trade in Practice

In practice, trade is based primarily on the following factors: volume of goods turnover in rubles, which is the chief and universal plan indicator at all levels of trade; overburdening stores and sales personnel with customers, which is aggravated by the low productivity of the sales personnel; and a number of noneconomic factors that create the atmosphere characteristic of trade services. All these factors play a daily role in Soviet trade and have become traditional.

The planned volume of trade turnover naturally creates an interest in it for the trade employees. It also creates a rather widespread indifference to the questions of selling what to whom, with what kind of service, and with what kind of quality. On the other hand, a very clear interest is created in selling as many and as expensive goods as possible in the shortest possible time period [proceeds have to be turned over to a *Gosbank* branch on a daily basis] with the least possible bother and with the smallest outlay of capital, energy, and labor. Industry is interested in producing the most expensive article in every commodity group. The situation with respect to trade discounts on various goods is also abnormal: "an increase in sales of these goods to the populace does not increase, but rather, significantly reduces the income of the enterprise [a store] causing it to sustain losses."[47] In this category of goods, "besides potatoes, vegetables, eggs, household soap, and children's clothes, we find fish, sausage, semiprocessed meat products, animal fats, milk products, canned vegetables and fruits, and fabrics."[48] It is the factory's income, its profit, that determines the size of its bonuses. In the eyes of the trade employees, therefore, the whole assortment of goods is divided into profitable and unprofitable. Thus, it is no accident that some essential goods (salt, for example) that are produced in sufficient quantity cannot be found in the stores. The unprofitablity of a commodity is also determined by possible losses in shipment and storage; the higher the risk, the more unprofitable the commodity.

At the top of this unique evaluation scale is "strong drink" such as vodka and brandy. Liquor is sold everywhere in the trade network and in public food service enterprises. It is possible to quickly "fulfill the plan without really trying" by selling liquor. That is why, for example, "the Workers' Supply Department of the Enakiev Metalurgical Plant [located in the Donetsk Basin area] accumulated four hundred thousand rubles worth of vodka and brandy in excess of their norm."[49] That is only *in excess* of the norm; the norm amounts exist as well. This is only for supplying the workers of one plant! Approximately a hundred thousand half-liter bottles! On a broader scale, "the offices of *Rosbakaleia* (Russian Federated Republic Groceries Organization) at times consider canned goods to be of secondary importance; wine and vodka are of primary importance."[50]

The highest levels of Soviet leadership are aware of all this. However, the assortment of goods in each type of store is based, not on demand or on considerations of giving the best and most comprehensive service to the consumer, but on norms from above that establish the mandatory assortment of goods. Even so, the mandatory assortment is violated regularly or is falsified. In a grocery store in Kurgan, for example, the management knowingly ordered milk at a rate of one-half of its demand (it is unprofitable and bothersome). "However, everything imaginable was done for show, including the alluring announcement: 'Milk for sale by the glass.' "[51] Such is the style of Soviet trade.

Indifference to the questions of quality in trade services is a broad, many-sided problem. In the just opinion of the chief of the planning department of the Ministry of Trade, it is "one of the main problems of trade," one which "is being solved exceedingly slowly.... "The reasons for this are shortcomings in organizing the work of trade employees and the low effectiveness of material incentives. The following also have a negative effect: the backwardness of the material and technical base, shortages in some goods, the inability to maneuver existing commodity resources, and the inadequate study of consumer demand."[52] Although the low quality of goods is not the fault of the trade organizations, it makes the already poor trade services even worse. Naturally, measures are taken to raise the quality of goods; "however, a general increase in the quality of consumer goods is still being attained slowly."[53] Low quality is the reason for overstocking (the accumulation of unsold goods). To combat overstocking, goods are transferred from large centers to medium and small cities and then into the rural trade network. At each of these levels, the buyer has a smaller choice and is himself far less demanding. However, even this measure does not always help, so for the first time in the history of Soviet trade, goods are being sold at sharply reduced prices. "In 1972 the state lost about 4 million rubles in price reductions on ready-made garments alone."[54] Nevertheless, the quantity of overstocked goods continues to grow.

The real attitude of the Party managers (*nomenklatura*) toward trade is shown by the fact that the worst economic managers are in trade, especially at the middle and lower levels of management. Their general educational level is insufficient. "At the beginning of 1966, of 1,400 directors of trade organizations and public food service trusts, only 68 percent had a higher- and middle-level special education; of 53,200 directors of stores and dining halls, the number was only 12,400, or 23 percent."[55] At the same time, "in 1968 over 37,000 trained specialists were working as sales personnel and cooks in the state trade organizations of the RSFSR alone."[56] This figure could be doubled for the whole country. It is self-evident that the Party managers, those specialists in shady dealings, are difficult to dislodge once they have secured a position. They naturally select lower-level trade employees in their own image. The people are firmly convinced that there are no decent, honest people in the trade network; they are all thieves, swindlers, bribe takers, or worse. Perhaps this opinion is overly categorical, but theft, false measuring, false weighing, and overcharging are widespread. There are sufficient examples of these practices; audits have uncovered them in one-third to one-half of the stores.[57]

The entire organization and condition of the trade network on the one hand and the opinion of trade employees on the other have created strained and extremely unpleasant personal relations in the trade services. "There are two hostile camps in stores: the store employees and the customers."[58] However, in reality, it is only rarely that rudeness to customers is *not* encountered. The customer often manages to hold his own, however, with the result that the trade services are a source of daily irritation and dissatisfaction, both of which are probably transferred to the Soviet system.

The Soviet leadership has been forced to pay more attention to the problems of domestic trade. In January 1972 the following resolution of the CPSU Central Committee and the Council of Ministers was published: "On Some Measures for Improving Trade and Its Level of Mechanization." The resolution admits in passing that "the condition of trade in the country still does not satisfy the demand made of it," that there are "immense shortcomings in the organization of retail trade," and that "in a number of instances there are low standards for trade services to the populace."[59] However, there have been no noticeable improvements since the resolution.

Notes

1. *Voprosy ekonomiki,* no. 8 (1966):141.
2. A.I. Levin, *The Socialist Domestic Market* (Moscow: Mysl', 1973), p. 24.
3. V.I. Moskvin, *Retail Commodity Circulation in the USSR and Its Planning* (Moscow: Vysshaia shkola, 1969), p. 46.
4. Ibid., p. 50.
5. Ibid., p. 51.
6. Ibid., p. 50.
7. Levin, *The Socialist Domestic Market,* p. 30.
8. Report at the All-Union Meeting of Trade Workers, 17 October 1953.
9. *Economic Reform and the Problems of Realization* (Moscow: Ekonomika, 1968), pp. 7-8.
10. *Voprosy ekonomiki,* no. 8 (1974):37.
11. *Sotsialisticheskaia industriia,* 17 August 1973, p. 2; 2 April 1974, p. 2.
12. *Sotsialisticheskaia industriia,* 17 August 1973, p. 2.
13. Moskvin, *Retail Commodity Circulation,* p. 82.
14. *National Economy of the USSR in 1972,* (Moscow: Statistika, 1973), pp. 598-599.
15. Moskvin, *Retail Commodity Circulation,* p. 13.
16. *The Socialist Domestic Market,* pp. 30-31.
17. *Economic Reform,* p. 8.
18. *Sotsialisticheskaia industriia,* 28 November 1972, p. 2.

19. *Ekonomicheskaia gazeta,* no. 32 (1971):17.

20. *Pravda,* 19 September 1973, p. 3.

21. *Ekonomicheskaia gazeta,* no. 41 (1971):17.

22. *Voprosy ekonomiki,* no. 4 (1972):96.

23. *Pravda,* 16 August 1974, p. 3.

24. *Voprosy ekonomiki,* no. 1 (1974):47.

25. *Sotsialisticheskaia industriia,* 20 January 1973, p. 2.

26. *Ekonomicheskaia gazeta,* no. 41 (1971):17; also *Pravda,* 16 August 1971, p. 2.

27. B.M. Lazarev, *Management of Soviet Trade* (Moscow: Iuridicheskaia literatura, 1967), p. 21.

28. *National Economy of the USSR in 1972,* p. 597.

29. *Ekonomicheskaia gazeta,* no. 24 (1970):17.

30. *Voprosy ekonomiki,* no. 9 (1973):47.

31. Ibid., no. 2 (1967):21.

32. Ibid., no. 8 (1959):55.

33. *Sotsialisticheskaia industriia,* 17 August 1973, p. 2.

34. Ibid., 15 January 1971, p. 2.

35. *Voprosy ekonomiki,* no. 4 (1969):52.

36. *Planovoe khoziaistvo,* no. 10 (1972):68.

37. *Voprosy ekonomiki,* no. 8 (1974):44.

38. Ibid., no. 4 (1969):53.

39. *Ekonomicheskaia gazeta,* no. 24 (1970):17.

40. *Pravda,* 20 February 1971, p. 3.

41. *Pravda,* 4 July 1971, p. 3.

42. *Pravda,* 20 February 1971, p. 3.

43. *Ekonomicheskaia gazeta,* no. 24 (1970):17.

44. *Pravda,* 20 February 1971, p. 3.

45. *Voprosy ekonomiki,* no. 10 (1969):54.

46. *Sotsialisticheskaia industriia,* 15 January 1971, p. 2.

47. *Voprosy ekonomiki,* no. 14 (1969):55.

48. Ibid., p. 56.

49. *Pravda,* 2 March 1975, p. 3.

50. *Pravda,* 14 May 1966, p. 2.

51. *Ekonomicheskaia gazeta,* no. 32 (1966):37.

52. *Voprosy ekonomiki,* no. 1 (1969):26.

53. *Planovoe khoziaistvo,* no. 6 (1974):9.

54. *Sotsialisticheskaia industriia,* 20 January 1973, p. 2.

55. *Voprosy ekonomiki,* no. 6 (1967):49.

56. Ibid., no. 10 (1968):57.

57. *Pravda,* 15 October 1968, p. 3.

58. *Pravda,* 16 October 1970, p. 1.

59. *Pravda,* 30 January 1972, p. 1.

19 Foreign Trade

"Foreign trade monopoly is one of the unshakable foundations of the Soviet government."[1] Although this principle was formulated long ago, it remains unshakable, regardless of the Soviet Union's trading partner.

Soviet foreign trade can be divided into two parts: trade with countries of the Socialist Bloc and trade with countries having a market economy. In trade within the Socialist Bloc, trade among the member-countries of the Council of Economic Mutual Assistance (CEMA) is considered separately. In trade with market-economy countries, a separate category is made for trade with highly developed capitalist countries. The main role in the USSR's foreign trade turnover is played by trade within the Socialist Bloc, but the proportion has dropped significantly in recent years: from 72 percent in 1960[2] to 55 percent in 1973.[3]

The total trade turnover has risen significantly only in postwar years. It was only in 1948 that the volume of trade turnover reached the level of 1913, but in 1972 it had exceeded the 1913 level by 10.7 times.[4] While this growth could be attributed primarily to trade within the Socialist Bloc in the 1950s and 1960s, at the end of the sixties and the beginning of the seventies the growth was due to rapidly increased trade with the highly developed capitalist countries. Thus, the trade turnover with seven countries (West Germany, Japan, Finland, England, France, the United States, and Italy) increased from 1.9 billion rubles in 1965 to 6.2 billion rubles in 1973, an increase of 3.3 times.[5]

Planning management in foreign trade is in the hands of *Gosplan*. The plan for foreign trade is an integral part of the national economic plan. The volume and structure of trade turnover for socialist countries and for market-economy countries are included in the general plan in different ways. Foreign trade management is handled by the All-Union Ministry of Foreign Trade and by the Council of Ministers State Committee for Foreign Economic Relations. Management and, partially, planning of foreign trade within CEMA are handled by that organization itself.

Under the Ministry of Foreign Trade and the State Committee for Foreign Economic Relations, there exist all-union associations having the rights of chief directorates and structured along the branch principle. In each of the 110 countries with which the USSR had trade relations in 1973, there are trade delegations (*torgpredstvo*) that handle trade transactions. There are two exceptions to this structure: the Petrozavodsk and Vladivostok affiliates of the ministry. The activities of the former are connected with trade with Finland; the latter is concerned with Japan. These affiliates have the right to seek internal export potential of specific regions and to conduct foreign trade with these countries over and above the plan based on the internal resources of the region. For the Petrozavodsk affiliate, this region is the European northwest. For the Vladivostok affiliate, it is eastern Siberia as far west as Lake Baikal. Soviet sources evaluate the work of these affiliates most positively; the first real decentralization in Soviet history has shown good results.

The quality of export articles is higher than that of articles made for the domestic market. These goods are supervised by the State Inspectorate for Export Goods Quality which is attached to the Ministry of Foreign Trade. However, the overwhelming majority of Soviet export goods are significantly inferior to the same types of products put on the world market by industrially developed countries. Even where a Soviet article is on the world level from a technological standpoint, it is usually inferior to articles made in other countries in terms of reliability and length of service.

Trade with Market-Economy Countries

In the eyes of the Soviet leadership, trade with capitalist countries is not an end in itself but a means to an end. For many years, this means was used only to the extent that the Soviet government needed certain goods that it did not produce or for which new production would have to be set up. Trade was also used to exert economic pressure for political aims, although the results were always insignificant. The goals of the Soviet leadership never included supporting and developing the world capitalist market by participating in it. Soviet leaders have always had a negative attitude toward any extended reliance on imports from capitalist countries. It was for precisely this reason that the foreign trade turnover with capitalist countries in 1961 was only 17.5 percent higher than that of 1913.

The scientific and technical revolution, however, and the increasing gap between the average scientific and technical level in the USSR and the level in the leading countries led to the appearance of new ideas. These ideas did not mean refuting old points of view, but the character of the new demands and the extended period of their expected effect led to the appearance of new views. Today it is stated that "only on the basis of widespread participation by all nations in the international division of labor will it be possible to really assimilate the worldwide achievements of science and technology and to ensure the further movement of humanity on the path of progress. Today no country can effectively develop the basic branches of production and science if it relies exclusively on its own assets and capabilities."[6] Objectively speaking, this is true, but in the case of the Soviet Union there remains the dilemma: is this a genuinely understood truth, or is it a new course for a comparatively long period of time?

At this new state of economic relations with the capitalist world, one is talking not just about trade but about broad cooperation in scientific, technical, and other fields. Licenses for patents held by various countries are being traded for more extensively. Soviet patent licenses are being sold to the leading technical countries of the world, although many of these patents have yet to be introduced in the USSR. The Soviet Union needs a wide variety of contacts today. Nevertheless, the Soviet Union "has rejected and will continue to reject in the future any attempt designed, under cover of economic cooperation, to lay 'ideological mines' or to attempt to shake the foundations of the socialist system."[7] The manner in which the ruling comrades think is such that they are ready to sacrifice economic reality to political fantasy. Do they really want to trade in the future, or is it only necessity forcing them to do so on a temporary basis?

"A new stage in the development of cooperation between socialist and capitalist countries is the conclusion of long-term (ten-year) agreements on economic, industrial, and technical cooperation. As a rule, these agreements are supplemented by detailed programs in production, science, technology, and trade."[8] Some long-term agreements are made on a compensational basis; these agreements have been developing rapidly in the 1970s and are usually large-scale, long-range transactions. They are based on agreements to assist in developing natural resources and to pay for this assistance either in natural resources (oil, gas, timber, and so forth) or in semifinished products. "Such agreements, incidentally, are a new type of tie between countries, ties in which state organizations participate to a significant degree. This makes it possible not only to establish long-term projects for developing trade and to give them a stable character but also to unify the efforts of the many firms in our partner countries which participate in the exchanges and to give them the necessary guarantees."[9] There remains only the question, Do these transactions give guarantees to the states involved and to their taxpayers?

In the eyes of many Soviet citizens, such transactions sell the natural resources of the motherland at giveaway prices. In one of its stories, the literary journal *Novyi mir* presents a conversation between two educated residents of Moscow:

"Pasha," I said, "we really don't have enough bread" [in the meaning of money].

"That's because we throw our money away! Catherine [the wife of one of the speakers, a geologist] discovered a new oil field. And then what? Shall we trade away the nice cheap oil? Specialist in selling resources! [One of them is a foreign trade employee.] Have you traded a lot away? ... We aren't so rich that we can sell cheap things. When will you understand that?"[10]

The same opinion is expressed more strongly in a joke from 1973:

At a newspaper stand:
"What newspapers do you have?"

"There is no more *Pravda* [Truth]. *Rossiia* [Russia] is sold out. We have only *Trud* [Labor] left."

The Soviet Union sells mostly raw materials to the leading capitalist countries and buys equipment, technology, and science from them. In the past, individual machines or comparatively short production lines were bought; now it is whole complexes (plants, factories, or, more rarely, production shops) with all basic and auxiliary equipment and technology, up to and including the calculation of the number of workers required.

It is obvious that Soviet leaders see the whole complex of economic interrelations, including trade, as the path to decisive and rapid acceleration of scientific and technical progress in the country, the chance for a sharp improvement in the technical level of industry, the means for a decisive increase in labor productivity, and, finally, the chance for a significant increase in the effectiveness of the national economy as a whole.

Once again, the Soviet leadership imagines that it has found the panacea for all its troubles. Psychological barriers prevent them from admitting and under-standing that something foreign, born of another type of organization and principles and transplanted into their system, will become subordinate to and be deformed by it, and will not produce the same effect that it gives in its own environment. Life and experience confirm this fact. It is sufficient to cite the story of the Zhiguli automobile, or the Lada, as it is called in its export version. Having earlier decided to break the agreement with Fiat forbidding export of these automobiles, the Soviet leadership counted on transferring the expensive and organizationally complex problem of service and supply of spare parts abroad to Fiat. A profitable export transaction was imagined. The auto was copied, but problems of raw materials, technology, equipment, and quality (that is, the internal peculiarities of the Soviet system) made it necessary to make changes in the automobile, changes that made it impossible to use Fiat spare parts and therefore virtually eliminated the possibility of exploiting Fiat service. The profitable export transaction did not take place.

It was not only a breakdown in the export plan that caused problems. The Soviet Fiats do not perform the same in the Soviet Union as Fiats do under normal conditions. It could be that such a goal is not even pursued. The main point is to satisfy the unmet demands of a populace with money to spend, to extract money from the pockets of Soviet citizens and put it into the coffers of *Gosbank,* and to the devil with the consequences. This is shortsighted shop-keeping; apparently, it has never occurred to the leadership how much an automobile normally raises the productivity of socially necessary labor, even if the auto is in private use.

No better results are obtained from factories bought to produce goods exclusively for domestic consumption. The Soviet press has cited an example of a chemical factory purchased in Holland. According to the Dutch plan, approximately 280 people were supposed to work in it; however, under Soviet conditions more than twice that number were employed. Consequently, the effectiveness of the factory was decreased by half. This is only one example, but a similar fate awaits any factory purchased abroad.

This, however, does not mean that huge purchases do not ensure a certain increase in the effectiveness of the Soviet economy and of industry especially. However, the Soviet leaders, as well as some people in the West, tend to greatly overestimate the possible effect.

Trade with developing countries should be considered part of trade with market-economy countries. The only difference is that the developing countries are in a position analogous to that of the Soviet Union in its trade with developed capitalist countries: first come credits and then purchases. During the 1960s and the early 1970s, trade with the developing countries has grown fastest of all, significantly faster than trade within the Socialist Bloc. Although in 1972 the trade turnover with these countries accounted for only 13 percent of all Soviet foreign trade, its volume increased 4.27 times between 1960 and 1972, while trade turnover within the Socialist Bloc increased only 2.28 times.[11] It is primarily in these countries that the USSR can sell finished industrial products, which is highly desirable from the standpoint of the Soviet export structure.

Trade within the Socialist Bloc

The percentage of trade within the Socialist Bloc, compared with the total foreign trade turnover of the USSR, has shrunk continually, particularly in the early 1970s. Total foreign trade grew 2.6 times between 1960 and 1972, while within the Socialist Bloc it has risen by a factor of only 2.28.[12] Over the last few years, this gap has widened still further.

The predominant portion of this trade is with countries that are members of the Council of Economic Mutual Assistance (CEMA). CEMA was created in January 1949 as an answer to the Marshall Plan for Western Europe. Its goal was to accelerate the postwar rehabilitation and development of the countries of Eastern Europe. The original, official goal of CEMA soon became the task of strengthening the economy of the Socialist Bloc based on mutual assistance. In the 1960s CEMA was additionally transformed into the chief instrument for integrating the economies of the Socialist Bloc.

The following countries originally joined CEMA: the Peoples' Republic of Bulgaria, the German Democratic Republic, the Hungarian Peoples' Republic, the Mongolian Peoples' Republic, the Polish Peoples' Republic, the Socialist Republic of Rumania, the Union of Soviet Socialist Republics, and the Czechoslovakian Socialist Republic. In 1972 Cuba was accepted into the organization. Representatives of the Democratic Republic of Vietnam and the Korean Peoples' Democratic Republic participate as observers. Thus, over time CEMA has been transformed from an organization of almost exclusively Eastern European countries into an economic organization of all communist countries with a Moscow orientation.

The highest organization of CEMA is its council, which meets periodically. Party and government delegations from the participating countries take part in the sessions. Party leaders of the participating countries also concern themselves with CEMA affairs. "During the Crimean meeting [July 1973], leaders of the communist and workers' parties" discussed progress in economic integration and problems of improving the work of CEMA and came to the conclusion that these questions "should remain the center of attention for the communist and workers' parties of the member countries of CEMA."[13]

The highest permanent organizations of CEMA are the Executive Committee and the Secretariat, both of which are located in Moscow. Besides these organizations, there are nineteen permanent commissions, as well as a total of six conferences and working groups and two committees whose importance continues to grow. The structure of the CEMA organizations is shown in figure 19-1.

Besides the integral organizations of CEMA, there are also intergovernmental organizations which are a part of CEMA or are controlled by it. These are the major organizations in this category (the year the organization was created is given in parentheses):

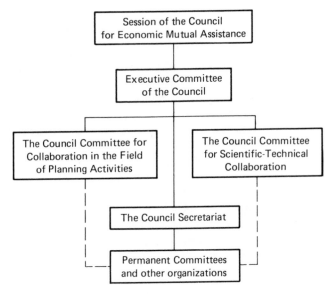

Source: *Ekonomicheskaia gazeta*, no. 50, December (1972):10

Figure 19-1. Basic Organizations of CEMA (Comecon)

International Bank for Economic Cooperation (1964)

International Investment Bank (1970)

International Center for Scientific and Technical Information (1969)

United Institute for Nuclear Research (1956)

Organization for Railroad Cooperation (1956)

Common Pool of Freight Cars (1964)

Organization for Cooperation in the Bearing Industry (1964)

Central Dispatch Directorate for the *Mir* United Energy System (1962)

Interkhim organization, for facilitating the production of equipment for the chemical industry (1969)

Intermetall organization, for cooperation in the field of ferrous and nonferrous metallurgy (1964)

Organization for Cooperation of Socialist Countries in the Field of Electrical and Postal Communications (1957)

Several other organizations, including only some of the CEMA members and having secondary importance.

The long-time chief representative of the USSR in CEMA is M.A. Lesechko, a deputy chairman of the Council of Ministers.

The main principle of relations in the Socialist Bloc is the principle of foreign trade, which is the result of cooperation in production and trade among the CEMA countries. The extent and character of this production and trade cooperation are based on coordinating the national economic plans of the participating countries. Work on coordination was begun in 1954; and since 1956, all Five-Year Plans (from the sixth on) have been developed according to plans that included coordination goals for CEMA. Naturally, these coordination goals are reflected in the national economic plans of the participating countries.

The goal of plan coordination is for individual countries to specialize in the production of a particular article, with an ensuing cooperation with the other CEMA countries. Since the USSR is the chief partner, specialization means that the other countries are becoming increasingly dependent on the Soviet economy. Specialization agreements are still being drawn up on a bilateral basis, sharply reducing the effectiveness of the undertaking. In addition, "it is difficult to increase specialization [both intra- and interbranch] due to the aspiration of each socialist country to satisfy its needs for machines and equipment, and for manufactured goods in general, with its own production."[14]

The shortcomings and failures in coordinating plans have caused the appearance of a new idea, economic integration. "International economic integration within the world socialist system is a special phase in the internationalization of economic life in which mutual complementation and mutual substitution of the national economies of the sovereign socialist states is strengthened in a planned manner and takes on a more economically expedient character."[15] In this way, the "national economies of the sovereign socialist states" are becoming significantly more dependent on the economic policies of the Soviet leadership. In order to understand an idea completely, it is sometimes useful to exaggerate it: ideal integration in the eyes of the Soviet leadership would be *Gosplan* planning the economies of all the countries, *Gossnab* distributing the resources of all the countries, and so forth.

By the mid 1970s, the idea of integration led away from coordination to the actual integration of national economic plans, and only the future will show the direction, level, and success of integration. For the time being, bilateral coordinated plans lead to the existence of bilateral trade agreements, which are usually long-term. Payments on the agreements are made by mutual deliveries of products valued according to improved world-market prices and are carried out as clearing payments through the International Bank for Economic Cooperation. The necessity for socialist trade to make use of capitalist prices is explained by the fact that "domestic wholesale prices were unfit for use as foreign trade prices, in view of great differences in production conditions, as well as in setting internal prices. Domestic wholesale prices in socialist countries are completely incompatible."[16]

Improving world prices basically means that prices on various goods are taken from different areas of the world market over an extended period of time and an average price is reached. "Thus, average world prices for 1960-1964 were used in the last review of contract prices in 1965-1966. . . . Prices remain stable for a lengthy period of time, usually for the duration of long-range trade agreements. This facilitates planning of the economy and foreign trade."[17]

In foreign trade within the Socialist Bloc, the primary economic problem is currently the problem of "a mutually advantageous exchange on the international CEMA market. . . . The tasks of extending socialist economic integration demand that the essence of mutually advantageous commodity exchange be defined, as must the criteria and factors involved in ensuring mutual trade advantage for the member nations of CEMA."[18] For the time being, there are no such criteria and, moreover, "reliable methods for calculating the effectiveness of the different variants of foreign economic contacts are necessary. These methods will have to satisfy the needs of the actual situation and will be based on correct theoretical premises. The creation of these methods is an extremely important task. The time has come to bring together the different viewpoints of economists in the field of estimates methodology, remembering that the best link between economics and the actual situation can be provided by creating a system of methods which gives practical economists reliable instruments for evaluating the decisions which have been made."[19]

As is obvious, the problem of mutually advantageous exchange is the result of planned price setting. For this reason, it becomes necessary to use world-market prices, but even the improved world-market prices must be further adapted to the specific conditions of the international socialist market. All this leads to the fact that "in trade among member-countries of CEMA contract prices for machinery differ from world market prices by at least 25 percent, and contract prices for industrial raw materials differ by a minimum of 15 percent."[20] Practically speaking, this means that machinery costs 25 percent less and raw materials 15 percent more than on the world market. The whole problem is complicated by the question of exchange rates, the proper solution of which should be "to ensure an economic basis for determining the profitability of export or import, and the mutual advantage of the underlying world price."[21]

The economic reasons for the inability to determine effectiveness and the degree of advantage of a given foreign trade transaction for each of the participating sides are reinforced by national and political considerations. As a result, each of the participating sides tends to consider itself the losing side in the vast majority of foreign trade transactions.

The general problem of mutual advantage in socialist foreign trade is directly connected to the most important specific peculiarities and circumstances accompanying foreign trade commodity exchange.

One of these peculiarities is the structure of trade turnover. To generalize somewhat, but without departing from the truth, one should note that in principle the Soviet Union is a supplier of raw materials, in exchange for which it receives industrial goods. The USSR is the only participant of CEMA that has huge natural resources, resources that other CEMA members either do not have or have in insufficient quantities. On the other hand, the Soviet Union does not want to permit a widespread and continual exodus of Eastern European countries into the world capitalist market. As a result, "socialist obligations toward friendly countries determine an unfavorable foreign trade structure for the USSR"[22] In 1968, for example, the suppliers of industrial goods had a positive trade balance of 1.3 billion rubles.[23] In addition, "in order to make a specific amount of money on the world socialist market, it is necessary to invest resources in production of iron ore, coal, oil, and cotton for export at a rate of five to eight times greater than in the production of machinery and equipment." To reduce the Soviet Union's own capital investments, "over the last few years, especially after approval of the Comprehensive Program, there have been an increased number of agreements which call for the CEMA countries to help finance the development of certain fuel and raw material branches of Soviet industry."[24] In some instances, CEMA countries themselves, with their own resources, extract raw materials from Soviet land (for example, timber). The growing number of deliveries of raw materials and fuel is a burden on the extraction branches of Soviet industry. For example, by 1968, the USSR was delivering 28 percent of its oil, 18.2 percent of its iron ore, and 17.5 percent of its manganese ore. According to preliminary estimates, by 1985 it will have to deliver more than 350 million tons of oil and 120 million tons of iron ore, which is simply impossible. "An analogous situation exists with many other types of raw materials, as well as with goods produced by the manufacturing industries." Therefore, there exists a very reasonable opinion that "the structure of import-export contacts which has developed has in many ways already exhausted its ability to support the existing rates of foreign trade turnover."[25]

The second important trait of foreign trade within the Socialist Bloc is that of transport. Trade is accomplished "in FOB port or FOB border prices of the exporting country." Considering the enormous distances (an average of 1,200 kilometers) and the predominantly rail shipment (66 percent), and "considering the relatively low cost per ton of the transported cargoes, transport costs reach 30 to 80 percent of foreign trade prices."[26] The corrections (that is, increases) of 15 percent in the improved world-market prices of raw materials therefore do not compensate for the transport costs in a large number of instances. The losing side here is the USSR. Moreover, the multimillion ton flow of cargo on the railroads puts an additional burden on the already overloaded mainlines. The *Druzhba* ("Friendship") oil pipeline has eased the situation somewhat, but this has turned out to be only temporary. The different railroad gauges cause additional difficulties and expenses. Large-scale organization of door-to-door truck deliveries requires that first-class highways be built.

The third important circumstance in socialist foreign trade is the question of the technical level and quality of the products delivered by one country to another. By 1969 M. Lesechko wrote: "The CEMA countries must solve crucial problems in increasing the technical level and quality of goods delivered to each other. While some mutual concessions by the socialist countries were to a certain extent explainable and justifiable in the initial period, ... under current conditions, the problem of technical level and quality has taken on primary importance and, in essence, determines the effectiveness of all social production of the council's community of nations."[27] This circumstance also determines the level of mutual advantage and the measure of satisfaction of each of the partners in socialist foreign trade. Economic planners in Eastern European countries probably reason that it is possible to sell industrial goods on the world market without discounts and to buy raw materials without price additions. Many Soviet managers reason that it is possible to sell raw materials on the world market, even if more cheaply, and to buy machines, even if at a little higher price; however, at least the machines will be of modern technical and quality level. There is dissatisfaction, but the reasoning about the world market is not very well grounded. First "it is necessary to raise the competitive capability of the CEMA countries on the world market."[28] Here the USSR has an advantage; it is simpler to sell raw materials than imperfect industrial goods.

The solution to all these problems always was and always will be impossible to attain along purely economic paths. Therefore, another path has been chosen, the path of cooperation through political and administrative coercion. Integration is the administrative and planning portion of the answer to the problem. The political considerations of maintaining and strengthening the unity of the Socialist Bloc, of the zone controlled by the USSR, reduce the economic problems of mutual advantage in this strange trade to secondary importance, at least in the eyes of the Soviet leaders. The idea has been repeatedly expressed that the political considerations of consolidating the socialist countries demand "the ability to subordinate to political goals when necessary the mathematical calculations of profitability in foreign trade."[29] Politics is in the foreground. "It is exceptionally important to consider the political aspect when analyzing the effectiveness of Soviet economic ties with the socialist countries."[30] Do the leaders of the socialist countries think the same way? And how long can trade be based on politics?

Notes

1. Joseph Stalin, *Problems of Leninism*, p. 179.
2. *Planovoe khoziaistvo*, no. 8 (1968):13.
3. Ibid., no. 12 (1973):3.
4. *National Economy of the USSR in 1972,* (Moscow: Statistika, 1973), p. 737.
5. *Planovoe khoziaistvo*, no. 12 (1974):7.
6. Ibid., p. 6.
7. Ibid., p. 10.
8. Ibid., p. 8.
9. *Sovetskaia Rossiia*, 27 March 1975, p.3.
10. *Novyj mir*, no. 2 (1972):121.
11. *National Economy of the USSR in 1972*, p. 737.
12. Ibid.
13. *Ekonomicheskaia gazeta*, no. 42 (1973):20.
14. *Voprosy ekonomiki*, no. 8 (1970):88.
15. Ibid., no. 3 (1971):101.
16. V.I. Zolotarev, *The World Socialist Market* (Moscow: Mezhdunarodyne otnosheniia, 1970), p. 185.
17. *Price Formation on the World Socialist Market* (Moscow: Ekonomika, 1968), p. 24.
18. *Voprosy ekonomiki*, no. 1 (1972):95.
19. *Planovoe khoziaistvo*, no. 12 (1974):27.
20. *Voprosy ekonomiki*, no. 12 (1967):67.
21. *Price Formation on the World Socialist Market*, p. 35.
22. *Voprosy ekonomiki*, no. 12 (1970):28.

23. Ibid., p. 100.
24. *Planovoe khoziaistvo*, no. 12 (1974):35.
25. *Voprosy ekonomiki*, no. 4 (1971):104.
26. *Planovoe khoziaistvo*, no. 7 (1969):16
27. *Ekonomicheskaia gazeta*, no. 10 (1969):5.
28. Ibid., no. 6 (1969):40.
29. *Voprosy ekonomiki*, no. 10 (1969):140.
30. *Planovoe khoziaistvo*, no. 12 (1974):20.

20 The Municipal Economy

In January 1974 there were 1,999 cities in the USSR and they accounted for 59.5 percent of the country's population. Two hundred and thirty-eight, or 11.9 percent of them had a population of over a hundred thousand, and 57.2 percent of the urban population, or 34 percent of the total population of the country, was concentrated in these large cities. Thirty-five, or 1.76 percent of these large cities, had a population of more than five hundred thousand and 27.9 percent of the urban population; in other terms, 16.6 percent of the total population of the country was living in them.[1]

The information cited is evidence of a very great population concentration in the large and very large cities. This concentration takes place because under Soviet conditions large cities offer considerably more amenities than small cities and towns. Some of these amenities are peculiar to the Soviet Union. As in other countries, the largest cities in the USSR offer a fuller cultural life and have more educational opportunities. However, peculiar to the Soviet Union are a better supply of housing, better supply of goods and services, and significantly greater chances to change one's place of work. All these things are enjoyed only by people in the largest cities of the USSR. Finally, a very important condition is that people in the large, and especially in the very large cities, enjoy greater freedom and independence because the inhabitants are better protected from the tyranny of the local bureaucracy and supervisors.

Administrative measures are being used to curb the growth of the large cities, but "administrative measures alone cannot restrain the excessive growth of the large cities. Moreover, such measures can have a negative effect. They lead to a situation where people not only cannot come to the largest cities for permanent residence but do not leave them for fear of losing their residence permit."[2] This fear sharply restricts the use of highly qualified specialists for work in remote regions. The author of the cited article quite properly sees a radical equalization of living conditions in all cities of the country as a solution.

Municipal economies are a significant portion of the national wealth. "At the present time, the fixed assets of municipal housing and services are valued at 240 billion rubles, or approximately *one-third* of the value of the fixed assets of the national economy."[3] The fixed assets of the housing sector, that is, residential buildings, alone totaled about 23 percent of the fixed assets of the country.[4] Consequently, the fixed assets of municipal services make up about 10 percent of the fixed assets of the national economy. It follows that the fixed assets of the municipal services make up about 30 percent of the total fixed assets of the cities. However, the official figures cited conform poorly to date on capital investment in municipal economies. As the journal *Voprosy ekonomiki* reports, "The lag in developing cultural and other municipal construction should be noted. The latter is only 13 percent of total capital investment, compared with 19 to 21 percent projected by norms for comprehensive city building."[5] The fact that norms are not adhered to in planned distribution of capital investment, together with the low level of the norms in general, leads to internal disproportions in city buildings and, most importantly, to insufficient development and neglect of municipal services.

This is perhaps most sharply felt in municipal transport, particularly in the largest cities of the USSR "where 40 to 60 percent of the workers spend up to one hour per day enroute to their places of work; 10 to 30 percent up to two hours; and 5 to 12 percent, more than two hours." Of course, they spend an equal amount of time on the return trip. The transport problem arises not only as a result of insufficient investment but also because "extensive territorial growth of populated areas persists" and because "on the average, the density of available housing at the beginning of 1975 is about 50 percent of the norm."[6] This significantly lengthens municipal transport networks. The extensive development is largely due to department-managed individual housing and, particularly due to inexpensive, single-story, individual housing that is transforming even large cities into something resembling huge villages.

City housing resources consist of socialized (that is, state-owned) resources and individual housing, that is, housing that is the personal property of the citizens. In 1973, 72.7 percent of the actual living space in city housing resources was in the socialized sector. This portion is divided into municipal housing managed by the city councils, and department-run housing, which is in the hands of the numerous departments and ministries. Thus, in 1965 there were 280 department owners in Moscow; and while by 1975 this multiownership was completely eliminated in Moscow, it still flourishes as before in other cities. Department-run housing "is 60 percent of all housing." This leaves only 12.7 percent of city housing in the municipal sector; however, with only a few exceptions, this sector controls the entire range of municipal services. Such a fragmentation of municipal economies and dispersal of housing is not justified from any point of view. This is especially true because "the buildings belonging to factories, institutions, and other organizations are operated at a considerable loss; and the level of service in them is, as a rule, even lower than in buildings assigned to the municipal sector." Although "the decision was made several years ago to gradually turn over department-run housing to the local councils, these resources have even increased over the last three years" in many large areas of the country.[7]

The urban economy developed at a very slow rate during the prewar years. Its development accelerated slightly during the first postwar years and only in the post-Stalin period did it attain high rates of development. This process is reflected indirectly but very revealingly in the rate at which residential buildings have been put in service. If the total area of completed residential buildings between 1918 and 1974 is taken as 100 percent, then from 1918 to 1951 a little over 18 percent was built (or 0.56 percent per year), and from 1951 to 1974, 82 percent (or 3.56 percent per year) was built.[8] Although this very rapid growth in housing was accompanied by a very rapid growth in urban population, the actual living space for one urban dweller only increased from seven square meters in 1950 to eleven square meters in 1970.[9] This figure reached almost twelve square meters by the end of the Ninth Five-Year Plan (1975). However, the urban housing problem is still far from solved, and it is precisely this problem that is one of the primary reasons for the sharp reduction in the birth rate over the last few years. Construction of residential buildings has considerably surpassed the increased amount of equipment available to municipal services. "For a number of areas of housing and municipal services, *the production of equipment is not centrally planned* [italics mine]. Equipment used for water and sewer purposes, for electrical energy and gas, and for tree and shrub planting in populated areas is produced in insignificant quantities and in limited variety at nonspecialized enterprises of twenty different ministries and departments. For all practical purposes, these organizations have no responsibility for the equipment and put almost no work into improving the equipment and into expanding its production."[10] "There is a lack of the necessary equipment for burning waste under modern conditions, as well as the equipment for mechanizing such labor-intensive work as washing windows and cleaning up courtyards, sidewalks, and stairwells."[11]

The director of the Academy of Municipal Services, F. Shevelev, states that "last year [1968] only 14 percent of the requirements of housing and municipal services in the RSFSR for sweeping and cleaning machines were met, 20 percent of the needed container-type garbage trucks, and 13 percent of the needed rotary snow-removing machines."[12]

"As a result of insufficient equipment at enterprises and organizations in the housing and municipal services sector of the country's economy, labor mechanization on the whole does not exceed 42 percent; and on jobs with unskilled labor, the figure does not exceed 2 percent."[13] For this reason, there were 3 million people working in the housing and municipal services sector of the economy in 1973, and "on the average throughout the USSR eighteen people are employed for every thousand apartments; while in East Germany, for example, there are 4.5 people per thousand apartments, or one-fourth of that number."[14]

The Organization of Municipal Economies

Municipal economies are divided into the housing sector, that is, residential buildings, and the municipal services sector, which encompasses everything else involved in running a city.

Approximately 60 percent of urban housing is currently in the hands of governmental departments and ministries which handle its operation and management themselves. The remainder of socialized housing is operated and managed by the appropriate departments of the city councils. These same organizations provide private housing with municipal utilities (water, sewer, and lights) and monitor the manner in which private owners observe housing regulations.

The city energy, water, and sewage systems, as well as streetcars and trolleybuses are almost completely under the control of the city councils. Strangely, with the exception of Moscow, city buses are controlled by the republic ministries of vehicle transport.[15] Under the city council are special organizations that manage large individual sectors of the municipal economy (energy, water and sewer, streetcars, and trolleybuses), usually having the status of trusts or directorates.

Housing run by city councils is managed by a system headed by the city housing administration. *Raion* housing administrations are directly subordinate to it. A building manager (*upravdom*), subordinate to the *raion* administration, manages several buildings and has charge of the service personnel: janitors, cleaning ladies, and stokers. Housing repair is accomplished by special repair offices run by the city housing administration and is carried out primarily through work orders submitted by the building managers. The building manager also monitors the manner in which the residents of his buildings adhere to the rules requiring police residence permits. He is therefore usually connected with the MVD (Ministry of Internal Affairs), and often with the KGB.

The whole system is unwieldy, bureaucratic, inefficient, and ineffective. The low rent, which is set for purely propaganda reasons, "covers only about one-third of the costs of maintaining the housing."[16]

As a rule, all socialized city housing is operated unsatisfactorily, and the buildings are usually "in a neglected state; the courtyards, stairwells, and entrances are littered, and the engineering equipment, drains, and roofs are defective. As a result, the buildings age prematurely, and the residents experience inconveniences."[17] It has come to the point that major repairs to old residential buildings are more expensive and the repair time three to four times as long as that required to build a new building of the same type."[18]

New Construction

Over the last four five-year plans housing construction has reached enormous proportions, and more than 200 million persons have been able to improve their living conditions during these twenty years. Many residential buildings have been built in the cities, with over two-thirds of the construction attributed to the socialized (state) sector. Multistory buildings, usually eight to ten stories high, predominate in construction within the state sector, but prefabricated large-block buildings may reach twenty-five stories. For the most part brick buildings are put up however, the course set during the Khrushchev era toward building large-block buildings is leading to a continual increase in their construction. In 1975 about 16 percent of all residential buildings erected were of the large-block type.

The quality of residential construction is too low to criticize. The highest Soviet leaders have tried to deal with this problem more than once and have demanded an improvement in construction quality, but positive results have not been forthcoming. A resolution of the CPSU Central Committee and the USSR Council of Ministers noted that "the quality of construction and installation work in residential construction is still low."[19] Six years later, in considering the same question, the Central Committee noted that "in some republics, *krais,* and *oblast's,* the necessary quality in public housing construction is still not being reached." The CPSU Central Committee also points out that "a significant negative effect on quality occurs by irregular completion of housing. A large portion of it is turned over at the end of the year under rushed conditions, with large quantities of incomplete and defective work. This requires numerous alterations and causes unproductive expenditures of considerable state resources."[20]

Large-block buildings are of especially poor quality. Despite sufficient experience in large-block construction, basic problems have not yet been eliminated, and "we do not have the right to go on building large-block buildings with ugly facades and leaking joints and windows."[21] Repeated checks of completed large-block buildings have shown that the metal parts that join the blocks are not protected against moisture. Over the long term, this problem will lead inevitably to major accidents as the joining braces rust through. Designed for the middle European area of the USSR, large-block buildings are built without modifications in regions with more severe climate (in Bratsk, for example), where it is almost impossible to live in them in the winter.

Apartment planning in new buildings is based on the demands of maximum economy. This, in turn, is based on the ratio of living space, that is, the area of the rooms used specifically for living purposes, to the whole useful area, that is, the total area of the apartment. "Based on this formula, in the majority of standard apartments we find cramped entryways, small kitchens, and a lack of closets."[22] Based on the same considerations of economy, "there are no basements in modern multistory buildings."[23] This creates immense inconveniences for residents, especially in storing supplies for the winter. This not only breaks the tradition of storing supplies by city families but also affects the family budget (potatoes, vegetables, and many other staples cost much more in the winter than in the fall) and significantly reduces the winter supplies of vegetables and potatoes for the city populace.

According to existing building norms, multistory buildings must be equipped with an elevator (two when the building is over ten stories). However, the elevators turned out by Soviet industry are of obsolete design, "and the elevators not only are slow and inconvenient, but also require frequent repair and adjustment. Repair and adjustment must be carried out after every thirty-five to forty hours of service."[24] In practice, the elevators "spend more time in repair than in service."[25] The general situation of the elevator problem and its influence on the living conditions of residents in high-rise buildings is conveyed by "a sadly humorous piece of popular folklore: Once upon a time, there lived a grandma and a grandpa up on the tenth floor; because the elevator worked poorly, they aren't around any more."[26]

New construction is improving municipal services and utilities somewhat, but at the beginning of the 1970s they were still on a low level. In 1962 a little more than one-third of city housing was equipped with city water and sewer and only one-fourth was equipped with central heating[27]; in 1975, depending on the area of the country, 51 percent to 70 percent of socialized city housing was supplied with city water, 48 percent to 66 percent with sewers, and 51 percent to 70 percent with central heating.[28] However, the picture in socialized housing is significantly better than the average for all city housing, for private housing is minimally equipped with these conveniences.

The planning and architecture of new construction is still another unsolved problem. The resolution of the CPSU Central Committee and the USSR Council of Ministers "On Measures for Improving the Quality of Public Housing Construction" notes that "in a majority of cities of the country, the architecture in areas of mass housing construction is monotonous and unattractive."[29]

Notes

1. *National Economy of the USSR in 1973,* (Moscow: Statistika, 1974), pp. 32-33.
    2. *Ekonomicheskaia gazeta,* no. 29 (1967):18.
    3. *Planovoe khoziaistvo,* no. 6 (1974):107-108.
    4. *National Economy of the USSR in 1973,* p. 57.
    5. *Voprosy ekonomiki,* no. 10 (1975):25.
    6. Ibid.
    7. *Pravda,* 1 February 1975, lead article.
    8. *National Economy of the USSR in 1973,* p. 608.
    9. *Voprosy ekonomiki,* no. 8 (1973):56.
    10. *Planovoe khoziaistvo,* no. 6 (1974):108-109.
    11. Ibid., p. 109.
    12. *Pravda,* 13 September 1969, p. 3.
    13. *Planovoe khoziaistvo,* no. 6 (1974):108.
    14. Ibid., no. 11 (1958):72.

15. *Pravda*, 28 October 1974, p. 2.
16. *Voprosy ekonomiki*, no. 2 (1973):41.
17. *Pravda*, 1 February 1975, p. 1.
18. *Pravda*, 1 July 1969, p. 2.
19. *Pravda*, 21 June 1969, p.1.
20. *Sotsialisticheskaia industriia*, 29 August 1975, p. 1.
21. *Pravda*, 26 November 1970, p. 2.
22. *Ekonomicheskaia gazeta*, no. 23 (1965):36.
23. *Pravda*, 22 March 1970, p. 3.
24. *Pravda*, 24 January, 1968, p. 2.
25. *Ekonomicheskaia gazeta*, no. 36 (1966):46.
26. *Pravda*, 30 November 1967, p. 2.
27. *Voprosy ekonomi*, no. 3 (1962):63.
28. *Planovoe khoziaistvo*, no. 1 (1975):60.
29. *Pravda*, 21 June 1969, p. 1.

Conclusions and Prospects

In recent years, it has been said more for the foreign than the Soviet audience that the Soviet economic system is the product of conscious, purposeful activity based on a study of the classic Marxist writers. Since Marxism is scientific, it is further stated, the economic system based on it is scientific. However, it is clear to the outside observer and investigator that this is an obligatory cliche; within the Soviet Union as well, not everyone has enough temerity to claim such a logical connection when speaking about manifestations of the system. They more and more frequently resort to the word established (*slozhivshiisia*) that is, in the sense of "which established itself" or "which turned out in a particular way." The word is used in combinations such as "the established methods of planning," the "established methods of management," the "proportions which have been established," and the "established distribution of industry."

Naturally, from the very beginning, the classic Marxists have been the basis for the development and established makeup of the system in many respects. This has been accomplished not only through direct instructions about the future socialist economy but also through developments that occurred during the implementation of these instructions. Thus, denying the market mechanism, which in the opinion of the classic Marxists enabled capitalists to achieve excess value, led to an "established" administrative planning and market substitute. Under this substitute, the system is unable to make use of the automatic mechanism of market relations and the functions of price in its own interests. This, in turn, inevitably led to a lack of concern for the questions of effectiveness and progress and to a rise in bad management practices. Marx's law of labor value becomes an element of this substitute and asserts that value is created exclusively by human labor. In the practice of Soviet management, this justifies the "established" practice of irresponsible exploitation of minerals, land, and timber on a massive scale.

The classic writers of Marxism also determined the planned nature of the Soviet economy. However, Soviet planning in practice has proved quite clearly that the classicists greatly overestimated the potential of the human intellect, and that they completely ignored the Leninist principle of material self-interest in every economic activity. These are the roots of the departmentalism (*vedomstvennost'*) that has "established itself" in the Soviet economy and which in principle represents an often successful attempt to simplify a complicated situation. These are also the roots of the formalism and apathy that characterize Soviet work.

The mixture of classicist assertions and the unexpected and unforeseen phenomena derived from them, together with the practical necessity to manage the economy under Stalin's methods of leadership determined the highly

241

centralized directive planning and rigid price-setting policies "that became established." The attempts to simplify an impossibly complicated situation in planning gave rise to its dominant principle, "from the attained level" and to rigidity, departmentalism, and bureaucracy in planning. Contrary to assertions about the advantages of socialism over capitalism, Soviet planning has to tag along and copy the development of the leading capitalist countries when it clearly becomes necessary to create modern branches of production and when modern forms and methods of management must be introduced. The established system, contrary to desires, commonly limits the practical potential of this copying. This is happening in the introduction of automated management systems, for example.

In established planning, economic incentives are in principle not applied to scientific and technical progress to raising the quality of production and labor, or to economizing in raw materials, production, and labor resources. Moreover, in production planning and especially in supply planning, the planning indicators are very often the main obstacle to a normal, effective organization of the economic system's work.

Primarily under the influence of planned price setting, the Soviet economic system became established not only as a system of chance proportions and relations but also as an economically blind system. It is impossible to calculate optimum economic effectiveness for making decisions in planning as well as in production and management. An economic analysis of decisions made primarily under the influence of noneconomic considerations is also impossible. At every point at which price and value enter into economic calculations, that is, in the calculations made for the national economic plan, those that are most important for the economy, it is impossible to use econometrics and computers because of planned price setting. In the mid seventies, attempts were made to substitute scientifically based norms for prices in these calculations, but these attempts were doomed to failure because the creation of genuinely scientifically based norms presupposes calculating the effectiveness of the norm itself. Using technical calculations as the basis for these norms will make it possible to evaluate the decision made, but it will not make it possible to actually make the optimum decision. This last factor is the most important. There is no chance to convert the norms into the mathematical language of computers. Making the decision remains dependent on the expert evaluations, intuition, and qualifications of the person making the decision. As is well known from Soviet economic management experience, however, departmental considerations that have nothing in common with national economic effectiveness often play a major role in decision making.

Because of their peculiarities, Soviet planning and the principles of economic management formulated by it, frozen as they were on the level of the first five-year plans, are coming into greater conflict with the urgent requirements of a greatly expanded and more complex national economy. Attempts to change the situation meet an insurmountable wall of conservatism, even when positive changes are both necessary and possible. Thus, the economic reform of 1965, which proclaimed the transition to economic levers for developing the economy, by the 1970s has returned to administrative means and the hackneyed socialist competition.

At the same time, these growing contradictions are the main source of disproportions whose negative effect on the economy and even on national policies is continually growing. The general disproportion between the development of industry and agriculture has become a factor in determining the policies and strategic capabilities of the Soviet state. As an old soldiers' saying maintains, "It's possible to fight without a gun, but not without a spoon."

Interbranch and intrabranch disporportions in industry are one of the main reasons for the failure of the course aimed at accelerating the development of group B industry. They are also among the most important practical reasons for the low effectiveness of the economy and the decreasing effectiveness of capital investments. The attempt to eliminate internal disproportions in so far as possible is the main reason for the predominant development of group A in the Tenth Five-Year Plan. This is quite clear from Kosygin's report at the Twenty-fifth CPSU Congress titled "Basic Trends in the Development of the National Economy of the USSR between 1976 and 1980."[1]

The Tenth Five-Year Plan, proclaimed as the Five-Year Plan of Effectiveness and Quality, finds its chief obstacle to attaining projected goals in established planning procedure itself. A survey of letters from readers, from simple workers to doctors of science, published in *Komsomol'skaia Pravda* on 14 March 1976 is evidence of this fact. The survey confirms that planning "unwittingly encroaches on the interests of the outstanding workers, (*peredoviki*) rewards those who lag behind, and gives rise to a striving for lower norms and plans." Such is the influence on effectiveness. Regarding quality the survey concludes, "Today it is clear that we shall not be able to make any serious improvement in production quality if the Tenth Five-Year Plan does not become a plan with a *qualitatively new approach to the principles of planning* material and technical supply" (italics mine).[2]

The profound defects in the principles of the economic system are well known to the Soviet leadership; they have been known for a long time, at least since the end of the Stalin period. In 1962 Liberman wrote about the intolerability of the situation and about the real necessity for making basic changes in the principles of the system. In 1964 Nemchinov proposed a new system of self-supporting (*khozraschet*) socialism which was essentially a market-economy system adapted to Soviet conditions.

However, from a certain point of view the existing system suits the Soviet leadership. It is not loyalty to the principles of Marxism-Leninism but fear for their power that forces the Soviet leadership to maintain the bankrupt system with its principle of Party spirit in the economy. They apparently understand

and believe that "political and economic freedom constitute a complex unity. It is unthinkable to remove one part without all the rest crashing down."[3] This means that after granting even relative economic freedom, it would inevitably be necessary to grant political freedom as well, or else the political freedom would be taken without asking. They also deeply believe, and not without reason, that only their system of nonfreedom makes it possible to create the desired level of military power at the expense of the living conditions of the people. This is an extremely important reason for maintaining power in their hands.

The actual economic situation is concealed by a gigantic system of lies, a system that has been raised to the level of a state virtue. This system includes false propaganda, unrestrained and groundless boasting, and the verbal shamanism of resolutions and decisions. It also includes "glossing over reality," the deceptive essence of "improvementism" (uluchshenchestvo) used within the country and abroad, "gigantomania," usually senseless and harmful (like KamAZ, the huge Kama River Truck Plant) but calculated for its external effect, and bluffing with the country's economic might in the international arena. It is primarily to advertise the advantages of its economic system that the Soviet leadership resorts to criminally trampling the vital interests of the young developing nations and insistently recommends its own path of economic development to them. Finally, a specific and significant role in concealing the truth is assigned to the science of economics and, strangely enough, to planning itself. Not everything has gone smoothly with science, as is evidenced by the purge of the Institute of Economics of the Academy of Sciences in the mid 1960s. However, with the recalcitrant broken and the pliant reoriented, it again became possible to write "scientific" articles in which desired effects are often passed off as actual fact. Gosplan processes millions of items of data and compiles thousands of balances. On the surface everything looks scientific and imposing; nonetheless, everything turns out to be a house of cards designed to depict the Soviet economic system as a new, progressive, scientifically based economic system with immense advantages over all previously existing systems, including capitalism, that is, over all market-economy systems.

The scale and range of these efforts, which all possess a demagogic, logical interdependence, have led to certain successes. It is not surprising that some people who have never observed the system from within believe the attractive fairy tale so diligently told, demonstrated at trade fairs, and finally instilled in them.

However, in reality the Soviet economic system is the fruit of an ill-considered, poorly thought out, and crudely conducted experiment. In the beginning it was entirely natural to have some hopes for it, despite all the brutality of its measures. These hopes are now groundless. Nevertheless, the experiment is not useless, in the same way that unsuccessful experiments in science are not useless. It demonstrates with utmost clarity that the chosen path is wrong. If experience teaches anything, then others should not choose to take the same erroneous path. It also gives us the opportunity to reach a number of important conclusions that are partly outside the framework of the Soviet economic experiment. Most important among the conclusions are the following.

1. Marx's economic theory, at the root of which lies his law of labor value, is basically erroneous. The economic practice of socialism has demonstrated that things other than those created by labor may have value and that the yardstick of value can be something other than labor. Surplus value, relegated by Marx to the capitalist method of production (the source of capitalist enrichment through exploiting the workers), is an essential element of any economic activity. Surplus value is essential for an expanded production and reproduction cycle; more important, it is the only index of the effectiveness of any economic activity. Moreover, surplus value (or its profit norm aspect) is an instrument for forming optimum proportions in the national economy. Marx's assertion about the possibility of successfully replacing the market mechanism with the planning process of the triumphant proletariat has turned out to be theoretical nonsense.

2. Directive planning of the Soviet type cannot ensure effective (optimum) and proportional (harmonious) development of the economy anywhere, at any time, or at any level of development of any country. A directively planned economy continually and inevitably creates disproportions because it inevitably becomes an object and instrument of politics and subjectivism.

3. Disproportionately high expenditures of labor and resources are required to attain the goals set by directive planning, because directive planning is organically incapable of foreseeing, coordinating, and ensuring the whole complex of resources and conditions essential for attaining goals by the most effective path. A vivid example of this is the mechanization and automation being introduced into the Soviet economy.

4. The problems indicated in points 2 and 3, along with other factors, determine the absence of freedom in economic activity and work and a low standard of living when compared to other systems on the same level of economic development.

5. Mankind has not yet invented a better instrument of economic activity than the market. Only the marketplace makes it possible to mutually regulate separate sectors of the national economic mechanism. Only the marketplace gives the economy the property of self-adjustment. Only market relations in all their complexity give prices and value the property of informativeness, for they reflect the actual situation in the economy and the tendencies of market changes, that is, the realities of economic life. Only in the process of free market relations do price and value automatically regulate the economy and encourage continuous growth of scientific and technical progress. The market mechanism itself does not predetermine the spontaneity of production. This idea is shared even by the deputy chairman of *Gosplan*, A. Bachurin,[4] although the official Soviet theory specifically attributes the property of spontaneity to the market. Spontaneity is created, not by the market mechanism, but by people trying to

act against the automatic mechanism of market relations, whether they are inspired by personal gain or have created the disgraceful edifice of centralized directive planning. The market mechanism has faithfully served various economic structures. The various systems of market economy are different from each other in the social character of the use to which the national product and profit are put. Therefore all future economic structures, whatever they may be called, must and will be based on market relations.

6. Only the market, "a unique mirror of consumer opinion, which shows the extent to which production is meeting consumption," can maximally draw together the state, group, and private interests in economic activity and can maximally satisfy the demands of all participants of this activity: the state, enterprises, and individual consumers.[5]

7. National economic branch (*otrasl'*) and territorial planning can be optimal only by using market prices. This is because market prices seek an optimum level, are comparable, reflect the reality of the ongoing economic process, and are therefore informative. The only possible alternative is not to let the plan suppress the market but to compile and carry out the plan through the market mechanism. This is the only real chance for using econometrics and computers to reach optimum solutions to the basic tasks of planning and management.

I have mentioned only the main conclusions that are possible and probably useful to make in objectively studying, not the prepared exterior, but the essence of the Soviet economy as it has developed up to the late 1970s. Ever-widening circles of Soviet economists and managers, as well as the thinking population of the country, have come to the same conclusions.

The general, long-term prospects under the present conditions are for the Soviet economy as a whole to work less effectively, increasing the gap between its scientific and technical level and that of the leading countries. All this will inevitably aggravate the existing polarization of viewpoints concerning that line that should be followed in the Party's economic policy. The conflict in viewpoints, continually inflamed by worsening economic management, will grow until an explosion, either inside the party or inside the country, destroys the present-day psychological barriers. An evolutionary path of economic development cannot, in theory, be excluded, but it seems that the best time for this path has already passed, and there are no strong individuals in view who are capable of conducting such an evolutionary process, a process bordering on revolution. A Peter the First is needed, but they have only Leonid Brezhnev.

Only large-scale foreign policy victories can postpone, but not completely eliminate, these historic prospects.

Notes

1. *Pravda,* 2 March 1976, pp. 2-6.
2. *Komsomol'skaia pravda,* 14 March 1976, p. 2.
3. L. Erhard, *Prosperity for Everyone,* p. 63.
4. *Planovoe khoziaistvo,* no. 11 (1965):8.
5. *Novyi mir,* no. 2 (1971):153.

Glossary

BAM Baikal-Amur Railroad.

Bedniak rural proletariat.

Berezka tourist shop where products are sold for foreign currency.

Bilet USSR Gosbank note.

Brigada brigade of workers in the shop of a plant.

CEMA Council of Mutual Economic Assistance.

Cheka Extraordinary Commission, Soviet secret police, established 1917.

Chervonets paper bank notes worth ten rubles during the NEP period.

Classicists Classic writers of Marxist ideology.

Comecon Council for Economic Mutual Assistance. Nations of the Soviet bloc are members.

CPSU Communist Party of the Soviet Union.

Dostaval procurers. They insure that a delivery is made within the agreed period of time; also known as *tolkach* (fixers).

Glavk Main Industrial Committee; unit of State industrial administration.

Glavkomplekt Chief Directorate of Assemblies.

Glavsnabsbyt Chief Supply and Sales Organization.

GOERLO State Commission for the Electrification of Russia.

Gosbank State Bank.

Gossnab State Committee for Material-Technical Supply.

Gosplan State Planning Commission.

GOST state standards for products.

Gosstroi state construction.

Gosstrakh state insurance organizations.

Inzhener-uskoritel' engineer-expediter who help plants fulfill the national economic plan.

Kampaneishchina system of working in spurts.

Kaznacheiskii bilet state treasury notes.

KGB Komitet Gosudarstvennoi Bezopasnosti, Committee for State Security.

Khozraschet independent, self-supporting organizations.

Kolkhoz collective farm.

Komsomol Young Communist League.

Krai district.

Kulak wealthy peasant.

Mestnichestvo giving priority to local interests.

MVD Ministerstvo Vnutrennykh Del, Ministry of Internal Affairs.

NEP New Economic Policy, which temporarily allowed free enterprise in the 1920s.

Nomenklatura lists of executives sanctioned by the Party.

Nomenklatura izdelii list of manufactured articles.

Ob"edinenie association. Part of the branch planning system.

Oblast' region.

Ochkovtiratel'stvo creating facade that business is going well.

Otrasl' sector of industry.

Peredovik outstanding workers.

Plan-proekt production draft plan.

Plan snabzheniia supply plans.

Plan-zaiavka plan-requisition.

Plenum committee meeting.

Pravlenie *Gosbank* board.

Predpriiatie enterprise, variously translated as plant, factory, or organization.

Prodnalog limited produce tax.

Prodotriad armed groups during War Communism who forced the peasants to relinquish their produce.

Prodrazverstka policy during War Communism forcing the peasant to supply agricultural produce to the state without compensation.

Raion region.

Rosbakaleia Russian Federated Republic Groceries Organization.

RSFSR Russian Soviet Federated Socialist Republic.

Rynochki marketeers, Soviet economists who advocate a market economy.

Sberkassa savings bank.

Seredniak peasants of average wealth.

Shturmovshchina rush work to fulfill the plan.

Soiuzsel'khoztekhnika All-Union Association for the Sale of Agricultural Equipment to Collective and State Farms.

Sovet soiuza Union Council.

Sovkhoz state-owned and state-managed farm.

Sovnarkhoz territorial principle of industrial organization.

Sovrabkop state trade during the NEP period.

Stakhanovite worker who sets records of production. Named after Stakhanov, a coal miner who broke records.

Stroibank Construction Bank.

Subbotniki volunteer Saturdays; when worker works for free.

Tekhpromfin Plan technical-industrial financial plan. Plant's annual financial production plan.

Tolkach see *Dostaval*.

Torgpredstvo trade delegations sent to the countries with which the USSR has trade relations. They handle trade transactions.

Torgsin Trade with Foreigners stores in the NEP period. Soviet citizens, surrendering valuables at 1913 prices, bought food and other goods.

Tovarooborot internal trade turnover.

TOZ Association for Working the Land.

Tsekh shop in a plant.

Trest   trust, part of the branch planning organization.

Uchastok   sector, part of the branch planning organization.

Uluchshenchestvo   campaign for gradual improvement in the economy.

Uluchshentsy   Soviet economists who advocate a planned economy in contrast to the marketeers.

Upravdom   building manager.

USSR   Union of Soviet Socialist Republics.

Vedomstvennost'   departmentalization. The departmental approach to working out state plans.

Vedomstvo   offices where the branch principle of planning is worked out.

VLKSM   Komsomol.

Vheshtorgbank   Foreign Trade Bank.

Voennyi predstavitel'   military representative system which checks on production of defense materials.

Voennyi priemshchik   same as *voennyi predstavitel'*.

Volost   smallest administrative division in czarist Russia.

VSNKh   Higher National Economic Council.

VTsSPS   leadership of the Soviet trade unions.

Index

agriculture, 157-180; collectivization, 8-9, 157; fixed capital, 160; labor force, 161-162; management, 164-168; NEP, 157, planning, 163-164; price setting, 158-159; production statistics, 170-172; War Communism, 157
amortization, 96-97
Antonov (Tambov) Revolt, 3-5
automated management system, 73

BAM (Baikal-Amur Railroad), 195
banks, 198-202; Nationalization Decree, 2
brigada (work brigade), 127

capital investment, 98-100
CEMA (COMECON), 225-231
Central Statistical Directorate, 66-68
Cheka (Extraordinary Commission), 2
collective farm. *See kolkhoz*
collectivization, 8-9, 157
Comecon (CEMA), 225-231
commodity production, 25-26
Communist Party, 81-82
computer technology, 73-75
"conference sitting," 77-78
credit, 196-198
currency, 185-191; circulation, 84, 188-191; reform, 6, 185-186
czarist debts, abrogation, 2

defense industry, role, 61-63, 111-114, 118-119
departmentalism (*vedomstvennost'*), 80
design bureau, 109-110, 113-114
domestic trade, 205-218; goods quality, 211, 215; management, 217-218; organization, 212-215; planning, 206-212; prices, 209; rural, 215; supply organizations, 212-213; trade organizations, 210-211, 214-215, 217-218; urban, 214-215
dostaval (procurer), 134

economic management, 77-81
economic reform, 13
economic self-sufficiency (*khozraschet*), 123-124
edinonachalie (one-man management), 127
"engineer-expediter," 135

factory, 127-128
finances, 185-202
Five-Year Plan: First, 8, 10, 77; Second, 8, 77; Fourth, 11; Fifth, 11-12; Sixth, 12; Seventh, 12; Tenth, 243
fixed assets, 93-98; active, 94; modernization, 97-98; passive, 94; structure, 95-96; use, 94-95
fixer (*tolkach*), 134-135
foreign trade, 221-231; capitalist countries, 221-225; socialist countries, 221, 225-231
formalism, 80

Glavsnabsbyt, 131-132
GOERLO, 38
Gosbank, 198-202
Gosplan, 38-42, 51-57, 130-133; coordination, 51-52; planning, 38-42, 54-57; supply, 131
Gossnab, 54-56, 130-133; planning, 54-56; supply, 130-133
GOST (state standard), 114-116

Higher National Economic Council (VSNKh), 2

improvers (*uluchshentsy*), 20
industrial association, 121-123
industrial development: extensive, 91-92, 97-100; intensive, 98
industrial enterprise, 127-128
industrial specialists, quality, 139-140
industry, 78-128; economic role, 83; Group A, 83-86; Group B, 83-86;

About the Author

Constantin A. Krylov was born in St. Petersburg, Russia, in 1914, and received a certificate in engineering from the Kiev Construction Institute. After World War II, he emigrated to West Germany. From 1949 until his death in September 1977, Mr. Krylov taught courses dealing with the Soviet economy and analysis of the Soviet press at the U.S. Army Institute for Advanced Russian and East European Studies, Garmisch-Partenkirchen, Germany. His first-hand experience as an engineer in pre-World War II Soviet industry and his continued analysis of Soviet economic periodicals contributed to his expertise on the Soviet economy.